NORTH CAROLINA DRAMA

by RICHARD WALSER

NORTH CAROLINA POETRY
NORTH CAROLINA IN THE SHORT STORY
LEMUEL SAWYER's BLACKBEARD (1824)
INGLIS FLETCHER OF BANDON PLANTATION
THE ENIGMA OF THOMAS WOLFE
BERNICE KELLY HARRIS: STORYTELLER OF EASTERN CAROLINA
NORTH CAROLINA DRAMA

NORTH CAROLINA DRAMA

with plays by

William Norment Cox

John W. Parker

Wilbur Stout

Thomas Wolfe

Bernice Kelly Harris

Charles Edward Eaton

Frances Gray Patton

Fred Koch, Jr.

and two comedies by Paul Green

Edited with an Introduction by

RICHARD WALSER

GARRETT & MASSIE   •   INCORPORATED   •   RICHMOND

1956

Library of Congress Catalog Card Number 56-8533
MANUFACTURED IN THE UNITED STATES OF AMERICA

PREFACE

THIS VOLUME IS INTENDED as a companionate volume to my two earlier published collections, *North Carolina Poetry* and *North Carolina in the Short Story.* For the reader, the editor hopes that the three present a fairly composite view of a regional literature. A book of essays would, of course, make the picture more unbroken. The novel, alas, cannot be anthologized.

A longer than usual Introduction has been provided for this collection; for the history of drama in North Carolina cannot be indicated by any reasonable number of short plays. For one thing, the one-acter as a literary type is of rather recent days, while the story of our drama reaches back hundreds of years. For another, the varied aspects of the theatre must be cited in order to show just what relationship the short play has to the whole. If the Introduction is still hardly more than a summary, it is—I believe—the first time that a general essay on the subject has been attempted.

When Frederick H. Koch died in 1944, North Carolina passed from one period in her drama history to another. Perhaps it is well, from this distance in time, to pause and consider and recapitulate—and also to see, if we can, in what directions the future lies. Through accumulation of data and in its endeavor to point out trends, the Introduction has tried to do this for the reader.

The ten plays which follow the Introduction are all from the Koch era. Though other short plays have been written in North Carolina at other times and under other influences, none of them are so characteristic of the state as those inspired by the little professor in Chapel Hill. Five of the ten are taken from Koch's *Carolina Folk-Plays* (1941); three were published elsewhere under his editorship; Paul Green's "The No 'Count Boy" is a ninth; and Charles Edward Eaton's "Sea Psalm" has never before been printed. While I conferred with Professor Samuel Selden regarding the selection of the ten, the final responsibility for their choice is my own.

v

If this book were the sort to be graced with a dedication, it should certainly be inscribed to the memory of that great teacher, "Proff" Koch. I sat in his classes and tried to write plays. That I, or any other student, did not succeed was never his fault. The wonderful thing is that so many did.

R. W.

Department of English
North Carolina State College
Raleigh, 15 March 1956

vi

CONTENTS

NORTH CAROLINA DRAMA

INTRODUCTION

The Story of Drama in North Carolina

THOUGH DISTANT FROM the theatrical centers of America, the state of North Carolina has a history of drama which reaches back several centuries. For most of that time, in fact until the arrival of Professor Frederick H. Koch at Chapel Hill in 1918, the years are uneven, especially in the composition of plays. Yet at an early date, traveling companies of professional actors were in the colony, and the interest in drama which our forebears had inherited from their English ancestors was kept alive. If an earnest movement in the writing of plays had to wait, perhaps it is well, for when it did come, it sprang forth vigorously almost in one leap. That first stride was a sure one; it left deep impressions in the cultural soil of North Carolina; it has abided. With it, a new life came to the tradition of theatrical production which began in the last half of the eighteenth century.

A FEW EARLY NAMES. The first footnote which connects the history of the theatre with North Carolina has to do with an English comedian, Anthony Alston, strolling player and composer of light opera. In 1702 on a voyage along the coast he was washed ashore during "a frightful Storm" off Cape Fear. He stayed with his rescuers for a month and then went on his way. Records do not tell us whether, on dull evenings, he entertained his frontier hosts with speeches from his comedy roles.

Even so, the earliest important connection of North Carolina with the history of American drama is not with the theatre itself, but with a playwright. In the spring of 1759, a 22-year-old Philadelphian came to North Carolina. Along with him he brought the first pages of a play he was writing, *The Prince of Parthia*. Thomas Godfrey took out time from his business as a mercantile agent and, in the little seaport town of Wilmington during the summer and autumn, completed his tragedy and then sent it north to be acted. Production was delayed, but years later on April 24, 1767, it was presented at the New Theatre in Philadelphia. *The Prince of Parthia* is noted in the annals

1

of literary history as the first American drama on record to be published in America (1765), as well as the first one written by an American to be produced by professional actors. Though Shakespeare provides the blank verse pattern and the gruesome events take place in ancient Persia, this first American play is a commendable effort. Godfrey was not destined to see his tragedy acted out. He died of a fever in North Carolina in 1763 and was buried in the old graveyard of the Church of St. James in the heart of Wilmington.

After Godfrey's death, dramatic composition languished till 1798, when Alexander Martin, ex-Governor of North Carolina, wrote a brief patriotic colloquy spoken by Genius and Columbus and titled *A New Scene Interesting to the Citizens of the United States of America*. Martin's poetic piece was designed as a tag to Thomas Morton's historical play *Columbus*, a popular attraction of the American stage and the first play in the English language in which the explorer appeared as a character. At the time of writing the epilogue, Martin, then a Senator, wished to spur the spirit of American nationality threatened by clannish factions. The title page informs that it was "performed with applause" in the Philadelphia theatre.

EARLY PROFESSIONAL COMPANIES. Though Charleston and Williamsburg had theatrical performances in the first half of the eighteenth century, the first record of actors in North Carolina carries the date 1768, in which year Governor William Tryon wrote from his seat at Brunswick on the Cape Fear to the Bishop of London in the interest of a young actor, Mr. Gifford, who was "engaged with a company of comedians" playing in that territory. Gifford had become wearied of the uncertain life of the theatre and wished to take holy orders in England, then return to North Carolina to instruct the youth. Tryon was not sure, however, that the Bishop would take a member of the stage into the church. As Gifford was under contract to the company in Brunswick, the Bishop probably never acted upon the petition. Tryon insisted that Gifford was "the best player on the American stage."

For the most part, the early companies had to be contented with makeshift staging; theatre buildings were few. At Edenton, for instance, performances were held in the large assembly room on the second floor of the handsome courthouse (standing today). A 1769 map of Halifax shows a "Play House," likely the first in the state; we have no information concerning its architecture. By 1787 there were facilities for an "elegant theatre" in Wilmington. Elsewhere, at New Bern and Fayetteville, strolling players performed in taverns and on improvised stages in public buildings.

Records for the early companies are sparse. In 1787 a group played Edenton with little success, and at Halifax a performance of Dryden's *The Spanish Friar* was cancelled when only five tickets had been sold by sundown. The players staged Molière's *The Miser* at New Bern. Of the performers Judge James Iredell wrote: "I never was so disgusted in my life. They are a most execrable set . . . and the great Mr. Smith appeared to me the greatest blockhead I ever saw. This opinion was pretty general." Nor was Iredell more pleased with *The Spanish Friar* when "two of the actors (Kidd and McGrath) fought behind the scenes; the stage was soon invaded by a crowd of people; the curtain was down at the time." A dramatic production in North Carolina in the eighteenth century was not without the action, excitement, and bombast characteristic of the frontier.

Indeed the life of an actor was a hard one. In 1793 John Bignall, joint manager of the Virginia Company which had toured both North and South Carolina, spoke a "New Prologue" to the entr'acte entertainment *Bucks! Have at Ye All*. In it he tells of the experiences of a traveling player in America. While his lot had not been easy, he was not entirely without gratitude to the Carolinas. In part, he said:

> To either Carolina, praise is due,
> Although from both with some disgrace I flew.
> 'Though in both I merited applause,
> Some queer ones talk'd of decency and laws.

In 1787 the American Company of Comedians performed in Wilmington, and during the following year they moved upstate and were in competition with other acting groups playing such towns as New Bern, Edenton, Windsor, Tarboro and Hillsboro. Then and for decades afterwards, the fare was primarily Addison,

Congreve, Dryden, Farquhar, Sheridan, Shakespeare, and other popular British dramatists of the seventeenth and eighteenth centuries; there was only an occasional piece from the pen of an American playwright. North Carolina produced no grist for the dramatic mill.

AMATEUR GROUPS. Whatever the fare or however inadequate the production, the strolling players left their mark on the communities they visited. Wherever the theatre went, there were left behind those who were inspired to emulate the professionals and to try their hands at amateur performances. As early as 1786 the students at the Hillsboro Academy were acting out dialogues. In 1793 the boys of the New Bern Academy, meeting in Tryon's Palace, gave "a dramatic piece in ridicule of scholastic pedantry"; one of the youthful actors was 15-year-old William Gaston, who was later to become a prominent statesman and the author of North Carolina's official anthem. The following year Thomas Pitt Irving, preacher and teacher, wrote an original skit for the students to perform at New Bern. On the other hand, when the two literary societies gave full-length plays at the commencement exercises at the University of North Carolina in 1797 as a method of speech training, William R. Davie protested and banned any such future activity.

Amateur theatricals became popular especially among the young gentlemen of the towns. In Edenton, on the departure of the troupe in 1787, the budding swells made immediate plans to distinguish themselves in the art. The first well-organized association, however, seems to have been in Wilmington, where the Thalians, a dramatic society which with several interruptions has been continued until the present time, was formed about 1788. Five years later "the Gentlemen of Fayetteville" presented a benefit play to raise money to repair the State House there. Also in 1793, to aid the local academy, the gay blades of Warrenton gave a Fourth of July performance of Susannah Centlivre's A Bold Stroke for a Wife. By 1804 the Raleigh Thespian Society was busy with "a Play or two," also benefiting the town academy. Two years later Halifax had a couple of rival amateur groups. The Salisbury Thespian Society, organized in 1812, not only raised money for its academy by producing plays;

it also ran a legalized lottery which cornered substantial financial resources for its pet project.*

FIRST DOMESTIC PLAYWRIGHTS. Perhaps within these early amateur organizations, some budding actor and writer was prompted to dash off an original script for his fellows. It is reasonable to think that this may have happened. If so, the record has not come down to us.

With the exception of Godfrey and Martin, whose efforts were hardly indigenous, local talent in playwriting began in 1809 when Everard Hall, a Virginia lawyer residing temporarily in North Carolina probably at Halifax, wrote *Nolens Volens; or The Biter Bit*. Published in New Bern by John S. Pasteur, it was called "the first *dramatic* performance, composed in North Carolina" by the editor of the *Raleigh Star,* who clearly did not know about Godfrey's work of a half century earlier. Of his play, Hall says that its "pages were written at night, for the sake of relaxation alone, without the smallest expectation of obtruding them on a discerning, but liberal and enlightened public." An undistinguished comedy of English life, it is concerned with varied love affairs reminiscent of eighteenth-century farce. The Epilogue tells, mistakenly, that with this play

> The Comic Muse long chain'd to Britain's shore
> At length has cross'd th' Atlantic's boist'rous roar,
> On plumy wings she leaves her sea-girt Isle,
> On Carolina's happy shores to smile.
> Clad in a homely garb, a *homespun* dress,
> She hopes her precepts will not please the less.

The Comic Muse, however, had been sporting in America long before this.

In 1823, another out-of-stater, schoolmaster Joseph Hutton of Philadelphia, arrived in New Bern to set up classes. Before coming to North Carolina, he had written quite a number of plays. In New Bern, we are told, he continued his playwriting with "a melodrama entitled *The Falls of Niagara,* and a trage-

---

*For a full discussion of this period, see Archibald Henderson, *North Carolina: The Old North State and the New* (1941).

dy on the murder of Colonel Sharp of Kentucky." Neither of them was published.

North Carolina's first native playwright was the prominent but eccentric Lemuel Sawyer of Camden County. Born in 1777, he early entered politics and represented the First North Carolina District in Congress for a number of terms. In May, 1824, he writes in his *Autobiography*, he "vamped up a manuscript comedy that I had laying by me, called Blackbeard, and paid a visit to my wife in Washington." With the help of his friends in Congress, including Speaker Henry Clay, he garnered more than sufficient subscriptions to pay for its printing, which was shortly ordered.

Blackbeard, by any but the most obstinate definition, is the first North Carolina play. It is the first play written by a native of the state, the first with North Carolina characters and with a North Carolina setting.* In spite of loose construction, the comedy is still highly readable and delightfully entertaining. It is surprising that it has never been produced, though there have been erroneous statements concerning its staging. The major plot relates the love affair of a certain Candid and his failure to be re-elected to Congress—the latter situation closely autobiographical. In the minor action two sharpers plan and consummate the fleecing of four Currituck County louts who hope to profit from the recovery of pirate Blackbeard's treasure. Sawyer is expert in satirizing the rustic coastal people of his day. Here are a few lines from a scene in which Mrs. Muley is told to expect a guest for dinner:

MRS. MULEY. Some dinner! Why, you know we've got nothing but pork and collards.

MULEY. But that won't do for Mr. Rogers; we must have something fresh; you must knock down the old rooster.

MRS. MULEY. The old rooster! Why, that's the only cock we've got on the land, and he'll be too tough.

MULEY. Never mind; boil him four hours; he'll make a good pot of broth, with comb, gills, and spurs; I'll buy a main of them tomorrow, if you want. Come, hurry, hurry; I expect old Rogers

---

*It was handsomely reissued in facsimile, with a full introduction, by the State Department of Archives and History, Raleigh, in 1952.

every minute;—set the dogs after him; I must go and get a turn
of wood.

MRS. MULEY. Yes, honey;—Here, boy, here; Tess, Tess, Tess.
(*Running off. Exit.*)

MULEY (*looking after*). Yonder he goes, head him;—(*running
out*) Tess, Tess-a-boy, hooye! (*Exit.*)

After this ridiculous colloquy, Sawyer appends the note: "If the
above scene is too vulgar for representation, it may be omitted."

Encouraged by the financial success of *Blackbeard*, Sawyer
issued another play in 1824, with subscribers again paying the
printer's bill. *The Wreck of Honor*, subtitled "A Tragedy," is
a bawdy drama of Parisian *affaires d'amours*. A minor plot, com-
pletely severed from the main one, concerns an American naval
officer in Paris and the attraction his forthright character has for
jaded Gallic noblewomen. *The Wreck of Honor* is a pretty
worthless effort.

A second native playwright of antebellum days was William
Henry Rhodes, born in Windsor in 1822. Educated at Princeton and Harvard, he accompanied his father to Galveston, Texas,
when the latter was appointed United States consul there. Un-
doubtedly he was familiar with the legend that Theodosia Burr,
daughter of the infamous Aaron, met her death at pirate hands
off Nags Head in 1812. His blank-verse play *Theodosia, The
Pirate's Prisoner* (1846) transfers the scene to Galveston where
Pierre Lafitte offers her love, but the heroic Theodosia refuses
and takes her own life. Rhodes' tragedy appeared as the second
section of his volume of poems *The Indian Gallows*.

THE PLATINUM AGE OF THE PROFESSIONAL THE-
ATRE. Shortly after the beginning of the nineteenth century
until the capitulation to the motion pictures 130 years later, North
Carolina passed through a period of an ascending and frequently
glorious professional theatre. The state, it must be candidly em-
phasized, was not unlike other parts of rural America. Everywhere in the young country, the inhabitants were eager for entertainment, and companies of actors and other performers set out
to provide it. Some of the most illustrious names of the theatrical
world visited North Carolina's small cities, and troupes of less

renown were constantly on the move. The need for a native drama was never apparent. In antebellum times, four towns usually made up the circuit of the professionals: Raleigh, New Bern, Fayetteville, and Wilmington. Drama was not the only offering of the entertainers.

Even before the turn of the century, there are records of sleight-of-hand performances in the State Capitol building in Raleigh. There in 1803 Davenport and Street's Wax Figures were on exhibit at the courthouse. Soon after the Masonic theatre was opened in 1815, a troupe of professionals delighted the citizens with "upwards of over 260" of the most wonderful and curious performances in Tumbling." A stock company arrived in 1818 with several plays. Five years later some English actors stayed for three weeks, among their offerings *The Forty Thieves,* a "Grand Operatical Romance." Popular plays of the day which Raleigh saw were *Pizarro* and *Damon and Pythias.*

Sometimes the theatre did not please the more provincial residents. One who signed himself "Abner" wrote in the *Raleigh Register* for March 7, 1823: "I cannot conceive that the charity of Corneille or Racine, is any apology for the lascivious French pantomine, or the sublime flights of Shakespeare, a defence of the obscene British comedy. Whoever has read Shakespeare cannot deny but that his low drollery and buffoonery are highly exceptional, and his brilliant efforts tarnished by improper and indecorous incidents."

Performances at the Raleigh theatres were not constant. Often, except for the productions of the amateurs, the playhouses would be dark for years on a stretch. Until after the Civil War, the companies usually timed their engagements to coincide with the meetings of the Legislature. One in 1835 remained for six weeks. A nostalgic enthusiast of the theatre wishes he might have been in Raleigh in 1849 for Signor Spinetto and His One Hundred Learned Canary Birds and Java Sparrows; or could have seen The Great Rhigas, Prince of Equilibrists from Paris; or bought a ticket in 1854 for Parrow and Company's Great Southern Burlesque Opera and Ballet Troupe; or again in 1854 been present at the Yarbrough Hotel for Madame Amelia Siminski, advertised as "The Greatest and most wonderful Flutist of the Age." On October 10, 1860, in a tent erected in Moore Square, Raleigh patrons saw *Our American Cousin,* the same play Lincoln was seeing when he was assassinated. The last entertainment to play the capital city before the war was later that year when a panorama of life-size figures stayed for two weeks: Moving Mirror of Bunyan Tableaux, a presentation of 60 scenes from *Pilgrim's Progress.*

New Bern, about 1804, had a Theatrical Society composed of "the Gentlemen of the town" and, soon after the building of the theatre in the Masonic Temple, performed a play there. In 1812 they acted out several scenes from *Hamlet.* The professionals came later. In 1820 a notice in the local newspaper advertised M. G. Lewis' *Adelgitha, or The Fruits of a Single Error,* followed by *The Wag of Windsor.* Three years afterwards, *Richard III* cost the playgoer $1 for upper and lower boxes, 50¢ in the pit, and 25¢ admission to the colored gallery. There were many performances in 1823 and 1824 when New Bern had a population of only about 4,000. Letters on the merits of the drama, both pro and con, appeared in the press. Though incomplete newspaper files tell only a partial story of the antebellum New Bern theatre, we can believe that it was reasonably continuous. *Hamlet* was being performed there in 1850. In 1863 the Federal press, set up during the military occupation, issued what is now a very rare item: *Il Recrutio, a Comic Opera, as Originally Produced by Members of the Forty-Fourth Regiment, in Barracks, at Newbern, N. C. . . . before Major General Foster, His Family and Staff.* Words were by Frederick Jackson, Zenas T. Haines, and William G. Reed, with music arranged by Charles C. Chickering. This lively little musical tells the story of a Northern soldier from the time of his enlistment in Boston through the trials of army life in New Bern and Plymouth. It is clearly a domestic product.

More fortunate than most North Carolina towns, New Bern had a handsome building during all the nineteenth century. The theatre of the Masonic Temple began showing motion pictures in 1917, and remains the oldest theatre in the United States still in regular use.

Professional actors came to Fayetteville before 1824 and returned there off and on for the next many decades. A typical troupe was Shadgett's company, which arrived in 1829 from Raleigh with plays advertised for Monday, Wednesday, and Friday evenings. On opening night, January 17, Mrs. Charles Kemble's *The Day after the Wedding* was presented, ending with a sailor's hornpipe and other miscellaneous acts. Such an evening's entertainment is an example of the British and American custom of the age, when a main play was followed by an afterpiece usually a short farce, with recitations, music, and dancing between the two. Crowds gathered at Fayetteville in 1850 when the stupendous extravaganza titled *Great Original Panorama of the Mississippi River and Indian Life, and Calhoun's Funeral Procession in Charleston* was unrolled in a continuous picture 1,800 yards long, accompanied by music and a lecture.

The panorama, like this, was one of the most popular of the stage businesses in the mid-century. Minstrels, variety shows, concerts artists, magicians, Scotch Pipers, and Swiss bell-ringers also came to North Carolina and competed with the actors' companies. The average Tar Heel clamored for the spectacular, and he got it. Plate-dancers, jugglers, trained dogs, sword-swallowers, glass-blowers, Siamese twins, ventriloquists, and Juvenile Comedians strode the North Carolina stage in the nineteenth century. A favorite attraction in the state was Colonel Chaffin, "the original American Tom Thumb," 27 pounds, 19 years old, 27 inches tall.

During this time the Moravians in Salem were troubled by the traveling performers and often exacted promises that no showing having a low moral quality be staged.

Charlotte seems to have been a mecca for the odd and curious. At the courthouse of the Queen City in 1855 the Mecklenburgers could view a combined attraction of The Infant Drummers, The American Mocking Bird, and Mr. James Sinclair Baker, imitator. Later in the same year Charlotte was entertained at Everett's Pavilion of Science and Art. The Celebrated African Twins were showing there at Spring's Hall in 1857.

By all odds, however, the city with the richest theatrical history in nineteenth-century North Carolina was Wilmington. Up until 1858 its fare was similar to that provided for Raleigh, New Bern, and Fayetteville. Even so, Wilmington was generally luckier than the others, for its easy access by sea brought into the town many stars who would not rough it upstate by the uncomfortable modes of transportation. Edwin Booth appeared there in 1850, and the great Joseph Jefferson a year later. The famed soprano, Mme. Anna Bishop, gave a recital in 1853, and the world-renowned Norwegian violinist, Ole Bull, paid a visit in 1856. On October 12, 1858, Thalian Hall, then as now one of the most beautiful theatres in America, was opened, and professional companies put Wilmington on the same circuit as New Orleans, Savannah, Charleston, and Richmond. On opening night the well-known Marchant's company staged Tobin's *The Honey Moon*. In its month's engagement, Wilmingtonians saw such classics as *The Taming of the Shrew* and *Macbeth*. Later Marchant brought an opera company with standard repertoire to the port city. The French Opera Comique and Operette appeared there in 1860.

During the war years, when professional entertainment all but disappeared from the inland towns, Wilmington had its most lavish theatrical era. The winter of 1863-64, at the height of the blockade and with military troops crowding this railroad terminus, the season was the greatest in the city's history. There were 285 theatrical entertainments in three different auditoriums; Shakespeare, Boucicault, and Hugo were often on the boards; and other favorites were Lord Byron's *Werner* and Mrs. Henry Wood's ever popular *East Lynne*. After the fall of Fort Fisher, there was a drastic decrease, but even in May, 1866, Carter's Grand Combination Troupe was showing there with "Fifteen Beautiful Young Ladies." The humorist Artemus Ward appeared in the same year. *Under the Gaslight*, by North Carolina native Augustin Daly, arrived in 1869 with "Engine and Cars and Railroad on the Stage."

For the next several decades, some of the greatest names of the stage visited Wilmington. The incomparable Edwin Forrest acted *King Lear* in 1870. In the following years Wilmingtonians saw P. T. Barnum's General Tom Thumb and His Midgets, and Buffalo Bill and his Wild West Plays with "real Indians." Joseph Jefferson returned in 1880 as *Rip Van Winkle* and again in 1884 in Sheridan's *The Rivals* with the noted Mrs. John Drew as Mrs. Malaprop. In 1894 Otis Skinner as Shylock and Mme. Modjeska as Portia acted *The Merchant of Venice*, and Richard Mansfield appeared as *Beau Brummel*. After the turn of the century, during a flush of religious presentations, *Parsifal,* advertised as "a sacred festival play," was twice given in 1907. The 1911-12 season accounted for 114 performances.

The story of the Wilmington theatre was matched somewhat in other North Carolina towns,* but without the intensity and frequency of professional entertainment in Wilmington. After 1870 the stock companies usually remained only a week, though the musical and operatic offerings increased. Soon, in between the stock engagements, came the nationally known stars, and later the "hit" plays with their own stars and their own scenery. Before the turn of the century the North Carolina playgoer was enchanted with such dramas as *Ten Nights in a Bar Room, Camille, Leah the Forsaken,* and *The Hidden Hand.* In the 1890's, after the introduction of electricity, musical comedy troupes were especially welcome.

The numerous Opera Houses which were building throughout the state in the previous decades provided for these attractions handsomely. When Tucker Hall opened in Raleigh in 1867, it had a "complete set of eleven scenes and 26 wings—all done in the best style" by a Philadelphia "scenic artist." Charlotte had an Opera House in 1874; the small piedmont town of Lexington, in 1885. The Opera House in Goldsboro, built in 1881, was supplied "with gas, opera chairs, a first-class stage, twelve changes of scenery, and a Mathushek grand piano. Dimensions of the building 56 x 110 feet." The stage had a curtain opening of 27 feet, and there were "four comfortable dressing rooms." Its seating capacity was 900. For the inaugural performance on December 21, Miss Claire Scott, English actress, appeared in *The Lady of Lyon, or Love and Pride.* On Christmas Eve, the fourth and final night of her engagement, she portrayed Shakespeare's Juliet. Railroads advertised reduced rates to attract out-of-town patrons. Thereafter, many traveling companies stopped over in Goldsboro, and amateur groups frequently mounted the stage of

———

*The excellent and detailed articles by Donald J. Rulfs on the Wilmington, Raleigh, and Fayetteville theatre (*North Carolina Historical Review,* April, July, October, 1951; July, 1952; and April, 1954) have provided much of the material for this section. Unfortunately there have been no comprehensive published studies of the theatre in North Carolina cities like Durham, Greensboro, Winston-Salem, Salisbury, Charlotte, and Asheville.

the Opera House with their offerings. Ziegfeld's money-makers Anna Held and Billie Burke paid calls at the Opera House, but for these stars the proper Goldsboro mothers kept their daughters at home.

An odd establishment for amateurs of the day was the third floor of the architectural freak, Körner's Folly, at the village of Kernersville in Forsyth County. Frequently the music room at the top of the house was converted into a "little theatre," with Mrs. Körner's original plays enacted by the local residents against scenery painted by the eccentric, wealthy Mr. Körner.

Throughout North Carolina in the early 1900's, popular plays were *Monte Cristo, Ben Hur,* and *Quo Vadis.* Cahn's *Theatrical Guide for 1904-1905* listed twenty-nine North Carolina towns having "opera houses." Among them were Beaufort, Mt. Airy, and Gastonia. Gilbert and Sullivan operas were in demand, and the Ben Greet Players came along with their repertoire of Shakespeare. Eva Tanguay, the most sought-after musical "queen" of the day, was in Wilmington in 1905. Later, Lillian Russell and her variety show also played the town. In 1916, when Maude Adams toured North Carolina in Barrie's *The Little Minister,* large and enthusiastic audiences greeted her. By the 1920's the smaller towns were treated by Redpath Chautauqua to such standard fare as Booth Tarkington and Harry Leon Wilson's *The Man from Home,* Martin's *Smilin' Through,* and De Koven's *Robin Hood.* Touring companies brought *Abie's Irish Rose* in the middle twenties; in the same years there were such horror melodramas as *The Cat and the Canary, The Bat, The Monster,* and *The Gorilla.* About this time Charles Winter Wood of Greensboro organized the first professional stock company in America composed entirely of Negroes. Keith's Vaudeville was established in many of the cities like Asheville and Greensboro. . . . But the theatrical pattern was already in jeopardy.

Even then, the movies were quickly changing the picture for actors, playwrights, producers, and playgoers. By 1930 the stock companies had all but disappeared. Lexington, as an example of the smaller towns, had a dozen touring stage attractions in 1923-24; by the end of the decade it had none. Even the perennial *Blossom Time* had called a halt. What injury the low cost of movie admissions did not wrack on the traveling actors, the Great

Depression did. By 1930 the professional companies were so rare—and how quickly they had become so!—that when Maude Adams, making her final tour, came to Greensboro with Otis Skinner in 1931 in *The Merchant of Venice,* it was almost as if a ghost had arisen. At this time only the most heralded plays could hope for success. Ticket demand was heavy for Marc Connelly's *The Green Pastures* in Winston-Salem in 1933, and for the Greensboro performance of Katharine Cornell and Basil Rathbone in *The Barretts of Wimpole Street* in 1934; but few patrons turned out for such mediocre entertainment as the 1934 Winston-Salem showing of Leonore Ulric in *Pagan Lady,* or the 1935 Durham engagement of the Earl Carroll Vanities. In 1936 Raleigh had a full house for the Pulitzer Prize drama, *The Old Maid,* with Judith Anderson and Helen Mencken. By 1939 bookings were gradually shifting to the college campuses, for in that year Eva Le Gallienne acted her memorable role in Ibsen's *Hedda Gabler* at the Duke University auditorium instead of a downtown Durham theatre. Tallulah Bankhead fared excellently in the local movie palaces when she played the "whistle stops" of North Carolina in 1941 with *The Little Foxes.*

Following the inactivity of the World War II years, the professionals attempted sporadic comebacks. A favorite like *Oklahoma!* sold out its tour of the state in 1949, but generally the road companies met with only meager reception. By the time the tooted Broadway plays reached North Carolina, the original stars had withdrawn and the production cut. Disillusioned diehards among the ticket-buyers almost gave up after shabby presentations of *Kiss Me, Kate* and *The Streetcar Named Desire* in the early 1950's. In spite of such fiascos, mobs stormed the doors of Memorial Hall in Chapel Hill for such pre-Broadway mouthfuls as the 1951 reading of George Bernard Shaw's *Don Juan in Hell* by Charles Boyer, Charles Laughton, Sir Cedric Hardwicke, and Agnes Moorehead; or the showing of Stephen Vincent Benét's *John Brown's Body* in 1952 with Tyrone Power, Judith Anderson, and Raymond Massey. These two productions showed that North Carolinians, like other Americans far from the large centers, were still theatre-minded and would support professional companies of high caliber. Even then, however, the imperative necessity of living theatre enacted by seeming experts was diminishing; the appetite for such provender was being amply satisfied by a native drama and an assembly of local actors who often outshone their so-called betters from the metropolitan areas.

PLAYWRIGHTS HERE AND THERE. The dewy attempts at dramatic composition by Godfrey, Hall, Sawyer, and Rhodes did not, as one might suppose, lead to increased playwriting activity in North Carolina in the 1800's. The three quarters of a century after Rhodes' effort in 1846 are distressingly indifferent as far as local dramatists go. Only a few names peep timorously from the creative wastelands.

For Augustin Daly and the de Milles, North Carolina can hardly take credit. It would be first-rate if she could, for they were destined to leave their names ineradicably on the pages of theatrical history.

Daly was born in the Washington County village of Plymouth in 1838, the same year his father, a sea captain, settled there to engage in the lumbering business. Neither of the child's parents were of North Carolina heritage. Three years later, when the father died, Elizabeth Daly moved to Norfolk, where the youngster was subsequently to see his first play. His youth was spent in New York, and there his fabulous career began. As both manager and playwright, he was a dominant figure of the American stage in the 1870-90 period, when his productions were noted for their scenic splendor and famous stars. He operated several theatres in London in addition to his American ventures. Though "author or adapter of more than 90 plays, most of which were radically altered from the original French or German, and often given an American setting," Daly is best remembered for a trio of melodramas: *Under the Gaslight, Horizon,* and *Divorce.* He is frequently called America's first cosmopolitan manager-dramatist.

The story of the de Mille family is somewhat different. In 1850 Thomas A. de Mille moved from Connecticut to the old riverside town of Washington in Beaufort County, where a son, Henry Churchill de Mille, was born in 1853. When the lad went to New York to study for the ministry, he was dazzled by the theatre and soon had sidetracked his energies to the stage. With David Belasco he collaborated on such successful plays as *The*

Wife, The Charity Ball, and *Lord Chumley.* The two sons, William Churchill de Mille and Cecil Blount de Mille, chose to follow in their father's footsteps. The former (1878-1955) was born in Washington, the three-year-younger Cecil in New England, though both always spoke of eastern North Carolina as "home"—naturally, since they spent most of their boyhoods there. As a young man, William wrote four plays for the New York stage: *Strongheart, The Warrens of Virginia, The Land of the Free,* and *The Woman.* Cecil, too, was actor, dramatist, and producer in the first ten years of his professional career, during which time he was associated with his brother and David Belasco. By 1914, when the infant motion picture industry was stirring vigorously in California, the brothers were in Hollywood. First Cecil went out to see what was going on, and eventually persuaded William to follow. From the beginning they were vastly successful as producers and directors, and occasionally prepared their own scenarios. Among the older brother's hits were *Craig's Wife* and *Passion Flower.* Cecil B. de Mille's name is almost synonymous with the colossal and the spectacular. From his father, who never lost the devout feelings which had for a while directed him toward the ministry, he inherited a deep religious sense evinced in his most glittering productions such as *The Ten Commandments, The King of Kings, The Sign of the Cross, The Crusades,* and *Samson and Delilah.*

The prolific writer of romantic fiction, "Christian Reid" of Salisbury, published *Under the Southern Cross* in 1900. A patriotic play with action in 1863, it had its setting at "Warrington Court, an old Southern mansion in the country."

The pomp of early Hollywood was not confined to the photoplays of Cecil B. de Mille. In 1915 Thomas Dixon, a native of Cleveland County, produced the scenario for the filming by D. W. Griffith of *The Birth of a Nation,* the industry's first large spectacle. Screening was based on Dixon's book *The Clansman.* Better known as a novelist and lecturer, Dixon found time to write nine plays, most of them taken from his own previously published stories. Their titles are *The Clansman* (1905), *The One Woman* (1906), *The Traitor* (1908), *Sins of the Father* (1910), *The Almighty Dollar* (1912), *Old Black Joe* (1912), *The Leopard's Spots* (1913), *The Red Dawn* (1919), and *A*

Man of the People (1920). Three of them, *The Clansman, The Traitor,* and *The Leopard's Spots,* are Ku Klux Klan problem-dramas based on North Carolina material. Dixon's plays toured the country successfully, and many productions of them came to North Carolina. When *The Leopard's Spots* appeared in Wilmington on October 16, 1913, Dixon proclaimed in a curtain speech that the Wilmington race riots of 1898 had given him "the idea upon which the whole structure of the book and play rests." At the Opera House in Goldsboro, the Dixon dramas were especially favored. One old playgoer there recalled that in *The Clansman* a horse was used on the stage of the second-story auditorium. How did he get there? "Easy," said stageman Fred Johnson, "we just marched him up the front steps." Between *The Birth of a Nation* and 1923, Dixon wrote six additional photoplays for the Hollywood studios.

In 1907 Mrs. Jane Yancey Harris of Henderson published a six-act melodrama of current life as she thought it ought to be represented on the stage, its title *Thoroughly Tested.*

A fresh cadence was sounded by the Summer School Dramatic Club at Chapel Hill on July 4, 1912, when a historical play was presented using such personages from the past as Governor Tryon, Edmund Fanning, and Herman Husband. At the suggestion that the North Carolina chronicles could provide dramatic material in bounteous measure, Adolph Vermont of Smithfield had written *Esther Wake, or The Spirit of the Regulators* especially for the occasion. Perhaps the playwright knew, or perhaps he did not, that he was forerunner of things to come.

PROFF KOCH AND THE PLAYMAKERS. The arrival of Frederick H. Koch at Chapel Hill in 1918 was a felicitous event on many scores. First, and most notable, was the exuberant, infectious personality of "Proff," as he was always called. North Carolina was lucky to get Proff. But Proff was lucky too. In retrospect, it seems almost as if the planets were right in the heavens. Second to the irrepressible Proff was the situation he found at Chapel Hill. He was invited to the University of North Carolina by Dr. Edwin Greenlaw, noted Spenserian and head of the Department of English there. Greenlaw had heard of Koch's work in North Dakota and felt that such a man could extract the unearthed drama in North Carolina soil. Unconsciously, perhaps, Greenlaw had prepared for the arrival of Koch. For many years he had been diffusing on the campus a burning respect for scholarship and good literature. Even then the University was turning into the great institution it was destined to be. Another figure on the campus, who along with Greenlaw was contributing to the germinating essence of the place, was philosopher Horace Williams. A Socratic questioner, he was continually preaching "that the material is vacuous and nebulous. The mind and the spirit are the imperishable citadels. Nothing is true because it is accepted as being true. Think! Investigate! There is no compromise. Never! Truth is the unravished bride of the Highest-Elect." Students wandering from the classes of Greenlaw to those of Williams heard and believed. Then Koch came.

A third influence had bearing on Proff's success. During the 1910's American drama was just beginning to break from the traditions which had fettered it since the time of Thomas Godfrey. Lonely brave voices had been scarcely heard in the grand sweep of conventionalism. But by 1918 such dramatists as Eugene O'Neill had spoken so loudly that they could no longer be ignored. In the next half dozen years American drama escaped into a freedom it had hardly dreamed of. Realistic American life, previously thought improper for representation on the stage, somehow came to the fore as dramatic grist. Koch, a participant in this new movement, was at the right place at the right time with the right associates, the right material, and the right students to work with. The confluence effected almost immediate achievement.

Frederick H. Koch was born in Covington, Kentucky, September 12, 1877.* The drama attracted him when he was a lad, much to the disappointment of his practical German father. He attended Caterals Methodist College in Cincinnati and graduated in 1900 from Ohio Wesleyan University. At the University of North Dakota, to which he went as an English Instructor in 1905, he staged plays by Shakespeare, Sheridan, and Barrie. It

*See the short biography *Frederick Henry Koch: Pioneer Playmaker* (University of North Carolina Library, 1954) by Samuel Selden and Mary Tom Sphangos; also *Carolina Play-Book*, Memorial Issue, 1944.

was at Harvard, where he earned a master's degree in 1909, that Koch came in touch with George Pierce Baker, famed drama teacher, and with the experimental work of the German and Irish playwrights. In 1916 he presented his first bill of original plays written by his students. Greenlaw was attracted to what Koch was doing. On coming to Chapel Hill, Proff taught Shakespeare, and Comparative and Modern Drama; but his principal efforts went into the new class in playwriting. Thomas Wolfe, seventeen years old, was the only male member of that first class of September, 1918.

Proff's classes, then as later, were informal gatherings. When a student suggested an idea, the others dived into a discussion to help him elaborate it. The method was out-and-out cooperative, with Proff being merely the mentor. Then came the writing—and rewriting. "Write about the people you know," he constantly told his students. "Do not search for characters and plots from far away. They are all about you. Open your eyes. Right back there in your home community is a play. All you need to do is to see it, to put it down." Not only did Proff *believe* his students could write these plays; he *knew* they could. Every man and woman has the creative spark within him—that was his philosophy. And this dynamic faith in people, he somehow got across to those who sat about his table. It is not surprising that the young writers often accomplished more than they thought possible.

In March, 1919, in the auditorium of the old Chapel Hill High School came the first of the many bills of Carolina folkplays. Thomas Wolfe's "The Return of Buck Gavin" (reprinted in this volume) was acted, and also "When Witches Ride," a play by Elizabeth Lay (now Mrs. Paul Green) about superstitions in old Carolina. When each one-acter was finished, Proff came before the curtain, and the audience were asked their opinions. With Proff leading the discussion and the neophyte dramatists standing by, the spectators-participants pointed out strengths and weaknesses as they saw them. It was a routine Proff followed for the next 26 years.

Though never pretending to be a playwright himself, Proff was called on to write a play almost as soon as he hit Chapel Hill. The tercentenary of Sir Walter Raleigh's death came in

1918; and while a production to signal the anniversary could not be mounted for that year, the promoters felt that it was better late than never. *Raleigh, the Shepherd of the Ocean* by Frederick H. Koch was given in the capital city in 1920, a pageant-spectacle with drama, music, dancing, and choruses—500 persons participating. If rather old-fashioned in style, it set the pace for the many other dramas celebrating events in North Carolina history which Proff was later to supervise.

By 1919 Paul Green was back from soldiering in France, and other budding playwrights were busy at work, sustained by Proff's enthusiasm. In 1921 the Playmakers made their first tour of original plays out among the people of North Carolina. From the first it was Proff's dream that the University was to be only a central point from which dramatic lines would lead out to all parts of the state, the South, perhaps the nation and abroad. Eventually he was to see the dream come true. In 1925 the tours expanded to South Carolina, Georgia, and Virginia; two years later the Playmakers were in Maryland, Pennsylvania, and New York. The end was not in sight, and always Proff traveled with the actors and talked to the audience between the plays.

In 1918, too, he had set up the Bureau of Community Drama, an agency employing a field agent to assist in playmaking anywhere, everywhere. In 1924 he spearheaded the forming of the Carolina Dramatic Association, an organization of amateur groups working together and meeting one another and seeing each other's plays, especially at the annual spring drama festivals in Chapel Hill. Young scene designers, actors, and playwriters worked all winter in order to deserve an April visit to the Playmaker Theatre, the beautiful little building opened in 1925. It was the first playhouse in America dedicated to the writing and production of plays by, for, and about the *people*.

In 1928, after ten years of pioneer effort, Proff Koch sat down and took stock. Besides an influence and enthusiasm which he had exerted wherever he went or wherever his words were read, he could count the production, under his supervision, of 59 plays by 42 authors, one of them, Paul Green, a Pulitzer Prize winner in drama. Proff decided it was time to hold a Southern Regional Conference, to which he invited representatives from other states. Present for the Conference was the honored drama critic of the

New York Times, Brooks Atkinson, who wrote reflectively that "what Professor Koch has accomplished, not only at Chapel Hill, but through the state, is nothing short of extraordinary. He has . . . brought into existence a non-professional theatre with fine individual tradition, in spite of the fact that a quarter of its personnel graduates every year. It produces ably. It has a printed library of its own plays. And in Paul Green, who expounds philosophy at the university and writes prolifically on native themes, it has a graduate who may be conservatively described as a genius."

During the next fifteen years Proff's broad program in playmaking was not diminished. Gradually, however, he collected about him a group of skillful assistants; and he was left with more time for his congenial tasks of editing, writing, and teaching. Among his early helpers were George V. Denny, later to make his name as president of New York's Town Hall, and Hubert Heffner, who went from Chapel Hill to become a distinguished professor of the theatre. Samuel Selden came to Proff's staff in 1927, and he was joined by many others who, like Selden, had been stirred by Proff's gospel of the people's theatre.

One of Koch's ways of disseminating his gospel was through the publication of the best folk-plays written in his classes. A first book was issued in 1922, a second in 1924, and the third in 1928. They were collected as Carolina Folk-Plays in 1941. Carolina Folk Comedies was published in 1931, and American Folk Plays in 1939. Koch also edited Josephina Niggli's Mexican Folk Plays, Bernice Kelly Harris' Folk Plays of Eastern Carolina, and Kate Porter Lewis' Alabama Folk Plays. The first issue of his beloved Carolina Play-Book, a quarterly which was charmingly Proff's own personal journal, appeared in 1928.

The 1930's saw the first of the Playmaker-staged symphonic dramas, and the initiation of work in radio. With the beginning of the War, Proff settled back to the writing of endless letters to his adored students all over the world. If the golden days had temporarily passed, not so the affections of the old teacher's heart. In 1943 the remodeled Forest Theatre, later renamed the Koch Memorial Forest Theatre, was dedicated in Chapel Hill; and in December he gave his 39th reading of Dickens' A Christmas Carol. On August 16, 1944, he died at Miami Beach, where he was on vacation with his family. "He tried to swim in a sea which his heart was no longer young enough to fight," his biographers tell us, "and the man of action had to stop."

The list of those on whose lives Frederick H. Koch made a lasting impression is a long one. It includes the names of all those dramatists represented in the present collection; there are actors like Shepperd Strudwick, Lionel Stander, Whit Bissell, Eugenia Rawls, Marion Tatum, David Hooks, and Robert Carroll; entertainers like Kay Kyser; writers like Jonathan Daniels, LeGette Blythe, Betty Smith, Joseph Mitchell, and Foster Fitz-Simons. It includes thousands of young people who came to know him and blossom under his praise and confidence.

By the time Samuel Selden took over the job which Proff had relinquished, new emphases in the work of the Playmakers were already noticeable. The short folk-play, significant as its role had been in the development of dramatic composition, was somewhat in eclipse. The original full-length play was being stressed; Koch had supervised such forerunners as Fred Howard's *Sharecropper* and Noel Houston's *The Marauders*. Production and acting were assuming almost equal status with playwriting; student dramatists were being encouraged to develop whatever material they found at hand, regardless of its folk or non-folk origin. With these new trends, Selden was in sympathy, although he did not attempt to abandon those qualities which had brought fame to the Playmakers. Moreover, he strongly supported the Bureau of Community Drama and the Carolina Dramatic Association, which reached into the heart of North Carolina. With Koch's death, however, an age had passed. The theatre cannot live if it becomes static.

PAUL GREEN. The most noted product of the Koch movement, as we have seen, is Paul Green. While the lines cannot be sharply drawn, his career as a dramatist may roughly be separated into three chapters. At first the Koch gospel of the folk-play was strongly influential, and this period is characterized by the one act comedies, tragedies, and fantasies.* The

---

*See pages 104-105 of this volume; also the biography by Agatha Boyd Adams, *Paul Green of Chapel Hill* (University of North Carolina Library, 1951).

period was climaxed in 1927 when he was awarded the Pulitzer Prize for his full-length folk-play *In Abraham's Bosom*, a stark drama of a mulatto who is defeated by his own inadequacy and racial frustration in an attempt to educate the Negroes of his locality. *The Field God* (1927), which W. David Sievers in *Freud on Broadway* called "one of the truly tragic and Aeschylean works in American drama," presents a hopeless conflict between reason and psychic guilt feelings in Hardy Gilchrist, a prosperous white farmer living among the narrowly religious people in eastern North Carolina. *The House of Connelly* (1931), generally considered Green's best play dramaturgically, portrays the decadence of the aristocratic Southern planter class and the rise of the robust tenantry—a problem he soon re-explored in his novel *The Laughing Pioneer* (1932). All three plays had successful runs in New York.

A second chapter—for lack of a better term, we may call it the experimental period—came after a year in Europe on a Guggenheim fellowship. In Germany, Paul Green was particularly enchanted by the art theatre, and he began to think of writing plays which blended music, mass formations, ballet movements, and pantomime with *the drama of the people*. All of these, he hoped, would expand the accepted concepts of time and space on the stage. A conscious poetic aura diffuses the plays of this period. *Tread the Green Grass* (produced 1932) was labeled by the author "A Folk Fantasy in Two Parts, with Interludes, Music, Dumb-show, and Cinema"; this brilliantly imaginative dreamlike work, composed in folk terms, symbolizes the sin-obsessed South in its struggle between paganism and asceticism. *Roll, Sweet Chariot* (produced 1934, a revision of the earlier *Potter's Field*) is a play without intermission detailing a composite Negro community which is being destroyed by the encroaching "civilization" of the white man. *Shroud My Body Down* (premièred in Chapel Hill in 1934) is a Freudian dream-play with poetry and music; it outlines the emotional terrors of a North Carolina farm girl and her indistinguishable notions of religion and love. A fourth experimental drama was *The Enchanted Maze* (1935), announced as "a satire on the American educational system," but unluckily identified as closely paralleling certain situations at the University of North Carolina in the mid-'30s. *Johnny Johnson* (produced in New York in 1936) is an anti-war play with pleasant satirical asides criticizing the growing field of psychiatry. Paul Green's next play written for Broadway was a collaborative effort with Richard Wright on the latter's novel *Native Son* (1941), in which a race-conscious Negro in Chicago murders his white employer's daughter, is caught and condemned. In 1951 he made an adaptation of Ibsen's *Peer Gynt*, which starred the late John Garfield.

The symphonic dramas, of which *The Lost Colony* (1937) was the first, have been Paul Green's latest contribution to the history of American playwriting. In a very real way, his symphonic dramas are the culmination of those years of working in the field of the folk-play and the experimental theatre. Here at last, on a huge outdoor stage, he could deal with a big subject to his satisfaction. From the beginning, he conceived of *The Lost Colony* as no historical pageant of Sir Walter Raleigh's colonists, presenting scenes from the past, but a play with a definite story line, with warm living characters, and with a plot mounting to dramatic heights. Here he could employ music and dance and sweeping movements, and here he could see fulfilled his ideas of vast panoramic effects. Here, through history, he could tell the people in the audience of the American Dream.

Two years after the success of *The Lost Colony* on Roanoke Island, Fayetteville saw Green's *The Highland Call*, a symphonic drama of Flora Macdonald. A third, *The Common Glory*, with Thomas Jefferson its leading character, played its eighth summer at Williamsburg in 1955. In 1950 *Faith of Our Fathers*, about George Washington, began a two-season run in the National Capital. In 1953 his fifth symphonic drama, *The 17th Star*, was produced at Columbus, celebrating the sesquicentennial of Ohio's admission to the Union. Also at that time he and Josephina Niggli wrote *Serenata*, a tale of Old California, given at Santa Barbara. In 1955 *Wilderness Road*, a drama of the Southern mountain people, opened in a huge forest theatre near Berea, Kentucky.

Though his interest in drama "for the people" has never flagged, recently Paul Green has been drawn to a study of the folk opera. Perhaps this will be the next chapter in the life of North Carolina's most versatile theatre man.

REGIONAL PLAYWRIGHTS. About 1920, as has been said, the American drama suddenly began extending its scope and horizons. Among the many elements which characterized this expansion was a new curiosity about regional varieties. Farmers, slum-dwellers, seafarers, Negroes, and others began to be considered as types for stage presentation. In this movement the hinterlands of North Carolina provided its share of folk material. In the early years of the decade, while Koch was developing his program at Chapel Hill, similar steps were being taken in New York and elsewhere by North Carolina writers not associated with the Playmakers. The simple truth is that the folk movement in drama was on the upsurge.

In 1923, if Broadway was not yet aware of Koch's work, it was quickly jolted into the realization that there were such people as the North Carolina mountaineers. On the evening of March 24, Lula Vollmer's *Sun-Up* opened; this melodrama of a North Carolina mountain mother was immediately successful and settled down for a lengthy run. Ma Cagle is a character whom no playgoer who saw her ever forgets. Grieved by the death of her son who had taken part in a "Gov'ment feud" and died in France—a place he thought to be " 'bout forty miles 'tother side o' Asheville"—she protects a deserter who she eventually learns is the son of the law officer who killed her "men" for moonshining. A last-moment realization that her son had died in the cause of peace and love prompts her to forego the revenge she had planned. For audiences the last act is a transcendent experience.

Born in Moore County, Lula Vollmer became acquainted with the North Carolina hills which as a child she visited with her father, a lumberman. Both at school in Asheville and later while working in Atlanta, she wrote mountain plays and short stories. Most of her life was spent in New York, where she died in 1955. Except for Paul Green, Lula Vollmer has had more plays produced professionally in New York than any other Tar Heel dramatist. After *Sun-Up*, though none ever matched its success, came five others, all but one dealing with the North

Carolina mountain people. *The Shame Woman* (1923) tells of two naive girls "wrecked by the same small-town Lothario." *The Dunce Boy* (1925) recounts the tragedy of a 19-year-old moron with, as Stark Young wrote, "the mind of a poetic boy, the innocence of a woman, and the body of a man." Young thought that of all the plays he had seen that year *The Dunce Boy* was "one of the most nobly and sincerely aimed." *Trigger* (1927) is a mixture of mountain religion and witchcraft. *Sentinels* (1931) unfolds the scandal touching a prominent family in a Southern city; the faithful Negro servant is willing to sacrifice her son to stay an impending tragedy, but the lynching is prevented. *The Hills Between* (1938) sets forth the story of a young man's return to his native hills as a doctor with a fashionable wife; his old love, Julie, after domestic difficulties, sends him away as she had done the first time. Besides these plays Lula Vollmer wrote copiously for the radio; her most popular program was *Moonshine and Honeysuckle,* a series of mountain sketches published in 1934 as a full-length play for amateur actors.

Hatcher Hughes, born in the foothills of Cleveland County at Polkville, attended the University before the Koch era. After settling down as a professor at Columbia University, he wrote *Hell-Bent fer Heaven,* a melodrama of western North Carolina which won the Pulitzer Prize in 1924. In it, the courtship of a returning War hero is complicated by a renewed family feud, a dynamited dam, and a competing lover, the religious fanatic Rufe Pryor. *Ruint* (1925), "A Folk Comedy in Four Acts," was also well received in New York. When pretty Many Jane Horton is reported "ruint," her mountain father and his friends blame a handsome young Northerner who is establishing a mission school nearby, but calamity is averted when it is learned that he only kissed her. *Ruint* has abundant folk humor, folk dialect, and comic situation. In Hughes' later plays, one a collaboration with Elmer Rice, he did not concentrate on the mountain scene.

An outstanding Broadway hit of 1927 was *Coquette,* the joint effort of Anne Preston Bridgers of Raleigh and playwright George Abbott. Helen Hayes was the star. Based on an actual incident in Richmond County, *Coquette* is a drama of small-town country-club life in the South of the 1920's. In this story of violence and lingering Confederate chivalry, the coquette's father kills her socially unacceptable suitor to protect, as he thinks, his daughter's honor. Anne Preston Bridgers later wrote two similar plays, *Quicksand* and *Carrie Was a Lady,* both presented by the Raleigh Little Theatre of which she was a founder.

Playmaker Loretto Carroll Bailey of Winston-Salem achieved some success in 1929, especially locally, with *Job's Kinfolks,* which dealt with a segment of North Carolina life previously ignored by the dramatists—the mill people in the small cities. Her play, enlarged from a one act version, is built around the contrasting points of view of three generations of mill women.

Asheville's Hubert Hayes, after several seasons acting with a stock company, wrote *Tight Britches,* a mountain comedy which opened on Broadway in 1934 after revisions by John Taintor Foote of New York. Like *Hell-Bent fer Heaven,* it is partially concerned with a mountain boy entangled in the maze of flesh and religion. Hayes' original version, somewhat uneven in its progression from high comedy to stark tragedy, is still given almost annually during the summer season in Asheville. *Smoky Joe* (1936) is a farce for amateurs set in eastern North Carolina among the wealthy pulp-mill owners. *The Red Spider* (1937), a full-length mystery play also for amateurs, deals with stolen jewels and amnesic patients in a sanitarium in the Blue Ridge. Other dramatic writings are *Blackberry Winter, Tiny Gets Her Man, A Womanless Wedding, Where Vanishes the Flame, Held for Call, Dear Tojo,* and several radio scripts. With C. R. Sumner of Asheville, he wrote *Foxfire,* a historical play on General Francis Marion. Hayes' most ambitious effort was *Thunderland,* produced on a lavish scale in the Forest Amphitheatre on the Biltmore Estate during the tourist months of 1952 and 1953. This outdoor drama with music by Lamar Stringfield followed the pattern used by Paul Green and Kermit Hunter elsewhere, and told the life story of frontiersman Daniel Boone.

Other mountain plays of the '30's are *King Cotton's Children* by George Tidd, Jr., a social drama of the hill people who moved to the piedmont textile industries to find work; Bertha Hester's realistic *The Harp of a Thousand Strings;* and Henry McIver's

The Conversion of Jed Efird, its theme education and religion. In 1938 James A. McLaughlin of Hendersonville published *Ra-cruits,* a War comedy with most of its scene in France; Private Oswald D. Biddy, a National Guardsman from North Carolina, is presumably a mask for the author. *The Belles of the Nineties* is a period comedy by Viola S. Burch and Ruth Dorval Jones, both of Raleigh. Another production of theirs is a musical pageant *Sir Walter and the Queen* (1956).

Homecoming, a comedy by Edward Peyton Harris of Greenville, was seen in New York in 1942. Based on the Biblical story of Noah, it relates in satirical terms the doings of Nate Eborn on the outskirts of the author's own eastern Carolina town. In 1947, Walter Carroll, a Koch alumnus of Durham, had his *Tin Top Valley* produced by the American Negro Theatre in New York. It delineates the vicious race hatred in a Southern mill village, and the tragic consequences for a white boy who becomes the friend of a Negro lad. In 1948 the Experimental Theatre of New York put on *A Long Way from Home,* a free adaptation by Walter Carroll and Randolph Goodman of Maxim Gorki's *The Lower Depths.* The violent action of the play, performed by an all-Negro cast, was transferred from Russia to "a basement lodging house, under a poolroom on the outskirts of Durham, N. C." Primarily it is a social protest against conditions of defeatism and squalor.

The most impressive Carolina play of the last decade is *Dark of the Moon* by Howard Richardson of Black Mountain and William Berney of Birmingham, Alabama. Also a Koch alumnus, Richardson is the grandnephew of Thomas Dixon and son of author-doctor Frank Howard Richardson. A poetic ballad-drama, *Dark of the Moon* is the story of John, the witch boy, and pretty Barbara Allen of Buck Creek, high in the Carolina mountains. In order to be with his love, John is changed by the Conjur Woman into a human being, in which form he will remain if Barbara Allen is true to him for one year. When their witch-baby is born dead, Barbara's religious friends coerce her into an unfaithful relationship with a former suitor; and John is then freed, to roam the mountain tops with no remembrance of his life among the human beings of the valley below. In 1945 this colorful fantasy began an entire season's run in New York, followed by a half year on the road. It had an unexpected triumph in London and has played Austria, Belgium, and Germany. The renowned French playwright Jean Cocteau did a translations for the theatre in Paris. The National Ballet of Canada transferred its story to the dance stage.

Richardson and Berney have written other plays: *Danny Goes to Hell* (1948), the Don Juan legend in terms of a Texas traveling salesman; *Design for a Stained Glass Window* (produced professionally in New York in 1950), based on a true story of a housewife's conversion to Catholicism in sixteenth-century England; *Sodom, Tennessee* (1950), a hillbilly version of the Biblical account with musical score by Lamar Stringfield; *Birds of Prey* (1951); and *Protective Custody* (1956). With Frances Goforth of Kings Mountain, a Playmaker alumna, Richardson has written *Catch on the Wing* (1947), folk comedy of a North Carolina mill town; *Maiden Voyage* (1948); *Widow's Walk* (1948), concerning an eccentric Charleston tearoom proprietress, later retitled *A Kiss beside Jordan*; and *The Cat in the Cage* (1952), which had a run in Paris.

Frances Goforth collaborated with Warren Anderson of California on *Whom the Angels Name,* a psychological thriller of New England in the early 1900's; and *Like Breath into the Wind,* a drama set in the Cape Hatteras lighthouse. The last has not had a professional production.

The Flesh of the Orchid, a thriller with a North Carolina setting by the English novelist James Hadley Chase, was shocking patrons of the Grand Guignol in Paris during the summer of 1955.

TODAY. The situation of the drama in present-day North Carolina is, in spite of the virtual disappearance of the traveling professional companies, a healthy and vigorous one. Drama, in whatever form, is necessary to the lives of all folk everywhere. In North Carolina, simultaneously with the vanishing career performers, there sprang up a people's theatre. The Carolina Playmakers, of course, provided the momentum for the awakening. Through the Playmaker-sponsored Bureau of Community Drama and the Carolina Dramatic Association, secondary schools and colleges enlarged their programs. The traditional Senior Class play became only one among many of the year's events.

Well-organized dramatic clubs with trained leadership, play-writing classes, production units, and radio stations made possible a varied student participation in all phases of the theatre. The Lee Edwards High School of Asheville, the High Point High School and the Goldsboro High School are among those who have provided themselves with elaborate physical facilities. Among the more enterprising and imaginative college groups are the Duke Players, the Playlikers of the Woman's College, and the Blue Masquers of Catawba College. During the 1930's the units of the Federal Theatre gave outstanding performances in North Carolina.

Taking the place of the old-fashioned and frequently drifting amateur organizations, the businesslike Little Theatres have been established on a firm basis. Today the Charlotte and Raleigh Little Theatres have their own handsome buildings, full-time paid directors, and heavy winter schedules. At the turn of the century William S. Hart, later the star of Hollywood horse-operas, organized a Little Theatre in Asheville; the Asheville Community Theatre of today is its descendent. The Thalian Association of Wilmington was revived in 1929 and now occupies its historic auditorium.

Though for the most part producing revivals and current Broadway successes, the Little Theatres have been energetic in staging original scripts. In recent years, for instance, the Raleigh Little Theatre has presented new dramas by Anne Preston Bridgers; by Anne W. Armstrong of Asheville, whose western Carolina play, *Mountain Ivy*, was given in 1951; and by Charles Aycock Poe of Raleigh, with his *Climate of Fear* (1955), a melodrama of political intrigue in Washington. Experimentally produced by the Raleigh Little Theatre in 1956 was *A Shout and a Cry* by Lodwick Hartley and Jack Suberman, both professors of English at State College. In 1950 the friends of Winston-Salem's Joe King provided for visiting Broadway dignitaries an extravagant production of his musical play, *Blood, Thunder 'n' Kathryn*, concerning some capering ghosts in a mansion high in the Blue Ridge Mountains. The Carolina Playmakers continue to encourage the staging of full-length original plays; in 1954 they gave Emily Crow Selden's *The Outsider* and Kermit Hunter's *Darkening Shores*. Kai Jurgensen of the Playmaker staff has written many religious plays. And meanwhile, two North Carolina housewives, Mrs. Beulah Bailey Woolard of Charlotte and Mrs. W. O. Kelley of Raleigh, have set up profitable businesses of writing and marketing class-night plays for high schools. In 1956 *The White Doe*, a play of pirates at Nags Head in 1718, was staged by Goldsboro amateurs from the original script by Carolina Playmakers' director Samuel Selden.

Not all North Carolina talent has remained at home. A list of those who have become prominent in the varied aspects of the entertainment world is a lengthy one. Some are natives; others received their training or beginnings in the state. It would be difficult to gather together an inclusive register. Bosley Crowther of Winston-Salem is motion picture editor of the *New York Times*. A recognized writer of the Hollywood scene is Charlotte's Cameron Shipp. In television production there is John Paul Nickell of Whiteville; in radio and other media, Andy Griffith of Mt. Airy. Norman Cordon of Washington and Anne Jeffreys of Goldsboro have had careers on the musical stage. Charlton Heston of High Point, Ainslie Pryor of Raleigh, Randolph Scott of Charlotte, Kathryn Grayson of Winston-Salem, and Ava Gardner of Rock Ridge have been successful in motion pictures. Richard B. Harrison of Greensboro and Raleigh gave his memorable impersonation as De Lawd in *The Green Pastures*. Robert Armstrong, a Playmaker product, and Sidney Blackmer of Salisbury are well-known names on the New York stage today.

For the past decade, the aspect of the theatre most characteristic of North Carolina is the outdoor symphonic drama. Paul Green set the style with *The Lost Colony* (1937). In 1950 *Unto These Hills*, a brilliantly effective historical play, opened at the Cherokee Indian Reservation in the Smoky Mountains. Its author Kermit Hunter is a West Virginia native then resident of Chapel Hill. His tragic and spectacular play had a drawing power unforeseen even by its most hopeful promoters. The following year his *Forever This Land*, an outdoor drama on Abraham Lincoln, began a two-season run in New Salem, Illinois. In 1952 Hunter's *Horn in the West*, a play of the western movement of the Southern Highlanders in the 1770's, played its first summer session at the Daniel Boone Theatre in Watauga

County. Hunter's central character in *The Bell and the Plow,* given in Tucson in 1954, was Arizona's Father Eusedio Kino. In 1956 Hunter had three presentations: *Voice in the Wind* at Tampa, Florida; *Chucky Jack,* on the career of Tennessee's first governor John Sevier, at Gatlinburg; and a play for the Woodrow Wilson Centennial at Staunton, Virginia. His festival play of the Moravians was groomed for production near Winston-Salem in 1957.

In 1951 a play somewhat less ambitious than these productions but constructed along their lines was *Then Conquer We Must* by Robert B. Osborne of Kings Mountain, celebrating the American victory at the Battle of Kings Mountain in 1780. The play was staged in an amphitheatre in the military park just across the state line in South Carolina. The next year, after business difficulties with the author, the promoters brought in Florette Henri of New York who fashioned for the same site *The Sword of Gideon,* based on her novel *Kings Mountain* (1950). The play was in its fourth summer season in 1955.

The trend set by Paul Green, Kermit Hunter, and Hubert Hayes' *Thunderland* was followed by many local groups who were eager to depict their county history. *The Duplin Story* by Tar Heel actor and bookwriter Sam Byrd was given at Kenansville in 1949 and 1950. For a Hillsboro celebration in 1953 John Ehle of Chapel Hill wrote *The Road to Orange,* emphasizing the Regulator troubles of pre-Revolutionary times. In 1955 *Thunder over Carolina,* an outdoor musical drama by Charles Loveland of Lincolnton, was acted out to signal the 175th anniversary of the Battle of Ramsour's Mill in Lincoln County. In the same year, Charlotte put on novelist LeGette Blythe's *Voice in the Wilderness,* showing the rise and growth of Presbyterianism in early Mecklenburg County; and *Queen Anne's Bell* by Edmund Harding of Washington celebrated the 250th anniversary of Bath. Governor Luther Hodges and other notables appeared in the cast of the Bath play.

A recent development has been the summer theatres with their schedule of plays for the vacationists. The most firmly established is the Flat Rock Playhouse near Hendersonville, whose director, Robroy Farquhar, is also an occasional playwright. At Burnsville, not far away, is the Parkway Playhouse. Both of these theatres have provisions for apprentices to work with professional actors. Greensboro, Wilmington, and Raleigh have also had summer productions from time to time.

In conclusion, it can be said that the story of drama in North Carolina is a checkered one, from the shipwrecking of Anthony Alston off the coast in 1702 down to the present day. Nor is it an isolated story; the North Carolina theatre has imported many of its performers and playwrights from outside, and in turn has sent its talent abroad. Except for the great cities, perhaps a somewhat similar story could be written of any section of the United States. Even so, the details, especially after the arrival of Koch, have, in their sheer and peculiar variety, a distinctness which is North Carolina's own. They are a part of the cultural history of a regional people who, like folks everywhere, love the theatre and will not do without it.

THE SCUFFLETOWN OUTLAWS

A Tragedy of the Lowrie Gang

BY

WILLIAM NORMENT COX

A PLAY OF THE CROATAN INDIANS

PERHAPS IT IS TRUE that the Croatan (or Lumbee) Indians of Robeson County are descendants of the survivors of Sir Walter Raleigh's Lost Colony, who disappeared from history in 1587 with Eleanor and Virginia Dare. Tradition holds that Chief Manteo led the English into the interior away from hunger, or hostile natives, or Spanish threats—maybe all three—and there they lived, peacefully hidden by the swamps. True it is that even in recent times many obsolescent English words and anti-quated English pronunciations have been noticeable among the proud black-haired Indians; and a similarity of names with those of the Lost Colony makes the tradition seem close to truth. There was, for instance, a Henry Berry on Roanoke Island in the sixteenth century.

In time the Scotch settlers who came to the Cape Fear found the Indians and intermarried with them. The Croatan's troubles with the whites started when, during the Civil War, they were pressed into service away from their homes. Retaliation began with minor thefts but broke into open warfare in 1864 when Henry Berry Lowrie's father was killed by law enforcement officers. Thereafter, for eight years, the Indians were a terror not quieted till the death of their leader.

Henry Berry Lowrie was a real man, as was John Sanders. Most of the events of "The Scuffletown Outlaws," though of course modified to suit the demands of stage presentation, ac-tually happened.

The play came to be written in this way: When young Bill Cox went to Chapel Hill, he became a member of Proff Koch's group, and toured with the Carolina Playmakers in eastern North Carolina. Once the company were near Scuffletown (now Pem-broke), and Cox asked Proff to go with him to visit an uncle who had taken part in the Lowrie war and loved recounting the exciting story. Cox's enthusiasm for the old history led him to exclaim that a "great play" could be written about it. "Well, Bill," said Koch in his usual way, "I guess *you'll* have to write it then." Cox had never before written a play; but the following year the author strode the boards as the Lowrie chief. The gun he carried on the stage had once belonged to Henry Berry Lowrie.

" 'The Scuffletown Outlaws,' " said the playwright, "was written to throw a true light upon the deplorable condition which
existed in Robeson County, North Carolina, immediately after
the Civil War. The question is a delicate one and it is well-nigh
impossible to present a just picture of the affair. I ask you not
to condemn the Croatan Indians too harshly nor to sympathize
with the good white people too freely. They were both right.
The trouble was kept alive by a pyramiding of circumstances
which the settlers as well as the outlaws would gladly have
removed if there had been any way to accomplish a mutual
settlement. I know the history of these people as well as any
one living today can be expected to know it. This is my excuse
for writing the play."

William Norment Cox was born in Norfolk, Virginia, on
August 3, 1902. He grew up in Robeson County, not far from
Scuffletown. After a year at Washington and Lee, he transferred
to the University of North Carolina, from which he graduated
in 1925 with a B. S. degree in Commerce. At Chapel Hill, besides his activities in the Playmakers, he inaugurated intercol-
legiate boxing and fought lightweight. He began his adult career
as a sports writer for the *Durham Herald,* moved to the *Greensboro Daily News* in 1929, and since 1931 has been sports editor
of the *Norfolk Virginian-Pilot.*

The Croatans have attracted many writers. Other one act plays
are Paul Green's "The Last of the Lowries" (1920) and Clare
Johnson Marley's "Swamp Outlaw" (1939). *The King of Scuf-
fletoun* (1940) by John Paul Lucas, Jr., and Bailey T. Groome
is a novel with Henry Berry Lowrie as the central character.
Cox's "The Scuffletown Outlaws" has been one of the most
popular plays of the Playmakers' repertory.

THE CHARACTERS

HENRY BERRY LOWRIE, *chief of the Croatan Outlaws*
STEVE LOWRIE, *Henry Berry's brother*
RHODY, *Henry Berry's wife*
JUNE, *Henry Berry's niece*
LUKE LOCKLEAR, *a young Croatan*
JOHN SANDERS, *a white man from Nova Scotia*
JAMES McQUEEN, alias DONAHOE, *a white man of Robeson County*

SCENE

John Sanders' shanty, in Scuffletown, the settlement of the Croatan Outlaws. A swampy region of Robeson County, North Carolina.

TIME

Scene 1. The evening of November 19, 1870, about eight o'clock.

Scene 2. The early morning of November 21.

SCENE 1

The scene is JOHN SANDERS' *cabin in Scuffletown Swamp—
the Croatan habitat. There is a barred door in the center of the
rear wall, and to the left of it a small window with a solid board
shutter. To the right, in the corner, is a cot piled with clothing,
a knapsack, and other camp equipment. Down-stage on the right
is a door, also securely barred. On the table in the center of the
room are a Bible, several other books, and two guns. There are
two splint-bottom chairs by the table. On the left down-stage is
a rough fireplace made of sticks and red clay, with a hand-made
bench in front of it. The room has a bare appearance as of
hurried preparations for departure.*

The rising curtain reveals HENRY BERRY LOWRIE, STEVE
LOWRIE, *and* JOHN SANDERS. HENRY BERRY *is about twenty-six
years of age and five feet ten inches in height. He is a rugged
man for his years—straight in the back, deep chested, his arms
and shoulders well-set—a well-proportioned figure. His hazel-gray
eyes dilate and flash when he is excited. A smile lights his face
sometimes when he is quiet, but when he is aroused it becomes
the smile of a demon. He is the clear-headed young leader of
his tribe. He never betrays to his enemies his real feelings. His
hair is straight and black, characteristic of the Croatan Indian.
He wears calf-skin boots, a woolen frock coat or blouse, breeches
of the same material (or Salem or Kentucky jeans) and a wide-
brimmed hat. He is seated by the table leisurely cleaning and
wiping his Spencer rifle.*

STEVE LOWRIE *is sitting by the fireplace, carelessly strumming
his banjo. He has been drinking heavily and gazes sullenly into
the fire.* STEVE LOWRIE *is six feet tall, thirty-four years of age,
and weighs one hundred and seventy pounds. He has great
muscular power and looks the Indian brigand more than any
of the other members of the gang. He has heavy black hair and
a dark thin moustache. The resentment of his race lurks in his
eyes. He is the robber and the murderer who needs little provo-
cation to kill his man.*

JOHN SANDERS *is a native of Nova Scotia. He has lived with
the Croatans for two years as a missionary, healer and teacher.
In this time he has won their confidence and their affection.*

39

He is a tall man, of winning manners, clear-blue, fearless eyes and alert mind—strikingly attractive in his blue homespun shirt, corduroy breeches, and calf-skin boots. He is busy packing up his outfit. He appears somewhat nervous and excited, but tries to conceal his anxiety under the show of preparations for the exodus. The room is lighted by the lightwood blaze from the fireplace and a single candle on the table.

HENRY BERRY. Mon, when first ye come to our swamp-land and begun a-talkin' about movin' to that Texas place, I thought ye a fool.

SANDERS. I reckon you did, Henry, for it did sound foolish at first.

HENRY BERRY. But I sees it now, mon. We can escape by traveling at night an' takin' it easy during the heat of the day. Course I hates to go like this—looks like the Lowries is a-runnin'. That's what them domn whites'll say.

SANDERS. Let them say what they want to, Henry.

HENRY BERRY *(bitterly)*. Yes, let 'em. Mon, ye know that it hurts me to go like this. But we are fightin' the whole State now. Outlawed—price on me, ten thousand dollars dead or alive. And a big price set on Steve over thar—on every last one of us. An' I see with ye that this is the way out.

SANDERS *(nervously, tying up a bundle)*. Yes, Henry, I believe this will come out all right. And you ain't showing the white feather by leaving like this. Besides, think of where we are going. *(With a show of enthusiasm.)* To a land where we can live as we see fit. A land that is not ruled by court-martial trials.

HENRY BERRY. Court-martial trials! Yeh ho, mon, it were at a court-martial trial that they murdered my pa for takin' a barrel o' molasses—killed him for takin' a barrel o' sweetenin'. Mon, that sweet killin' ha'e been as bitter as gall-berries to them what done it. Spite of that, we ain't gettin' nowheres. I'm ready to leave it all behind. I feels kind o' happy on my last night in Scuffletown.

STEVE *(breaking in)*. Me, too, mon. Hurrah for Texas! Domn Robeson County! *(STEVE has been striking meaningless chords on his banjo. His instrument seems to be out of tune. He strokes it carelessly, not paying much attention to the conversation.)*

Kind o' hate to slip off in the night like a domn sheriff's force, though.

HENRY BERRY (*going up to him*). Steve, quit yo' thumpin' that thing. Mon, I believe ye're drunk again. An' this night o' all nights for ye to be a-drinkin'. We need live men for the start, Steve; and you know it. (*He turns to* SANDERS.) Mon, see if ye can fix for him some o' that thar drink ye sober him up with.

SANDERS. Good. There's a little left, I think. (*He mixes a drink. The bottles on the fireplace are easily reached, because they are often used.*) Here you go, Steve, drink it down; it will make you feel better. (STEVE *drains the gourd dipper without changing his expression.*)

STEVE (*dully*). Mon, I'm all right.

HENRY BERRY. That's good. (*To* SANDERS.) Mon, brother Steve owes ye a lot on account o' what ye done for him during his drinkin' spells.

STEVE. Henry, I'm all right, I tell ye. Dunno be all lickered. I was thinkin' how much I'd give for one more shot at that domn Donahoe. Just one more, afore we leave.

HENRY BERRY. It's too late now, Steve. But, mon, let me tell ye, just one more shot at Donahoe, and he'd bleed.

STEVE (*now more mentally and physically alert*). Luck ha'e been agin me with that mon. Everything bein' ready to leave when the moon sets, think I'll strike ye up a tune or two afore we go. (*The meanest and most bloodthirsty of the Lowries is lost for the time being in the plaintive melody of an old ballad.*)

To the pines, to the pines where the sun never shines
And I'll shiver when the cold wind blows.
The longest train I ever seen,
Was the train that killed my gal.

To the pines, to the pines where the sun never shines
And I'll shiver when the cold wind blows.
Her hair was caught in the driver's wheel;
Her body has never been found.

(HENRY BERRY *and* SANDERS *go cleaning their guns while* STEVE *is singing. At the conclusion of the song* STEVE *goes to the window, throws open the shutter, and peers out into the swamp.)*

HENRY BERRY *(rebuking him and closing the shutter)*. Steve, ye domn fool, shut that thar window. Old Donahoe's rifle will bark out thar in the night and ye won't be a-goin' to Texas.

STEVE *(going back to the fireplace)*. An' what'll they be a-sayin' when we do go off to Texas?

HENRY BERRY. Dunno be no help for what they'll say, Steve. Dunno do no good to think about what they'll have to say.

STEVE. Domn 'em! They'll say we run—like women.

SANDERS *(cheerfully)*. Oh, it won't matter what they say after we get there. And it won't be long before nine o'clock will be on us. *(To* HENRY BERRY.*)* And you are sure that everything is ready?

HENRY BERRY. Yes, everything is ready, Sanders.

SANDERS. Have all the wagons been greased?

HENRY BERRY. Yes, every one o' them is fixed right. There's a-plenty o' feed for the mules—everything is ready.

SANDERS. What about my share of the grease for my wagon?

HENRY BERRY. Time Rhody and Luke's here with it now.

SANDERS *(nervously)*. Who you got out watching the roads tonight, Henry?

HENRY BERRY. That's all fixed, mon. Don't ye worry about that.

STEVE. We got 'em watched all right. Thar's William Chavis down by the crick bridge, an' George Applewhite is a-watchin' the big road to come this way. Brother Tom's over to Red Banks station to see if some of them domn deputies from Lumberton gits off the train. *(Footsteps are heard outside.* STEVE *and* HENRY BERRY *seize their guns, spring to their feet, and stand ready to fire. A signal of three short whistles is heard.)*

HENRY BERRY. Hit's Rhody and Luke. *(*HENRY BERRY *answers the signal and* STEVE *opens the door.)*

STEVE. Come in. *(*RHODY *and* LUKE *enter.* RHODY LOWRIE *is the wife of the robber chief,* HENRY BERRY LOWRIE. *Her figure and countenance mark her as somewhat older than her years. She is dressed poorly, but wears a bright-colored shawl about her shoulders. There is something in her voice which reveals the constant anxiety of her existence and a stoic attitude toward life.)*

RHODY. Everything with us is ready for the start far as I know. (*Turning coldly to* SANDERS.) Here's your grease, mon. (*Going to the fireplace she sits there silently, betraying no emotion.* STEVE *closes the door after* RHODY *and* LUKE, *and bars it.*)

SANDERS. Well, I'd better grease my wagon right now. Can any of you help me?

HENRY BERRY. Come on, Steve, we can holp him.

SANDERS (*to* LUKE). Here, lad. Sit down by the fire with Rhody and rest a bit. (*As they leave* HENRY BERRY *warns them.*)

HENRY BERRY. An' keep that window shut.

RHODY (*darkly*). Hit may be a good thing, but I fear it. Who knows what may happen on the road to Texas, and that mon Sanders a-leadin' o' us. Boy, don't ye never trust a white mon —never, I tell ye.

LUKE. (LUKE LOCKLEAR *is a fearless young outlaw-in-the-making. A handsome tall lad of eighteen, of keen and bright eye and graceful bearing. He is in love with* JUNE LOWRIE, HENRY BERRY'S *niece.*) I ha'e watched him. I ha'e trailed him like a hound-dog, and I aims to keep on his trail. He ain't a-lyin', Aunt Rho'; he means to take us some place far away. Uncle Henry and the rest ain't blind.

RHODY. I dunno be sure, Luke. I dunno know.

LUKE. Hit dunno be the plan, Aunt Rho'. . . . I—I could kill the mon like a moccasin for a-comin' betwixt June and me. But I can't do hit. I can't do hit, 'cause Uncle Henry and Steve and all of 'em don't put no faith in what I think.

RHODY. Boy, I ha'e argued for ye. But June won't listen to me lak she used to. She aims to marry him when we gits to Texas (*doubtfully*)—if we ever git thar. God help 'em. A Lowrie a-marryin' a white mon! (*A low whistle is heard outside.* LUKE *answers the signal.*)

LUKE. Hit's June, Aunt Rho'. (LUKE *goes to the door, unbars it, and lets her in.*)

JUNE. (JUNE LOWRIE *is a Croatan girl. She is well formed and fair to look upon, just turned twenty. Her eyes are dark; her skin is smooth and firm. In the sordid background of a Scuffletown cabin she appears fresh, clear and lovely. She wears a scarlet swamp flower in her hair. There is a wistful quality in her voice which is gentle and low—in marked contrast with the*

abrupt staccato speech of the men and of her Aunt Rhody.)
We ha'e everything ready to leave over our way and I thought
I'd run over and see if I could help John pack some of his things.
(*Looking around the room.*) But he's pretty nigh got his house
cleaned out.

Luke. Yes, and he don't need your holp. No white mon does.

June (*fiercely, her eyes shining*). He needs my holp and I'm
goin' to he'p him, too.

Luke. Well, he'p him if ye want to, and domn ye for it.
But it's agin your blood—and him a white mon! (*He goes out,
slamming the door.* June *bars it.*)

Rhody. June, thar goes the best boy in Scuffletown—and him
a Locklear, too. Luke would be good to ye, lass, and ye dunno
do right by throwin' him off.

June. But, Aunt Rho', I love John. He will be good to me, too.
But that good part don't make so powerful much difference. I
love the mon—here. (*Placing her hand over her heart.*)

Rhody. Lass, ye dunno know white people lak I do.

June. But, Aunt Rho', John is the same as one o' us.

Rhody (*bitterly*). If ye had been with us in that cold and damp
jail in Lumberton ye would not be for a-lovin' any white mon.
They thought they'd take Steve's wife, and Boss Strong's wife,
and me—Henry Berry Lowrie's wife—an' all the wives from Scuffletown, and make our men stop takin' what they wanted and
a-killin' them what was a-huntin' of 'em. Hit did no' work. I
would ha'e kilt myself if Henry Berry had give up on account of
my bein' in jail.—Bless God, no Lowrie has ever touched a white
woman!—An' ye go agin your blood, lass, when ye talk o' marryin'
this white mon. I dunno trust none of 'em, in spite of what the
rest thinks. I dunno forget them nights in that jail, with them
cold iron bars a-shadowin' on the wall. An' who knows but what
he's a-settin' to ketch us—him a-comin' away down here from
that Nova Scotia place.

June (*soothing her*). But, Aunt Rho', ye dunno forget, too,
how gentle and kind John has been to all o' us these two years
he's been here. He's doctored us for fever, tended the men when
they were shot up, and held preachin' for us every Sunday—and
all kinds o' things for us he's done. 'Twas a lucky day, I tell ye,
for Scuffletown when John Sanders was found out'n his head

with swamp-fever, and I brung him back to health. (*She takes up* SANDERS' *coat from the chair and fondles it.*) An' I love him, I tells ye!

RHODY (*despairing*). I understand what ye say, lass; but the day will come when my words'll sound like buryin' hymns to ye! I dunno be able to trust the mon like ye do. (*She rises.*) I must go home now, so as to be good an' ready for that nine-o'clock leavin' time. There don't seem no sense in a-arguin' with ye.

JUNE (*calling after her*). I'll be along in a little while, Aunt Rho'. (*Alone in the cabin,* JUNE LOWRIE *remains seated by the fireplace. She is gazing intently at the smouldering coals when* JOHN SANDERS *enters. She goes to meet him.*)

SANDERS. Hello, June. I thought you had gone.

JUNE. No, John, that was Aunt Rho'. I just thought I'd stay a little bit longer. You don't care if I do, do ye?

SANDERS. You should be at home resting. Didn't I tell you to get all the rest you could? The road to Texas is hard and treacherous and you should rest now as much as possible.

JUNE. I know that's what ye said, and I love ye John for a-sayin' it; but I couldn't keep from comin' over just for a minute.

SANDERS. Well, young lady, if you love me so much you had better obey me. (*He goes on with his preparations for the leaving.*) I know what's best for you.

JUNE (*coquettishly*). You dunno be able to make me go right now. Let me stay just a little while, John. I'll no' be in the way.

SANDERS. Oh, all right. Make yourself at home. (SANDERS *goes on with his packing.* JUNE *watches him closely—happy to be near him.*)

JUNE. John, where's Uncle Henry and Steve? Ain't they a-comin', too?

SANDERS. They've gone on down to their wagons to see that everything's ready for the start. (*There is a moment of silence.*)

JUNE. John, we be all by ourselves. . . . Won't you do something for me?

SANDERS. June, you know I would do anything for you.

JUNE. John, tell me more about that wonderful country we be a-goin' to—that country where everything is peaceful and happy, where there will be no more killin' and a-robbin' of folks. Where Uncle Henry and the rest can go to town without fear o' bein' arrested. Where the babes and the chillun can play and laugh knowin' that their pas will come home to the cabin of a night. Oh, John—John! It's good to dream about that country. It makes me believe on that hymn ye taught us to sing on Sundays. "Thar is a happy land, fur, fur away!" Mon, I tell ye one of them miracles is about to happen. Seems jus' lak one o' them you used to preach of.

SANDERS. Yes, June, it is a good country, and a free land. Texas is as big as half a dozen of our states out here. There will be plenty of land for everybody. We can begin at the bottom and build the Croatan nation over again. This trouble will be forgotten in a few years. The sun will shine on us tomorrow—I know it will, June.

JUNE. An', John, ye'll marry me when we get there; an' we can grow old together in that young country.

SANDERS. Yes, June, we'll marry when we get there.

JUNE. John, if ye knew how happy it makes me to hear ye say that, ye wouldn't ever stop sayin' it.

SANDERS. But you must run along home now, June, and try to rest. This escape is mighty serious business, and I must finish the packing right now.

JUNE. I dunno want to go—but I will, since ye say to. (Lightly.) I'll see ye at Uncle Henry's, John.

SANDERS (following her to the door, SANDERS impetuously draws her to him). June, I love you, girl. Tell me, would you always love me . . . even if something terrible should happen?

JUNE (quietly). Mon, I will love ye forever and ever—it matters not what happens.

SANDERS (he kisses her). Go on, child; go on. . . . (JUNE leaves and JOHN is alone. Now he appears tired and worried—unsettled in his mind. A sudden tapping at the side door interrupts his thinking. He listens. Again the tapping. He walks stealthily to the door and gives a signal. It is answered and he opens the door, admitting DONAHOE. JAMES McQUEEN, alias DONAHOE, is a tall eccentric figure—a gaunt "gawky Scotchman," swift and sure in every movement he makes. Each looks inquiringly at the other. SANDERS bolts both doors. Then DONAHOE strides to the center of the room and speaks.)

DONAHOE (in a repressed voice). Everything all right, John?

SANDERS. Yes, I think so—not much danger. They all left a few minutes ago. They won't be back soon. Make yourself comfortable. (SANDERS *pours out a glass of whiskey, which* DONAHOE *accepts gratefully.*)

DONAHOE. Thank'ee, lad; that tastes good! This business of crawling through Scuffletown swamp like a snake calls for some kind of a nerve settler.

SANDERS. I don't see how you do it, Donahoe. You must be a ghost. God knows they hate you since you killed Boss Strong. You run in Steve Lowrie's mind all the time.

DONAHOE. An' he runs in mine, the dirty skunk! I'd love to shoot him.—I don't want to see him hung like he will be when we catch 'im. (*A pause.*) Is everything all right, John?

SANDERS. Yes, I reckon so. . . .

DONAHOE. We got our end fixed all right.

SANDERS (*evasively*). Have you?

DONAHOE. Oh, yes. You can count on us. Tell you what we done. We got Wishart's Company, all the sheriff's force from Lumberton, and all the good shots from up Philadelphus way and tried them bridges the other day just to make sure. An' it'll work! You see, some of our men will be under the bridge on scaffolds fixed for it; the rest will be on the dam at both ends; you all drive on the bridge, and we'll close in and catch every damn one of 'em!

SANDERS (*vaguely*). Sounds all right, Donahoe.

DONAHOE. Yes, by God, and it is all right. (*In his enthusiasm his voice rises and* SANDERS *cautions him to speak more quietly.*) We got 'em now (*grimly*)—the rusty swamp-devils. They'll never git away alive if our boys surround 'em. Tell you what you can do, Sanders. Try to call Henry Berry and Steve and the other leaders up to the head wagon for a conference about the time you git to the bridge. They'll be easy to catch up there.

SANDERS (*evasively*). All right. . . .

DONAHOE. I bring ye good news, lad. The Governor has raised them rewards. You stand to clean up nigh on to $52,000.00 on this deal. God knows you deserve every penny of it for what you've been doing here. And I want to shake hands with the bravest man in North Carolina—no—in the United States! (*He offers* SANDERS *his hand, but* SANDERS *does not accept it.*) Oh, come on, John. I mean it, and there ain't no use beatin' 'round the bush.

SANDERS (slowly, with determination). Donahoe, I can't shake hands with you on this deal.

DONAHOE. Why, what's the matter, John? Seems to me you ought to be the happiest man in Robeson County.

SANDERS (walking away from him). But I'm not happy. I'm miserable. Donahoe, you call me a brave man. I tell you I'd rather be called the biggest coward in the world and have this thing off my hands. (Resolved.) I don't believe I can see it through.

DONAHOE (amazed). What do you mean about not seein' it through?

SANDERS. Man, you won't be able to understand it when I tell you. For two long years I have lived here with these people. I know the atrocities they have committed. I know things they have done that you will never know. You should go to their cabins as I have done, when their men are away hiding in the Swamp, and see their wives and little ones—wild-eyed, nervous, unable to sleep—listening, eternally listening, for the sound of a gun somewhere far off in the swamps. They can't understand it. The white people tramped on them and they had to strike back in their own way. I've lived with 'em, doctored 'em, taught them—and they have come to put a damning trust in me, in everything.

DONAHOE. John, have you gone crazy? What does this mean?

SANDERS (firmly). Donahoe, I mean, that with God as my judge, I swear to you I can't see this thing through. (He takes from the Bible on the table a faded photograph and observes it intently.) How could I ever face my wife and children—and me a traitor. . . . Donahoe, man is a queer mixture.—God knows how I can face them anyhow.—What's $50,000.00 for selling the lives of men who trust me as they have never trusted a white man before?

DONAHOE (facing him). Sanders, I warn ye not to put any confidence in their trust.

SANDERS. You don't know, Donahoe. Even their suspicious women trust me. There is one girl, June Lowrie—that girl loves me. I began by playing with her so as to make everything run smooth for me in Scuffletown. One little slip and I would have been a dead man. . . . Donahoe, what would you think of me if I told you that I love that girl?

DONAHOE. Good God, man! You are crazy!

SANDERS (*pacing up and down restlessly*). Maybe I am, but I can't help it. I hate to think about it. My two years here make me appreciate affection even from what you call "a damn Croatan."

DONAHOE. Man, don't talk to me about Croatan affection. How much would your trust be worth to Steve Lowrie? I know, and you know, that they would kill you like a dog if they knew what you were doing.

SANDERS. I don't believe they would, Donahoe. They have a keener sense of justice than you give them credit for. I can better stand the wrath and ridicule of North Carolina than to be forever tormented by a guilty conscience. (*Decisively.*) I can't see this thing through.

DONAHOE (*advancing to him*). John, I've listened to all this talk. You must be out of your head. I know it has been a great strain on ye, but try to buck up, man.

SANDERS (*resolved*). Donahoe, I stand by what I told you, so help me, God!

DONAHOE (*challenging him*). John, have you forgotten the eleven good and honest citizens that these hellions have murdered? Those men they waited on in ambush and blowed their heads off with buckshot? Tell me, have you?

SANDERS. No. . . .

DONAHOE. Have you forgotten so soon Owen Norment, who was shot down in his front yard, with his wife and children looking on and pleading for mercy? Old Sheriff King—they murdered him by his own fireside. Old man Barnes—shot down on his own mill dam. You know all this, Sanders. It's true, isn't it?

SANDERS (*evading him*). Yes, but. . . .

DONAHOE. Look at the terrified district—white men can't move from their firesides for fear of bein' shot down. White women and children pray that God Almighty'll take care of them through the night—and you talk like this.

SANDERS. Well. . . .

DONAHOE (*rebuking him*). And the whole country is laughing at us—saying that the people of Robeson Country are cowards. You can't pick up a newspaper but has something to say about the cold-footed North Carolina people who let a handful of Indians run wild, murdering and robbing. Well, you know it takes more than talking and even fighting to clean out this gang.— That's the reason we got you, John Sanders.—Tod Caldwell has power as Governor to clean out the gang for us; but he ain't helping any. The Freedmen's Bureau is helping *them;* the Republican troops what was here has helped 'em. You admit this, don't you?

SANDERS (*weakening*). Well, yes. . . .

DONAHOE. Sanders, you've done more by yourself toward ridding the earth of this running sore than all the rest of us put together. Think, man, of the suffering you will rid this country of when your plans go through—I'm Presbyterian, I am, an' it seems to me that the good Master sent you here to do your work. You've done it well, lad. You deserve—

SANDERS. Don't tell me that again.

DONAHOE. I know how you feel, boy. Brace up. . . . We'll be waitin' for ye.

SANDERS (*resigned*). I'll do what I can.

DONAHOE (*his hand on* SANDERS' *shoulder*). Man, I knowed all the time you was troubled by the strain. You are doing the right thing, and a great thing, for mankind.—We'll be on the bridge. I'll tell the boys that our troubles will soon be over. Guess you'll be along about three o'clock?

SANDERS. If nothing happens. . . .

DONAHOE. Well, good luck, boy; and God guide ye. (*He gives* SANDERS *a warm hand-shake, and slips out by the side door of the shack.* SANDERS *sits down by the table, deeply troubled.* LUKE LOCKLEAR, *who has been spying outside, now opens the shutter softly, and peers in. He watches* SANDERS *take up the photograph, study it intently, and place it in his bosom; then take a sheet of paper from the table, write something hurriedly on it, and leave it by the Bible. Then, with a last look about the walls of the cabin* LUKE *sees him sling a bundle over his shoulder and go out hurriedly by the side door.*

(LUKE LOCKLEAR *now slips in at the rear door as stealthily*

*as a cat. He goes swiftly to the table, takes up the written paper
—but he cannot make it out. He looks puzzled, places the paper
in his shirt and hurries out.)*

SCENE 2

*The setting is the same. It is early morning of the second day
following.* HENRY BERRY LOWRIE *is pacing the floor with evident
excitement.*

RHODY *(grimly)*. I told ye, Henry—many a time I told ye not
to trust that white trash. 'Tis a wonder ye ain't cold-dead right
now.

HENRY BERRY *(bitterly)*. 'Tis the truth, woman, if ye ever
spoke it.

RHODY. He fooled ye onct, Henry.

HENRY BERRY. Yes, but domn my hand to the bone *(holding
up his hand in front of him)* if ye ever hear o' this mon a-foolin'
me twice. A dead mon fools no mon.

RHODY. Ye remember of him a-preachin' to us out'n that book
—and him all the time no better'n a stray dog.

HENRY BERRY. Luke and Steve'll get him. They'll get him,
I tell ye. They'll run him until he's so tired it'll hurt him to close
his domn eyes.—Mon, I kin see ye a-bleedin' on every bush betwixt here an' your stoppin' place—a-bleedin' and a-sweatin'
drops o' blood.

RHODY *(sullenly)*. I dunno trust no white mon.

HENRY BERRY. I tol' Steve to bring him here for me to make
up my mind about what to do with him afore I turns him over to
the rest of 'em for trial. They ought to be here with 'im by this.
*(Outside footsteps, guttural commands, and the clanking of guns
are heard.)* They're here, Rhody. *(He goes to the door.)* Woman,
ye'll stand over thar *(pointing to the fireplace)* an' dunno move
your tongue. *(*STEVE *and* LUKE *enter with* SANDERS. *He is
bound and bleeding, and nearly exhausted. He reels and sinks
to the floor.* STEVE *and* LUKE *kick at him viciously, and jerk
him to his feet.)*

STEVE. Stand up, ye son-of-a—

HENRY BERRY *(sternly)*. Mon, if ye ha'e strength in ye to
breathe, ye ha'e strength enough to stand up and hear what I

ha'e to tell ye. Stand up!—for Henry Berry Lowrie—afore I nails ye to that wall with hickory pegs. (SANDERS *braces himself with a frantic effort, and stands erect.*) Mon, I got ye! I got ye afore ye could git away with your lyin', dirty scheme. An' till now I ha'e not decided what to do with ye; but I ha'e some notion what it'll be.

STEVE (*casually*). Ye'll remember, Henry, how ol' mon Norment looked when Jack McLaurin blowed his jaw off'n him with them number ten buck-shot. (RHODY *and* LUKE *nod agreement, but* HENRY BERRY *continues calmly.*)

HENRY BERRY. Mon, for two years ha'e I been fooled into trustin' ye. I trusted ye with things that the others'll never know. I thought ye my friend, a-workin' to help me and the rest, when every other domn white mon was a-workin' to kill us. Mon, ye ha'e been brave, but the brave mon most times gits shot.

RHODY. I dunno lak to hear ye speak so, Henry.

HENRY BERRY. Woman, you keep quiet, I tell ye. (*To* SANDERS.) Mon, I hate to see ye there a-whimperin' and a-shiverin' like a cur-dog. Hit's your own doin' though, and I reckon ye kin stand it. What do ye mean o' this? (*He reads the note* SANDERS *had left behind him, studying his face intently as he does so.*) "Good-bye, good friends. Don't follow plans made for to-night and you will be safe from any danger." What do ye mean by that?

SANDERS (*with great effort*). For God's sake, Henry . . . let me tell you. . . .

HENRY BERRY. I tol' ye to speak, mon.

SANDERS (*breathing hard*). I . . . I . . . I came here with a plan for capturing you and the whole Lowrie gang. You know I don't belong to this part of the country . . . and I swear to you that I came all the way from Nova Scotia . . . just for the rewards. I . . . I had you in my power tonight. . . . I could have sold you to the white people of this section . . . for $50,-000.00 . . . but I couldn't do it. . . . My two years here with you have made me understand your true feelings so much that on this very night, I couldn't see it through. . . . Before God, I swear that I'm telling you the truth—I am. . . . (*He is about to sink exhausted to the floor.*)

STEVE (*forcing him to his feet again*). Mon, ye'll stand up, if ye know what's good for ye.

SANDERS. God have mercy. . . .

HENRY BERRY. Don't call on God, mon. Little holp he will ha'e for ye now. 'Tis better you waste your cryin' on me—'twill do ye more good than a thousand a-prayin' for your soul.

RHODY. Ye speak the truth, Henry.

HENRY BERRY (speaking calmly and coldly). Let me tell ye. One day I went to my fish-box in Drowning Creek to git some fish for Rhody, and one pore little perch had his head all e't away and his fins gone—a jack-fish done it. I can see ye, mon, with your head gone and your body a-bleedin' and a-drippin' lak a stuck hog.—One day, while I was a-watchin' McNeill's dam by myself, I saw a king snake squeeze the life out'n a moccasin. He wropped himself around the other snake and he squeezed, and he squeezed till he mashed the life out'n that moccasin.— Mon, let me tell ye, I could do thot for ye with my own hands and I—(The door is opened suddenly, and JUNE rushes in.) June, you go home. You—

JUNE (rushing to SANDERS she helps him into the chair). I know ye tol' me to stay home, Uncle Henry, but I couldn't do it. I had to come. I stayed outside and listened as long as I could stand it; and I tell ye I had to come in. (Observing SANDERS' weakened condition.) Get me some water quick! (No one responds. She gets the water herself and lifts the gourd dipper to JOHN SANDERS' lips.) Doesn't that feel better? (SANDERS can only look at her, gratefully.)

STEVE. June, why don't you keep your domn mouth shut and go home where you belong?

JUNE (fiercely). I hear you, Steve; and I ain't goin'. Can't you see he's too weak to talk for himself? He tried to tell you, but ye wouldn't hear him.

RHODY (grimly). He's had too much of a chance already.

JUNE. I'm goin' to speak for him.—You, Steve, what's he done for you? How many times has he saved your life when you were too drunk to move? How many times has he gi'e you medicine to sober you up so you could go to Back Swamp and hide, when the deputies were hot on your trail? How many times, I ask ye? —You, too, Uncle Henry. (Her voice changes; she speaks with a tone of respect.) He's been a help to ye; 'cause look how many times he's advised ye about what to do. I know, Uncle Henry, that you are too wise and too brave to ever be caught, but you know what he's done for the rest of the men. *(She turns fiercely now on* LUKE, *with a sneer.)* You, Luke, where'd you be if John Sanders hadn't been here when you broke your leg over at Brown's Grist Mill. Ye'd be walkin' on a wooden peg right now! *(To* RHODY, *reproachingly.)* And you, Aunt Rhody, what did he do for you when you was down with chills and fever? Ye remember how ye tol' us all good-bye, and how ye was ready to die, and John saved you.

RHODY. I dunno trust him in spite of it.

JUNE *(pleading)*. I ask all of you to think of the good things he has done for all of us. He has been a guardian angel for Scuffletown for two long years, and now you talk of killin' him.

HENRY BERRY. But I tell ye, he betrayed *me*.

JUNE. But, Uncle Henry, you know that nothing has hurt us for what he has done.

HENRY BERRY. Yes, June . . . that's the truth. But he ain't what we thought he was, and no white mon can be. It's just like a great river a-tween us. Them over thar on the one side and us over here on the other. And there ain't no endin' to it but by killin'. *(Gravely.)* An' killin's don't end nothin' neither. *(A pause, then he turns quickly to* SANDERS.*)* Mon, I gi'e ye six hours to be out'n this territory. If ye're no out by then, and if I ever see ye or hear of ye in Scuffletown again—God help your soul!

SANDERS *(dazed)*. You mean . . . I can . . . go? . . . Free? . . . Thanks. . . .

HENRY BERRY *(indicating the door)*. Go, go! Don't thank me. Go, I tell ye!

JUNE *(rushing up to* SANDERS*)*. And I'm goin' with ye.

SANDERS. No, no. . . .

JUNE. I am.

HENRY BERRY. Go! Go!

LUKE *(flashing out)*. Who you goin' with?

JUNE. You know who I'm goin' with.

LUKE. You wouldn't go if ye knowed what I know. I ain't tol' ye all there is to know, yet.

JUNE. What do you mean?

LUKE (*his eyes flashing*). I mean that he's been a-lyin' and a-foolin' ye. He's been betrayin' ye all along. He tol' ye he loved ye, and he promised to marry ye, jus' so's he could stay on the good side of Uncle Henry.

JUNE (*savagely*). You're a domned liar, Luke Locklear!

LUKE. I ain't neither; I know.

JUNE. How do you know?

LUKE. He's married, and he's got two chilluns—that's how I know!—Last night I crawled up to that thar window just in time to see him a-lookin' at a picture, and a-talkin' to himself. —Wish to God I had knowed it were Donahoe I seed goin' down the path. I thought it was one of our folks.—(*Crossing over to* SANDERS, *he draws out the photograph from his shirt bosom, and hands it to* JUNE.) And here it is for ye to see for yourself. (JUNE *snatches the picture and stares at it fixedly for a moment. Her expression changes. She is puzzled, hurt, afraid. Then she goes slowly over to* SANDERS *and hands the photograph to him.*)

JUNE (*quietly*). Will ye tell them what this is? Whose picture is this? What are they to ye?

LUKE (*savagely*). It belongs to him—they're his wife and chillun. That's what they are.

JUNE (*still very calm*). Is it so? Is this your picture? Does this be your wife and chillun?

SANDERS. (*Erect. He speaks quietly and firmly.*) Yes . . . they are mine . . . my own!

JUNE *is transformed. Her eyes burn with the hate of the diamond-back when he is about to strike. Her face is set, motionless as a mask shadowing a presentiment of tragic fury.*

HENRY BERRY (*grimly*). My word stands; ye can leave, mon.

JUNE (*coldly*). Then, go! Get out of my sight, ye white trash, with your lyin', dirty heart! (*She walks slowly to the table, takes up a large knife she finds there and fondles it distractedly.*) I could cut it out o' ye, mon, just like ye cut the heart of a melon . . . but I don't want to see how filthy it is. . . . I want to kill ye so bad, it makes my heart ache. (*She hesitates a moment, then goes up behind him, and—cuts his bonds.*) Go, you white Judas! (SANDERS *staggers out. There is a pause.*)

HENRY BERRY. I dunno be sure whether I done the right thing or no.

JUNE. Uncle Henry, I pray that God Almighty'll strike him dead, afore he goes a hundred yards! (STEVE *on the instant, takes up the rifle, throws open the shutter and takes aim to shoot.* JUNE, *seeing this, fiercely springs at him and shrieks out.*) No! No! ! No! ! ! (*But* STEVE *has pushed her aside. He takes careful aim and fires to kill.* JUNE *stands, staring blankly.*)

CURTAIN

THE CROATAN DIALECT

In preparing the text of "The Scuffletown Outlaws" the aim of the Editor has been to preserve the natural speech as far as that is possible. The spelling of the dialect has been simplified as much as is practicable, without destroying the local characteristics of the language.

It is difficult to represent the spoken dialect in print. Below is a list of words, commonly used by the Croatans, which will be of interest to the reader and serve the actor as a guide in the pronunciation.

Man, Can, That, Damn, Land , Swamp, Stand are pronounced Mŏn, Cŏn, Thŏt, Dŏmn, Lŏndt, Swŏmp, Stŏnd.

Time , Strike , Right are pronounced Toime, Stroike, Roight.

There, Where, Here are pronounced Thär , Whär , Hyär.

Do not }
Don't know } ....Dunno
Plenty ......Plain-tee
Brother .....Bruvver
Mean ......Mäne
Liquor .....Licker
Leave ......Läve
Because ....Becäze
Onion ......Inyun
Creek ......Crĭck
    ("Swamp" is often used)
Woman ....ŏŏman
Fire ....Fär
Sack, or Bag . Wallet (of meal)

Help (noun) ....Hōlp
Help (verb) present . Hĕp
            past .... Hōlp
Wagon ....Waggin
Window ....Winder
Afraid ....Afeard
Between ....Betwixt
Bring ....Fetch
Carry ....Tote
Marry ....Merry
Argue ....Argy
Good ....Gŏot

F. H. K.

SLEEP ON, LEMUEL

A Carolina Negro Comedy

BY

JOHN W. PARKER

A PLAY OF FOLK SUPERSTITION

In the lives of all people, superstitious beliefs play a part—but among no other group of people in America is it greater than among the Negroes of the South. The belief in conjuring, for example, is still wide-spread, and even today the newspapers occasionally carry stories of witchcraft. Often the conjuring concludes with unhappy results, though this is not true in the present play. To serve the purposes of comedy, the playwright has written of a conjure doctor who performs her tricks in order to bring two lovers together. Against a macabre background, which contrasts with the romantic events going forward up front, the old woman Louisa delights the audience with the way she handles a difficult predicament.

It has not been necessary for the author to invent unusual superstitions to lend a touch of the grotesque to his play. What he has written about, he learned first-hand in his boyhood days in "the quaint old town of Murfreesboro situated on the Meherrin River in eastern North Carolina. Here a unique remnant of slave days still exists," wrote Professor Koch when the play was first printed. "Behind the street of 'white houses' formerly occupied by the Southern aristocracy sprawl the slave quarters, separated from the more pretentious dwellings by the spacious gardens of plantation days. So close are the cabins to the 'big houses' that, sitting on the back porch, one may still hear the plaintive songs of slave days or the jazz tunes of the present time on any warm night in June. Today the cabins are still occupied by the Negro folk, who serve now not as slaves but as household servants. The author, having lived all his life in close proximity to the Negro, knows him as he was and is—his social and religious life, his fears and his dreams. The language used in the play is the speech he has heard from his earliest childhood."

Perhaps no name connected with amateur theatricals in North Carolina today is better known than that of John W. Parker. For more than two decades, from his post in the Department of Dramatic Art at the University of North Carolina, he had been encouraging young actors, playwrights, and directors all over the state. His job at Chapel Hill is a four-fold one: director of the Bureau of Community Drama, secretary of the Carolina

Dramatic Association, business manager of the Carolina Play-makers, and professor of theatre administration, playwriting, and the teaching of dramatic art.

Parker was born on October 16, 1909, in Murfreesboro, un-doubtedly the scene of "Sleep On, Lemuel." From the local high school he went to Wake Forest for a year, then shifted to the University, from which he graduated in 1930. In 1936 he was awarded a master's degree. Earlier he had taught at Four Oaks High School for a year, then three years at High Point High School. In 1934 he went to Chapel Hill to work in the Extension Division and, except for four years in the Army, has been there ever since. At Chapel Hill he met his wife, Darice, at that time Proff Koch's secretary; they have one son.

"Sleep On, Lemuel" was followed in the spring of 1934 by "Itchin' Heel," a full-length Negro play which Parker wrote and produced in High Point. It was a tremendous success—the first all-Negro play ever given in the South with an all-Negro cast.

Since then, his energies have been turned away from actual dramatic composition of his own. Even so, the reader of "Sleep On, Lemuel" will wish that John W. Parker had continued to write of the engaging Negro of eastern North Carolina—a personality whom he knows so well.

THE CHARACTERS

Louisa, *an old conjure doctor*
Collin, *a young Negro man*
Lucy, *a Negro girl*
Sipp, *Lucy's father*
Parson Baton, *the preacher*

SCENE

The yard in front of Lem's cabin in eastern North Carolina.

TIME

A summer night. About two o'clock.

60

The scene is the yard before an old weatherbeaten two-room Negro cabin dimly seen at the right. An umbrella china tree in the background is silhouetted vaguely in the soft moonlight of a warm night in June. Yellow lamplight shines from the front window of the cabin.

As the eye becomes accustomed to the scene, a penthouse porch is observed, and a door leading into the lighted room of the cabin. On a shelf, which reaches from the far porch-post to the house, is a battered water bucket and an old wash-basin. Under the window is a goods-box which serves as a bench, and barely visible around the corner of the cabin is an old wash-barrel with a pestle in it.

At the left is a thick cape jasmine bush with a rough home-made bench beside it. In the left background a chicken-house is dimly outlined, an old black rusty wash-pot on its bed of ashes, and sagging clothes line extending from the chicken-house to the porch.

If we could look through the window we should see a rather repellent sight. The corpse of an old Negro man is stretched out on a "cooling-board." Breath left the body late yesterday afternoon, but the undertaker will not arrive with the coffin until dawn. The corpse is clothed in a cheap black suit and is bootless. The sparse gray hair is combed out into a kinky pompadour. Two shiny nickels press down the eyelids and a saucer of salt has been placed on the stomach to keep the body from purging. A pan of ashes on the floor under the cooling-board absorbs the disease of the dead man. In one corner of the room, on a small pine bed, the bed clothes are rolled up in a knot and placed in the center of the mattress. A mirror, hanging on the wall, and two pictures have been turned to face the wall. On a small table near the bed there are still two half-empty medicine bottles and a lamp burning smokily.

As the curtain rises, the voice of PARSON BATON *is heard finishing a lengthy prayer for the spirit of the deceased and invoking a blessing on the remaining "loved ones."*

PARSON BATON (*inside*). . . . And, Oh Lawd, ef it be dy will, O Lawd, hab' mu'cy on dis po' sorrow-stricken fambly. As de pitcher was broken at de well, O Lawd, so is deir hearts crushed

61

and bleedin' as de result ob our po' brudder's death; and now we is all pantin' atter de goodness ob dy healin' love. O Jesus, Lawd, Gawd, turn our hearts from sin and let dis heah man's death and burial help us to convert more chillun into de kingdom ob de Lamb. Amen.

And the voices of the other brethren and sisters who are sitting up to comfort the family of the deceased mumble out "Amen." A sigh of relief, the blowing of noses, and the muffled scraping of chairs comes from within. The parson starts a hymn and the others join in.

> I ain't got nobody but de Lawd, Lawd, Lawd;
> I ain't got nobody but de Lawd;
> I ain't got nobody but de Lawd, Lawd, Lawd;
> I ain't got nobody but de Lawd.
> I's so full ob tears, I cain't he'p cryin';
> I ain't got nobody but de Lawd.

During the song, LOUISA *comes in from the left. She is an old Negress, past sixty, her face gaunt and wrinkled, and her head covered by a faded purple bandanna. Her dress, of plaid homespun, is billowy and ragged, and her shoes are slit for comfort. On her left arm she carries a small basket filled with wild roots and herbs, and in her right hand a stick, upon which she sometimes leans rather heavily. She pauses a moment as if to take in the situation, gazes at the house, then hobbles over to the window and looks in. She does not seem surprised at what she sees, for she chuckles to herself and mumbles.*

LOUISA. So dere you lies stretched on de coolin' bo'd, with nickels on yo' eyes, and a plate ob salt on yer. Well, you ain't de fu'st un to be laid stretched dat-a-way, Lem, an' you ain't gwine-a be de las' un, I reckons.

A MOURNING VOICE (*inside*). All dat I's gots done gone. O Lawd! Hab' mu'cy on me!

LOUISA (*turns away from the window and speaks as if talking to the dead man's spirit*). You's been a moughty good nigger, Lem, an' you done me some ra't good turns in time, so I'll wu'k my cha'ms, an' make it rain, so yo' sperit will be at res' an' won't go screamin' up an' down de woods o' nights, pesterin' de res' un us.

The door opens and the old woman hobbles quickly behind the house out of sight as LUCY, *a young Negro girl of eighteen, enters, followed by* COLLIN, *a mulatto of twenty-one. They are dressed in their Sunday finery for two reasons: first, because of the nature of the function which they are attending; and second, because they knew they would see each other tonight.*

COLLIN. Reckon it's too chilly-lak' out here for you, Lucy? Ef 'tis, I don't want you to be coming out wid me.

LUCY. Chilly? Lawd, now! (*She inhales deeply.*) It feel a heap sight betterer out here dan it does in dat dere shet-up room wid Parson Baton rantin' aroun' an' everybody hoppin' fu'st up an' den down—singin' an' prayin' an' sich lak'. I plumb lose patience wid all dese wakes. Cain't nobody die no mo' widout a 'laborate settin'-up party.

COLLIN. I's glad you didn't stay 'way from dis un, Lucy. I mought not a-got a chance to a-seed you dis week.

LUCY (*goes over to the cape jasmine bush at the left and plucks two of the blossoms. She smells them, and pins one on her dress and the other on* COLLIN'S *coat*). Yeah, I had a time gittin' Pa to come. He held out a long time, but I finally recomembered him ob de seed taters dat Lem gin him t'other day, and I 'low dem taters ain't lackly to do so well if Lem's sperit gits riled wid him an' makes dem sprouts to rot in de groun'. Dat fixed him. He'd do anything to keep on de good side ob a sperit.

COLLIN. You got a head on yo' shoulders, Lucy. You has fo' a fact, now.

LUCY (*takes* COLLIN'S *hand and leads him over to the bench beside the jasmine bush. They sit down and there is a slight pause*). Boy, you sho' is takin' a heap o' chances, sittin' here holdin' my han' an' 'pearin' so romantic-lak'. S'pose'n' Pa would step out on dat po'ch an' get a look at you. He'd be gunnin' fo' you tomorrow.

COLLIN. Has he said anythin' else 'bout me lately, Lucy? He ain't spoke to me since I got dat job o' sexton dat he'd been holdin' fer twenty years over at de white folks' church.

LUCY. Dat's what turned him agin you, I reckon. The white

folks knowed Pa was gittin' too old to clean up dat church lak' it or't to be, so dey had to git a spry young man lak' you, Collin. But Pa thought you lied about him or somethin' jest so as you could git de job, an' he never forgive you. Pa always was proud ob being app'inted to sweep dat church. He thought he ranked wid Preacher Baton in church affairs den; but now what wid him losin' de job an' all, an' you gittin' it, it's made him take a back seat an' he's kinder hurt.

COLLIN. I'd ruther mos' anybody'd be mad at me dan yo' pa, Lucy, 'cause after I marries you I don't want no trouble in de fambly.

LUCY. Don't look lak' dere's gonna be no marriage lessen yo' does sumpthin' to make Pa lak' you betterer. He said he'd ruther see my soul roastin' in hell an' my body floatin' roun' in a watery grave wid worms crawlin' over it dan to hab' me married to a low-down dirty liar lak' you. But I don't keer; I lak's you just de same.

COLLIN. Lawd, Lucy, do he hate me *dat* bad?

LUCY. Dat he do, an' he said ef he caught you 'round our place agin he'd shoot you so full ob holes you'd look lak' a 'tater grater.

COLLIN. I 'specks I better keep out'n his way, den. I noticed how he kept eyein' me in de house dere wheneber he'd ketch me lookin' at you. But dey was so busy havin' silent prayer when we come out I reckon he didn't notice us.

LUCY (*catching hold of* COLLIN'S *arm and listening intently*). Collin, did you hear anythin' in dat room? (*She points to the room in which the dead man is lying.*)

COLLIN. Naw, I didn't hear nothin'. You ain't gittin' scared out here, is you? (*He laughs.*) Lem's dead, an' his sperit ain't gonna bother us. (*He pauses a moment, listening.*) Lucy, dere is somethin' makin' a noise 'round dat winder! (*He rises, goes over to the window, and peers in. In the meantime,* LOUISA *comes from behind the house with her basket and stick.*) It must-a been our imaginin', honey; dere ain't nothin' in dere to make a noise.

LOUISA (*who is standing behind them*). Evenin', folks.

LUCY (*jumping up*). Aunt Louisa!

COLLIN (*wheeling around*). My Gawd! The conjure woman!

What you doin' progin' 'round here dis time o' night? An' scarin' folks half to death? Ain't dere enough trouble aroun' here widout you messin' roun'?

LUCY. Now, Collin, you hush; you ain't got enough sense to bell a buzzard. (*In an undertone.*) You don't know what she'll do if you— (*To* LOUISA.) How do, Aunt Louisa—how you come on?

LOUISA (*still glancing at* COLLIN). Kind-a po'ly, thanks, but so's to be about. How's you an' yo' folks?

LUCY. Well as common, I reckon. Don't hear no complaint. Won't you set a spell wid us?

LOUISA. No, thankee, chile, I got to be movin' along. I been out eber since de moon riz, collectin' plants an' weeds fer my medicines, an' 'twon't be long befo' daylight; an' I got a ra't fur piece to go 'twixt now an' then.

COLLIN. Aunt Lou, do you know what's in dat house?

LOUISA. Sho', I knows. Lem's body is in dere, but not his sperit. His sperit is hangin' aroun' out here waitin' fer de three days to be up so it kin go wanderin'. Down at de crossin' I met an' talked wid Lem's sperit, an he told me things. Told me things dat was meant for no mortal years but ol' Louisa's. De Great Un sont me a heap o' comfort an' power through him. Comfort fer de weary an' oppressed in de world, an' power, to oberthrow de wicked jes' as I pleases.

COLLIN. Say, Aunt Louisa, you can do mos' anythin' you wants to, cain't you? I mean anythin' anybody axes you to?

LOUISA. You ain't got much faith in my wu'ks, has you? Well, my ma was a conjure doctor, an' her ma befo' her. Dey taught me what I knows, an' now dat dey're dead, dey's taught me mo' dan dey did when dey was livin'. I kin talk to sperits an' dey kin talk to ol' Louisa. I knows whar de sweet healin' an' killin' plants grows, an' I knows all de cha'ms to give people to keep 'em out o' trouble or to make 'em hab' trouble. Dere ain't no man, woman, or chile dat can resis' when my spell is cas' on 'em.

COLLIN (*hesitantly*). How much do you cha'ge to put cha'ms on people, a r'al easy cha'm dat wouldn't hurt none?

LUCY. Now, Collin, what you up to? Dere ain't nobody you wants to hab' conjured.

COLLIN. Honey, maybe dis lady could holp us out ef she got her mind set on it.

LUCY. What do you mean?

COLLIN. I means fix yo' pa so's he would let us git married widout no row or us havin' to run off.

LUCY. Naw sir! Ain't nobody gonna pizin *him* or nuthin', ef I has any say-so about it.

COLLIN. Why, she wouldn't pizen him, honey chile. She could give him somethin' mild-lak', so he wouldn't be mad at me. (*To* LOUISA.) You could do dat, couldn't you?

LOUISA. It would be ra't smart harder to give him a mild cha'm, but I guess we could fix it, somehow.

COLLIN (*eagerly*). Let her do it, Lucy, let her do it. Just think, we'uns could get married—maybe nex' Sunday—an' we could move ober to dat little house on de far side o' Mr. John's field —an' . . . oh, come on, honey, let her try it anyway. It won't cost much.

LUCY (*doubtingly, to* LOUISA). You shore you ain't gonna hurt Pa, or nothin'?

LOUISA. Lawd, chile, I neber hurts nobody less I got cause to, an' yo' pa ain't neber done nothin' agin me.

LUCY. How much you gonna cha'ge us?

LOUISA (*to* COLLIN). How much money you got wid you?

COLLIN (*emptying his pockets*). Eighty-six cents. (*Hastily.*) But I mought be able to git you a little mo' in de mawnin'.

LOUISA. Dat's enough in money. How about a ham or a shoulder o' meat? Do you reckon you could bring me one down to my place dis week; my meat's runnin' short.

COLLIN. Yes'm, I kin. I tell you what. If you does dis fer us, I'll bring you a ham an' some fresh chitlins to boot. How's dat fer a bargain, now?

LOUISA. Uh, dat's enough from you. Now (*to* LUCY), what has you got to help pay fer your pa's consent to you marr'in' dis boy?

LUCY. I don't know. I ain't got nothin'.

COLLIN. Look-a-here. How much more you want? You must think we're rich, or somethin'.

LOUISA (*to* LUCY). Ain't you got nary ol' quilt? Dat would complete de bargain betwixt us.

LUCY (*hesitantly*). Yes'm, I could give you a red tulip quilt Miss Katie gint' me last year.

LOUISA. Uh-hum—well, you gimme dat money now, an' both of you kin bring me de odder things nex' Thursday evenin'. An' be shore you bring 'em because. . . .

COLLIN. Oh, we'll git 'em dere, all right.

LUCY. Yes, Ma'am, we won't go back on our word.

LOUISA. Uh-hum. Le's see, chile, is yo' pa in dere wid de res' ob de mourners?

LUCY. Yes'm, he's in dere now.

LOUISA. Well, you step in dere an' tell him a friend's out heah, an' has a message fer him.

LUCY (*steps up on the porch, hesitates a moment*). You plumb sho' you ain't goin' to hurt Pa none?

LOUISA. Run along, gal. I knows dis bus'ness better'n you does. (LUCY *goes into the house.*)

COLLIN. Wheah mus' I go? One thing shore, I better not git too close to Lucy's pa befo' dat cha'm start wu'kin'.

LOUISA. You stay heah, boy. Stay heah an' keep yo'self quiet. (*Inside the house the Negroes begin to sing again, and shouts of "Hallelujah" and "Amen" are heard. Old* LOUISA, *lifting her head, sniffs at the breeze with a keen nose.*) A little bitsy breeze is 'ginnin' to rise—an' dat breeze goin' to rise high by an' by. I smells rain in de air. It'll be good fo' yo' sperit, Lem. Yeah, dis rain be good fo' yo' sperit. (*She places her basket beside the jasmine bush and draws out some herbs from its contents. She gives the herbs to* COLLIN.) Here, boy, go put dis in dat bucket o' water dere on de shelf.

COLLIN. It ain't pizen, is it?

LOUISA. You git a move on yer befo' dey git back. You wants dis done proper, don't yer? (COLLIN *drops the herbs into the water-pail.*) An' put dis under de step dere. (LOUISA *unties a small flannel bag from around her neck.*) All dis will he'p us some. Dese heah cha'ms don't nebber fail. (COLLIN *puts the bag under the doorstep.*) Don't you an' yo' gal say much whilst he's out heah, er he's lak'ly to git mad. He's got 'ligion in him now, an' 'ligion make him mad; an' conjure medicine don't mix wid it no mo'n oil an' water.

COLLIN. No'm, but I's 'fraid dey goin' to mix lak' fire an' dynamite. (LUCY *appears in the doorway, followed by* SIPP, *her father, an old Negro past fifty, neatly dressed for the occasion. He comes out blinking his eyes to accustom them to the uncertain light and wiping them with a red bandanna handkerchief. He is visibly affected by the emotional strain of the settin'-up.*)

SIPP. What dat you sayin', Lucy? Look like you done lost yo' manners, de way you actin' dis evenin'.

LUCY. I done tol' you, Pa, somebody wants to see you out heah.

SIPP. Who in de name ob Gawd could be a-wantin' to see me at dis time ob night.

LUCY. You go see. Dere dey are—waitin' fo' you dere in de yard.

SIPP. Huh! Dey's cain't be much if dey out dere skulkin' around in de dark. (*He peers out suspiciously.*) Huh! Mus' be dey don't want no good.

LUCY. Pa, I do b'lieve you're plum' scared to go see who 'tis.

SIPP. You hush yo' sassy talk, gal. I reckon ef dey's waited dis long dey kin wait till I wet my whistle wid some well water. (*He goes to the well and takes a big drink from the bucket, swallowing noisily, all the time keeping an eye out in the dark yard. But* LOUISA *and* COLLIN, *concealed in the shadow of the jasmine bush, make no movement. Finally having no reason for a longer delay, he calls out from the porch.*) You, out dere. Step out wheah I can see you. I ain't goin' messin' aroun' in de dark wid no strangers.

LOUISA (*stepping out of the shadow*). You's ra't sma't chicken-hearted dis evenin', Sipp.

SIPP (*boldly descending into the yard*). Huh! What you up to, Louisa? How come you keep yo'se'f so secret?

LOUISA. I ain't lak' some to make a big noise ober de dead. Let 'em sleep, I say.

SIPP (*catching sight of* COLLIN *for the first time*). Collin! I reckon it was you done sent fo' me! Well, I ain't got no mo' jobs fo' you to take away from me, an' I ain't come heah dis evenin' to fight ober de daid.

COLLIN. No, suh. I ain't wantin' to see you about nothin'—leastways. . . .

LUCY. Now, Pa, you and Collin keep still. Aunt Louisa's got somethin' to tell you, Pa.

SIPP. Well, spit it out. I's got business in dere comfortin' dem dat mourn, an' I cain't be bothered wid standin' out here in de night air talkin', lessen you got somethin' special to say.

LOUISA. Sipp, take stock o' what yo're sayin', fer dere's mo' people an' things listenin' to you than you can see.

THE VOICE OF THE WIDOW (inside). Po' Lem, yo' had to go leab' yo' home life! What's I gwine do widout yo'!

SIPP. What you tryin' to do, Louisa? Conjure me? I ain't neber gin' you no cause to git riled wid me, so I'd just thank 'ee to move on an' let me go back to my business o' healin' dem dat need comfort.

PARSON BATON (inside). Lawd, hab' mu'cy on dis man at de bar o' jedgment! (Cries of "Amen" from the Negroes in the house.)

LOUISA. Sipp, you listen to me befo' it's too late. I ain't goin' to conjure you; you's already conjured! Somebody else done conjured you, an' bad luck's follerin' you around jes' like a calf follerin' a cow. Why you reckon you lose dat job o' sexton ober at de chu'ch? Why you think yo' bes' Polo Chiner hawg died las' week? Man, you ought t' a-been t' see me long afore now t' git a cha'm agin dis conjurement.

SIPP. What yo' mean, Louisa? Who been conjurin' me? Tell me his name so I kin bus' his skull in. I mought be gittin' old, but I ain't so weak I cain't frail a low-down sneakin', leather-neck, son of a tree-toad to death!

LOUISA. Ca'm down a minute, an' let me ax you a few questions, Sipp. Yo' spell is sho' wu'kin' ha'd on yer tonight. You ain't got much furder to go afore hell breaks loose in yer. Atter that won't no cha'm do yer no good. Fu'st, answer me dis: why does you hate dis boy Collin so bad?

SIPP. Why does I hate him? Ax me how bad I hates him. (He glares at COLLIN.) Nigger, I tol' yer de next time I seed yer wid my gal, you an' me was goin' to git togedder and dere wan't goin' to be but two licks passed. I'm goin' to frail you ra't now, an' you're goin' to hit de ground. Why fo' yer always hangin' roun' here, nohow? Anybody wid a yaller streak in 'em lak' you cain't mean no good.

COLLIN. Mr. Sipp, it's dis-a-way. You is mad at me 'ca'se I got your job as sexton, but I don't want de ol' job. It kin go ter ballyhack fer all I keers. But I loves Lucy an' she loves me, an' we'uns wants ter git married.

SIPP. Why, damn your dirty, rotten, lyin' soul! (*To* LUCY.) What you mean puttin' up wid any sich thing as dis fer? Ain't I done tol' yer what I'd do fer yer ef I ketched yer traipsin' roun' wid him? Anybody dat would lie 'bout me so's he could git my job ain't goin' to hab' nothin' to do wid me or mine.

LUCY. Oh, Pa, he didn't lie to get your job. Aunt Louisa done tol' you how you is conjured.

THE MOURNERS (*wailing inside*). Jesus, forgib' our sins! . . . We ain't nebber had so many! . . . Hallelujah! . . . Amen! . . . Sabe us from a burnin' hell, Lawd! . . . Amen, Jesus!

SIPP (*bristling*). Ef I's conjured, he's de nigger dat done it. You let me git my han' on dat clothes passel ober dere, an' I'll see who he conjure.

LOUISA. Wait, Sipp! You ain't goin' to git in no roucus here in de presence ob death, is you? Listen to dis: all day I been a-hearin' voices. Dem voices tol' me to come an' warn you 'fore it were too late, an' your soul was los' forebermo'. An' jest dis evenin' whilst I was out a-gatherin' yerbs, I seed a black crow settin' in a ol' daid tree. He looked so f'miliar dat I went up close; an' shore enough 'twas Lem' sperit turnt inter a crow an' he was a-moanin', an' a-groanin'; an' dat's a bad sign dat he's displeased wid somethin' here in dis world.

SIPP. But how you know Lem's displeased wid me? I ain't nebber done nuthin' agin Lem.

LOUISA. I's comin' to dat part now. Whilst I was lis'enin' to de crow, I looked through de woods an' seed a great ball ob fire rollin' along. So I ups and follers it to de clearin', an' from dere it went a-floatin' along easy-lak' 'twell it stop. It stop off short —an' wheah you reckin dat ball ob fire stop at? (*Pointing a bony finger at* SIPP). It stop at yo' house!

SIPP. O Lawd, I sho' mus' be conjured, fer a fac'. (*There is the sound of wailing and chanting inside the house.*)

LOUISA. Whilst I was a-watchin', dat ball ob fire git tired ob settin' in front ob yo' house, Sipp, and all of a sudden it shoot up in de air. It kep' a-gettin' smaller an' smaller an' smaller— 'twell it went clean out o' sight!

SIPP. Dat low-down Collin done put a spell on me. He's jes' dat kin'. But I fix him. What else you seed? Tell me eberthing you seed.

LOUISA. I cain't tell you no mo', but it's turrible de things I been seein' an' hearin' lately—an' all ob 'em p'intin' to you. (A faint breeze stirs the jasmine bush.) Lawd, look!—Dere's a sperit in dat bush right now! Don't git near it, Sipp! Don't git near it!

SIPP. Oh, Jesus, what's I gonna do? Gib' me a cha'm to break dis spell, Louisa. What's I gonna do, tell me quick!

LOUISA. You must a-been doin' a powerful sight ob meanness lately fer de sperits to be atter you dis bad. What you been doin'? Tell me so's I kin fix you a cha'm.

SIPP. I ain't been doin' nuthin,' I tells you. (The curtains blow slowly out of the window and the lamp light flickers in the room.)

LUCY. Don't you lie, Pa. I don't want nuthin' bad to happen to you. Maybe Aunt Louisa can fix it now if you tell her.

SIPP. Lucy, chile, I ain't done nuthin', I tell you. What you reckon I done? (THE MOURNERS inside are wailing and shouting.)

THE WIDOW'S VOICE. Why you take him away, Lawd? We was so happy. . . . Jesus, what I gwine do? (Suddenly the wind blows the lamp out. This is too much for the old SIPP, who drops to his knees and begins praying.)

SIPP. Lawd, de sperit done got de light! Dey mus' be fixin' to get me sho' now. O Lawd, hab' mu'cy on me! Hab' mu'cy on me, Jesus! I'm sorry fo' what I done. It wa'n't nuthin' so bad, but I'm sorry fo' it, Lawd.

LOUISA. I knowed you been up to some meanness fer de sperits to be atter you! What you been doin', Sipp?

SIPP. Fix me up dat cha'm, Louisa. Yeah, gimme dat cha'm quick.

LOUISA. How I goin' to fix you a cha'm 'lessen you tell what you been up to?

SIPP. Yes, Lawd—I'll tell eberthing—I didn't mean to do nuthin' sinful. I jes' found one little dollah bill under de chu'ch pew—I didn't know it belong to nobody. . . .

LOUISA. Lawd, man, you done stole a dollah bill outen de chu'ch?

SIPP. I take back every cent ob dat money, Louisa. I didn't mean to keep it, Lawd! Honest I didn't.

LOUISA. You sayin' honest! Man, take dat word "honest" outen yo' mouf.

SIPP. Gimme dat cha'm, now, lak' you promise.

LOUISA. Here, you take dis cha'm. (*She feels in her pocket and produces a gray sack filled with some smelly concoction.* SIPP *takes it, and rubs it between his hands.*) Now, de Lawd ain't goin' to answer nobody's prayers widout deir heart's free from malice. Hab' you forgib' Collin? Does you know why you los' dat job ob sexton?

SIPP (*kneeling*). Yes, yes, Lawd! I knows, an' I axes you to forgib' me!

LOUISA. Does you agree to Lucy an' Collin gittin' married?

SIPP (*protesting*). Heah, now, what's dat got to do wid dis conjurement? What dey got to git married fo'?

LOUISA. Uh-huh, I see you ain't ceased from yo' sinful thoughts yit. (*She gravely draws a large circle around him with her stick, while* SIPP *looks on panic-stricken.*)

SIPP. Look out, look out, heah, Louisa! —What you up to? Don't you put no mo' cha'ms on me!

LOUISA. I's got you hemmed in, Sipp, an' you cain't go free 'twell yo' heart is cleared o' malice.—Now then, is you ready to cease from yo' sinfulness?

SIPP (*walking gingerly about in the circle, afraid to cross the line*). Heah, heah, Louisa! You come back heah and git me out o' dis picklement.

LOUISA. You do what yo' conscience tell you, Sipp.

SIPP. O Lawdy, Lawdy! Come heah, Collin; come heah. Lucy. I won't stan' in yo' way no longer. (*He puts* LUCY's *hand in* COLLIN's *hand.*) Don't you cross dat line—I don't want you to be in torment 'cause o' me.—Collin, boy, I must a-been doin' you wrong, but now you an' me is going to hit it off togedder. I ain't goin' to stand in yo' way no longer—naw, suh! (*He turns to* LOUISA *piteously.*) Now, den, Louisa, you git me outen dis mess.

LOUISA (*spits impressively into the circle*). Now, den. You is free, Sipp!

SIPP (*steps gingerly out of the circle, being careful not to touch the line*). Does you reckon dat'll fix me, Louisa? Reckon dis cha'm will keep off de sperits? (*He holds up the conjure bag.*)

LOUISA. Sho'! Ain't nuthin' goin' to bother you so long as you wear dat medicine sack, an' cease from yo' sinful ways. But if I was you, I'd git back in dat house ra't now an' git to prayin'.

SIPP (*edging toward the house*). Yeah, yeah, I'm a-goin' now. An' I's goin' to take dat dollah bill back to Mistuh Larkin fu's' thing in de mawnin', an' ax him to let me he'p clean up dat chu'ch fo' nothin'. Yes, suh, I'll do it fo' nuthin'.

LOUISA (*calling after him*). Sipp, you wear dat cha'm three days an' nights, an' den go chunk it in de branch, at sunset, at de end ob de third day.

SIPP. Yeah, yeah—I'll do it, Louisa, I sho' will! (*He disappears in the house. The Negroes inside are singing "Swing Low, Sweet Chariot."*)

COLLIN. Lady, we sho' is indebted to you fo'. . . .

LOUISA. You shut up, now, an' git home. Pair o' young folks in love ain't got no reason fo' hangin' aroun' de daid, nohow.

LUCY (*as the two go out, LUCY calling a shy good-bye to the conjure woman*). Good-bye, Aunt Louisa.

LOUISA (*grunts by way of reply, picks up her basket and goes over to the window to look in on Lem's dead body.*) Sleep on, Lemuel. It'll rain tomorrow, an' den yo' sperit'll be free to go roamin' through de world. (*She chuckles to herself and, spitting over her shoulder, goes off.*)

CURTAIN

IN DIXON'S KITCHEN

A Comedy of a Country Courtship

BY

WILBUR STOUT

(Written in collaboration with Ellen Lay)

A PLAY OF THE LATE HORSE-AND-BUGGY DAYS

"I know about a country boy's courtship which ought to make a play," student Wilbur Stout remarked in Professor Koch's playwriting class one morning. "The old man used to stamp on the floor of his bedroom upstairs as a signal for the boy to go home. One night the boy—we'll call him Lem—conceived the idea of pretending to leave. He called out to the girl a loud 'Good-bye,' and banged the outside door. Then after a little he slipped in through the window in his stocking feet to finish saying 'Goodnight.' But the father came in and discovered his trick."

Such was the germ of the comedy which follows. Proff Koch always suspected the incident was autobiographical, though the author never admitted it. Later, at suggestions from the members of the class, the Little Brother was added, and also a rival suitor who never appears on stage. The older brother's theft of the shoes was a final touch, except for the phrasing of Annie Lee's speeches by classmate Ellen Lay. Author Stout protested that he could never make a girl-character talk naturally.

The amusing comedy which resulted is an example of Professor Koch's method of teaching. If a young playwright had an idea, the class was urged to help him develop it. For the language, however, the writer depended upon his own recollections of dialect, and Wilbur Stout maintains that much of the conversation "was set down verbatim." He dedicated his comedy "to the real Annie Lee, and to all others who have been courting in the country and have contended with the perplexing problem of the Little Brother."

Wilbur White Stout was born September 27, 1898, at Farmer in Randolph County. From Burlington High School he entered the University of North Carolina, from which he has three degrees, an A.B. in 1921, M.A. in 1922, and Ph.D in 1926. His career as head of English Departments and director of dramatics has been varied: first, three West Virginia colleges—Davis and Elkins, 1927; Concord State Teachers, 1927-29; and Morris Harvey, 1930. Between Kentucky Wesleyan College in 1931 and back to West Virginia at Kanawha College in 1933, he served as a free-lance director of dramatics and later as assistant to a literary agent in New York. He was at Mercer University for seven years, 1934-1941, during which time he was married. In 1941 he moved to Virginia Polytechnic Institute, and a year afterwards to Southwestern at Memphis. In 1944 he went to Mississippi Southern College at Hattiesburg, where he is now chairman of the English Department.

To all these posts, Dr. Stout carried the gospel of playwriting which he learned at Chapel Hill. In 1955 he was busy, for instance, spearheading the building of an outdoor stage near Hattiesburg for the presentation of historical drama along the lines developed by Paul Green and Kermit Hunter. He had interested the whole town in the project by helping in the organization of the Hattiesburg Community Drama Association.

Dr. Stout has had a hand in writing other plays besides "In Dixon's Kitchen." Another of his country comedies, "Dogwood Bushes," was published in *Carolina Folk Comedies* (Samuel French, 1931). Perhaps it too has an autobiographical pigment; it tells about the rural boy who dreams of the day he will burst upon the world as a book-writer.

Dr. Stout says that his acting roles have been most unusual ones. They include the braying of a "jack-ass," none other than the off-stage noises made by Old Bob in the original production of "In Dixon's Kitchen."

For a long time "In Dixon's Kitchen" held the record among the Carolina folk-plays for number of performances, both in and outside the Playmakers. Perhaps its popularity is due to its being a play of *action;* there is nothing static, even for a moment, about "In Dixon's Kitchen."

THE CHARACTERS

HIRAM DIXON, *a dour old farmer*
MA DIXON, *his wife*
ANNIE LEE DIXON, *their daughter*
GIL, *their son, aged 16*
JACK, *their son, aged 12*
LEMUEL ISLEY, *Annie Lee's "special" friend*

SCENE

A country district in the Piedmont section of North Carolina.
The Dixons' kitchen.

TIME

An evening in June, 1921.

The kitchen of the Dixons' home is a very neat, clean room, supplied with the furniture ordinarily found in a comfortable farmhouse. At the rear, left, is a long table set with an abundant country supper. A kitchen safe is at the right, and a small cook-table. At the left, front, is the stove, with the usual pots and pans, a woodbox, and a blue stone jar of cream covered with a white cloth. At the rear, right, is a window hung with a sash curtain; the waterbucket is in this corner. A door, at the center, opens on the side porch, and one at the left leads to the other part of the house. The unpainted walls of the room are of yellowish-brown color, presenting a rather attractive appearance in the glow of the shaded lamp.

The Dixons *are sitting at the supper table, all eating heartily.* Lem Isley, *who is "company," sits next to* Annie Lee *at the rear of the table.* Ma *is on the right side, with* Jack *close beside her;* Gil *is opposite her and* Pa *is seated with his back to the audience.*

Lem *is dressed up for the occasion in his Sunday blue-serge suit, new flowered necktie, and tan oxfords. The members of the* Dixon *family, with the exception of* Annie Lee, *are in their everyday work-clothes. (*Annie Lee *does not usually wear a pretty white dress when cooking supper, but tonight she wishes to appear at her best; and* Ma *wears a small white sewing apron over her faded gingham dress.)* Jack *wears overalls and has already started going barefoot, although the weather is still a little cool for that. There is hearty laughter from all the family when the curtain rises.* Jack *has crammed more chicken into his mouth than he can properly manage, and* Ma Dixon *gives him a reproving yank by the ear, which calls forth a loud guffaw from* Gil. Lem *cannot refrain from laughing heartily too. But* Ma, *unperturbed, turns sweetly to* Annie Lee's *"company."*

Ma. Have another piece of chicken, Lem. You're not eatin' any supper at all.

Lem. Thank you, ma'am. I believe I will. (*By this time* Pa *has finished eating and settled himself in a chair by the stove, where he puffs away comfortably at his pipe.*)

Gil. Pass it down this way when you get through with it, Lem. The rest of 'em has quit; I reckon it's up to us to clean out the dish.

79

ANNIE LEE. You oughtn't to eat so much supper, Gil, if you're going to the candy pullin' over at Carrie's tonight.

GIL. I was about to forget that. (*He eats with renewed energy.*) Annie Lee, it's too much trouble to move that dish. Pitch me one of them cowcumber pickles over here by the tail.

ANNIE LEE. Why, Gil! I never heard such talk! (*She is somewhat embarrassed, but forces a laugh and tosses a pickle across the table to him.* JACK *giggles.*)

GIL. That's the stuff! (*He pushes back his chair, takes the pickle in one hand, reaches with the other halfway across the table for a piece of chocolate layer-cake, crosses to the cook-table and cuts a generous slice from a gooseberry pie which* MA *has left there to cool.*) I'm in a rush! You-all can set and eat as long as you want to; I got somethin' better'n eatin' comin' to me. (*He hurries off to dress up for the party.*)

ANNIE LEE (*with mock formality*). We will excuse you, Gilmer.

GIL (*at the door, with exaggerated politeness*). Thank you, ma'am.

ANNIE LEE. Have another biscuit, Lem. Don't stop eatin' just 'cause Gil did.

LEM (*glancing at his plate and helping himself*). Thank you, Annie Lee.—Did you eat my biscuit, Jack? If you didn't, I'm afraid this makes about six for me.

JACK. Six? Is that the best you can count? You've done e't ten!

LEM (*glancing at* ANNIE LEE). Well, maybe I have, Jack, if you kept count. It's mighty good bread all right.

MA (*smiling*). Yes, Annie Lee is gettin' so she makes right good biscuit.

LEM. Did Annie Lee make these biscuits?

MA. Yes. I had some sewin' to do today, so I let Annie Lee do most all the cookin'.

LEM. No wonder I e't so many of 'em. That accounts for me likin' 'em so well.

JACK. You didn't cook enough, Annie Lee. He's hungry yet.

GIL (*from the other room*). What you-all done with my necktie?

MA (*raising her voice*). It's on the foot of your pa's bed, Gil.

I pressed it out for you this evenin' when I had the iron on the fire.

JACK. I got a necktie.

LEM. You have?

JACK. Uh-huh. (*Rummaging in his overalls pocket, he produces a bright red one.*) Ed give it to me.

LEM. Who's Ed?

JACK. Ed? Ed Nicholson. He's got red hair and he comes out from town to see Annie Lee sometimes. (ANNIE LEE *knowing* JACK's *propensity for making disconcerting remarks, glances anxiously at* MA.)

LEM (*worried*). Oh, I see. . . . Does he come often?

JACK. Ed was out here the other day in an automobile. Wa'n't he, Pa?

PA. Uh-huh.

JACK. And Annie Lee said she'd rather ride with—(MA *silences* JACK *by putting her hand over his mouth.*)

ANNIE LEE (*flurried*). Do you know Mr. Nicholson, Lem?

LEM (*coldly*). Just know him when I see him. (*There is an awkward pause. Then he pushes back his plate.*) Well, I ain't e't so much supper since old man Simpson's corn-shuckin'. I knowed you was a mighty fine cook, Annie Lee, but I didn't know you could cook like this.

ANNIE LEE (*blushing at* LEM's *admiring glance*). Oh, I like to cook.

MA (*as they rise from the table*). You-all go in the other room now. I'll wash up the dishes this time.

ANNIE LEE. You better try to get that dress finished, Ma. Lem and me will wash the dishes, if he don't mind.

LEM. I don't mind a bit. I'd like to help you. (MA *takes down the dishpan and pours out the water from the kettle on the stove.* LEM *and* ANNIE LEE *clear the table.*)

MA (*pointedly to* PA, *who is still sitting by the stove, smoking contentedly, absorbed in his own thoughts*). The paper come today. It's in yonder on the bed. Don't you want to read it?

PA (*fumbling for his glasses*). Bring me that thar paper, Jack. I'll read a little 'fore I go to bed. (JACK *goes and brings in the newspaper;* PA *settles comfortably to read it.*)

MA. You better go in the other room to read that paper. They'll be washin' the dishes in here. (PA *reluctantly resigns his ease and starts off.* LEM *and* ANNIE LEE *are busy with the dishes but they watch anxiously till* PA *has quit the room.* MA *turns to* JACK *as she goes out.*) Jack, you got your kindlin' to get in for the mornin'.

JACK (*taking a chair at his post of observation, beside the door at the left*). All right, Mom.

PA (*meeting* GIL, *who now returns from the other room*). Gil, you better let the horse git done eatin' 'fore you catch out.

GIL (*pulling at his necktie in an effort to adjust it properly*). He ought to be done eatin' by now. (PA *grunts and goes off.* GIL *begins to rub off his shoes with his handkerchief.*)

JACK (*sniffing the air and crossing to* GIL). Annie Lee, he's been usin' your perfume!

ANNIE LEE. Gilmer Dixon! (*She looks at him severely a moment, and then laughs.*)

LEM (*holding his nose*). You smell like the "Breath-of-Spring" all right; but I think you better take yourself out to walk 'fore you go to the candy-pullin'. How much of it did you use, anyway? (*They all laugh and* GIL *covers his embarrassment by hunting for his hat.*)

GIL. Oh, 'bout a spoonful, I reckon. Some spilled while I was messin' round in there. I wa'n't aimin' to use no perfume. (*He finds his hat on top of the kitchen safe, and starts to leave.*) That horse is done eatin' by now, I know.

PA (*reappearing at the door*). Now, Gil, don't you come blunderin' back in here, 'way late at night, wakin' us all up. Remember the rest of us wants to get a little sleep, even if you don't.

GIL (*in the doorway*). All right, sir. I won't. (LEM *and* ANNIE LEE *have finished clearing off the table and are preparing to wash the dishes on the cook-table which they have moved out into the room.* LEM *takes off his coat and* ANNIE LEE *arrays him in a big pink gingham apron.* JACK *lingers in the room doing nothing in particular.*)

MA (*coming to the door*). Jack! Jack! Come on out of there. I got somethin' I want you to do.

JACK. I'm not botherin' them, Ma. They're not doin' a thing! (*Nevertheless* MA *pulls* JACK *out of the room.* ANNIE LEE *follows them to the door and closes it. She begins washing the dishes, passing them to* Lem *to be dried.* Ma *comes back quietly to turn down the lamp which has begun to smoke, beams on them with approving affability, and goes out closing the door softly after her.)*

Lem. I wanted your Ma to get her sewin' done, Annie Lee, but that wasn't the main reason I wanted to help you.

Annie Lee. Why, what was the main reason?

Lem *(after a pause)*. Oh, . . . just for fun. *(There is another pause.)* Annie Lee, did Ed Nicholson help you wash the dishes when he was out here?

Annie Lee. No, he wasn't here for supper. But I reckon he would have helped me.

Lem. Huh! He never had an apron on in his life. He thinks folks wash dishes with a vacuum cleaner.

Annie Lee. Now, Lem! You're just runnin' Ed down 'cause he's a city boy. If you knew him like I do, you'd like him fine.

Lem. Oh, I know him well enough. He's just not worth a— much.

Annie Lee. I'm sorry you feel that way about him, 'cause I kind o' like Ed.

Lem *(forgetting the dishes and coming close to her side)*. How much?

Annie Lee *(pushing him away and indicating the unwiped dishes)*. Oh, now, Lem. Don't get jealous. Just look how far behind you're getting. *(They work in silence for a time. . . . Shyly.)* I wonder if you'll be willin' to help like this when . . . .

Lem *(alert)*. When, when?

Annie Lee. Oh, you know when . . . when you . . . get married.

Lem. Do you think she'd want me to? *(In taking up a wet dish, he fumbles and lets it slip and fall to the floor.)*

Annie Lee *(amused)*. No. I don't think so. Not if you drop them around like that. *(She picks up the pieces of the broken dish and puts them in the woodbox.)*

Jack *(bursting into the kitchen)*. Say, Annie Lee, come on out here! That old cat's got kittens and they ain't got their eyes open yet. Come on out here and see 'em!

Annie Lee *(shocked)*. Don't bother us, Jack. Can't you see we're busy? *(She goes to the table, gets a plate of scraps, and gives them to him.)* Now, you take this to the cat, and you go look at them.

JACK. Aw, you come on, Annie Lee.

ANNIE LEE. Now, run on out, Jack. *(Reluctantly he goes and she closes the door after him.)* I'm much obliged to you, Lem, for helpin' me wash the dishes. I wish I could help you some way.

LEM. Well, if you don't, it won't be because you don't get the chance. *(They continue. When* ANNIE LEE *reaches for the last dish, her face comes temptingly near to* LEM's. *He starts to kiss her, but misses by a few inches.)* Dad gum it! I almost caught myself kissin' you when you leaned over to get that dish.

ANNIE LEE *(carrying a pile of the dishes over to the safe).* That's all right, so long as you don't let me catch you doin' it.

LEM. Um . . . m . . . m . . . I wish I knew whether . . . whether. . . .

ANNIE LEE *(shyly).* What did you say? (PA *enters in his yarn socks—he was warming his feet by the fire in the other room. He says not a word, but crosses the kitchen, gets himself a drink of water at the bucket, turns and walks deliberately back the whole length of the room.* LEM *and* ANNIE LEE *pretend being very busy.* LEM *gets into his coat, preparing to leave.* ANNIE LEE *puts the last of the dishes away in the safe.)*

PA. We all want to get to bed pretty early here tonight; Annie Lee, you know what we got to do tomorrow.

ANNIE LEE *(obediently).* Yes, sir.

PA. And I don't want to hear no such racket as you and Jack was a-makin' last night. I got to get a little sleep sometime.

LEM. Yes, sir. I was a-thinkin' it was about time for me to be wakin' up old Bob.

PA. Well, I 'spect you better do it then. *(He makes this suggestion half under his breath, and goes off, leaving the door wide open behind them.* ANNIE LEE *hastens to close it.)*

ANNIE LEE. Now, you put the table back in the corner, Lem. *(He does so while she takes off her apron and hangs it up on a nail. She hesitates a little, then draws a chair toward him.)* Do you want to go in and talk to Ma awhile, or would you just as soon stay out here in the kitchen?

LEM. Naw, I come to talk to you—in the kitchen, or outdoors, or anywhere else. *(They sit down with their chairs not too far apart.)*

ANNIE LEE. Now, don't talk like that, 'cause I know you don't mean it.

LEM. I do mean it, too. I'd swear it on a stack of Bibles a mile high.

ANNIE LEE. You talk like you'd said that before. How many other girls have you said that to in the last month?

LEM. Nobody else. But if I could just say what I'd like to, you'd be surprised.

ANNIE LEE. Say it. I like to be surprised. *(She puts her hand on his arm. He takes it up, impulsively, and kisses it. She breaks away.)* Why, Lem! I wouldn't have thought that of you. I thought you were more of a man than to take advantage of me like that. I'm not that kind of a girl and I thought you knew it.

LEM. But that's nothin' to get red about. *(Rising to go.)* If you're goin' to cloud up and storm. . . .

ANNIE LEE. Well, if it's nothin', what was you tryin' to do it for? I don't intend to do anything like that till I'm engaged.

LEM. I'm sorry, Annie Lee. I reckon I did sort o' act the fool. . . . I'm sorry. . . . I'm not that kind of a fellow either. I wouldn't go with a girl that would let anybody kiss her till they was engaged. *(There is a painful silence.)* I feel awful mean about it, Annie Lee. . . . I'll try to do better—next time.

ANNIE LEE *(going to him and putting her hand softly on his arm)*. It's not all that bad, Lem. It's just your doin' it without. . . .

LEM *(vastly relieved)*. Well, let's forget about it and start all over again. *(He takes her impulsively by the hand and leads her back to the chair again.)*

ANNIE LEE *(mischievously, drawing her hand away)*. Do you feel any better now?

LEM. Lots better! Folks always feel better after a little spat.

ANNIE LEE. What makes a boy want to kiss a girl for . . . like that, anyway?

LEM. Dad burn it, I don't know! Durn the fellow that invented kissin' anyway. He caused more trouble than anybody else.

ANNIE LEE. Oh, I don't know. It's all right . . . in its place.

LEM. Where is its place?

ANNIE LEE. It's not . . . on the hand.

LEM. Generally speakin', is it—in the kitchen?

ANNIE LEE (*wistfully*). Generally speakin', it's anywhere that a boy and girl . . . love each other. . . .

LEM. I could fill my side of a bargain like that.

ANNIE LEE (*breathlessly*). But you don't love me.

LEM (*boldly now, he puts his arm over the back of her chair*). I do too. I love you, Annie Lee.

ANNIE LEE. No, you don't. You just say you do.

LEM. Maybe that's the way Ed talks. But I mean it. How can I prove it to you?

ANNIE LEE. Not by sayin' so. You just said that . . . to get a chance to . . . kiss me.

LEM. I always thought kissin' was the way to prove it.

ANNIE LEE (*shaking her head*). Nh . . . nh. . . .

LEM. What's the use for me to say it? What do you reckon I rode over here for? To sit around and talk? No! If there's any way to prove it, I'll do it, if it's to swallow old Bob! (*He is down on his knees when* JACK *reappears suddenly at the door.*)

JACK. Annie Lee, get me a drink of water.—What you-all sayin' your prayers for? (ANNIE LEE *gets him one and holds the dipper for him while he drinks long and thirstily. Then he grins.*) Mama said I could stay in here a little while, if you-all would let me.

ANNIE LEE (*coldly*). Just a little while, Jack. It's most time for you to be in bed. (*They resume their seats while* JACK *tries to entertain them.*)

JACK. I can stand on my head. . . . Hold my feet up, Lem. Now see if I can stand. (*He stands inverted a moment,* LEM *assisting him. A shower of marbles, nails, etc., descends from his pockets to the floor, He makes haste to recover his possessions.* LEM *resumes his chair, but* JACK *persists, following him.*) Wa'n't that good?

LEM (*glumly*). Good a-plenty! (*Now* JACK *climbs up into* LEM's *lap, and* LEM, *hard-pressed for a way out, scrubs his chin on* JACK's *face.*)

JACK (*gleefully*). Gee whizz, Annie Lee! Does it hurt you like that?

ANNIE LEE (*at her wit's end*). You'd better go to bed now, Jack.

JACK. No, I'm not sleepy. (*He feels something in* LEM's *pocket and whispers to* ANNIE LEE.) He's got some candy in his pocket! (LEM *pulls out a paper bag of candy and passes it to* ANNIE LEE. *She offers him some but he refuses; she gives* JACK *a piece and then forces him out of the room.*)

ANNIE LEE (*timidly*). Have you got over your scare yet?

LEM. I wasn't scared. I was just tryin' to convince you. (JACK *has come back for more candy.*)

JACK. I believe I could stand on my head again, if I had another piece of candy. (LEM *is now exasperated—quite.*)

ANNIE LEE (*speaking with authority*). Jack, it's time you were in bed. (*Calling.*) Ma, why don't you put Jack to bed?

MA (*at the door*). Come on out of there, Jack. (JACK *not minding her, she comes into the room after him and leads him out by the ear. He begins to cry and* ANNIE LEE *gives him the rest of the candy to quiet him. Now* PA *appears.*)

PA. Hush up that cryin', Jack. Mind your Ma. (*He directs a meaning glance at* LEM *and retires. In the confusion the door is left open.* ANNIE LEE *slams it to.*)

LEM. Confound it! Every time the signs get right, something has to go and happen.

ANNIE LEE (*they sit down and try again*). Something has happened. I don't know whether to believe what you said awhile ago or not.

LEM. Drat it! I don't believe all the preachers in the world could make you believe that Jonah swallowed the whale. (*There is an awkward pause.* ANNIE LEE *feigns indifference.*) Well, if it's goin' to be like this, I guess I'd better go. (*Starting up.*) You and Ed done got it all fixed up, I reckon. . . . (*He gazes longingly at her.*) I better be goin' on. . . . I got to get up soon in the mornin'. Got to hold the governor cords over the business end of an old jarr-head. (*The mule brays outside.*) There's old Bob callin' me now. He knows when it's time to leave.

ANNIE LEE. 'Tain't worth while to rush off. . . .

LEM. Yeah. . . . I got to be goin' on. . . .

ANNIE LEE (*pursuing him*). No, don't. Set awhile longer.

LEM (*relieved*). Well, if you want me to.

ANNIE LEE. You ought to know I want you to. (*He resumes his seat closer now to* ANNIE LEE *than ever before and takes her hand.* PA *pounds on the floor overhead.*)

LEM. I would like to convince you before I go. (*Before she can reply,* PA *pounds the second time.*)

ANNIE LEE. There's Pa again. I reckon you had better go now.

LEM. Yeah, I reckon I had better. . . . (*He is loath to go.* ANNIE LEE *stands looking blankly at him. Then she has a brilliant idea.*)

ANNIE LEE. Wait! I've got an idea! Let's. . . . (*She takes him by the hand and whispers something in his ear. He seems doubtful at first, glances at the window, then grins broadly, and strides heavily to the door.*)

LEM (*in a loud voice*). Good night, Annie Lee.

ANNIE LEE. Good night, Lem. (*He is heard walking across the porch outside. She closes the door with a bang, goes to the window, raises it, and lets him in that way. He enters noiselessly, in his stocking-feet, carrying his shoes in his hand. They tiptoe back to their chairs.*)

LEM. Well, Annie Lee, I guess we slipped one over on the old man, that time—if that blame mule will just keep his mouth shut. (*With suppressed laughter she picks up the shoes and is about to set them aside.* LEM, *however, makes for them.*) Better let me get into that pair o' gun-boats. I want to be ready to move off from here at about half-a-second's notice.

ANNIE LEE. But Pa might hear you movin' round. Hadn't you better wait?

LEM. Well, I better keep 'em handy, though. (*He puts the shoes to the rear of his chair. They sit very close together now, talking in subdued voices.*)

ANNIE LEE. You never did get it done. . . . (*He is about to kiss her, when* GIL *bounds up on the porch and breaks in on them. They jump apart.*)

GIL. Howdy, folks! What you-all doin'?

ANNIE LEE. Just talkin'—don't you want an apple?

GIL (*hilarious*). Naw! I ain't got no more appetite than a snake's got tail-feathers. I just e't thirteen in a contest. I couldn't eat no more—that's the reason I came home so early. . . .

ANNIE LEE (*knowingly*). I guess there was some other reason than that.—But don't talk so loud, Gil. Pa said not to wake him up comin' in, and he thinks—

Gil. Say, you-all ought to have been at the candy-pullin'! We made some molasses candy and it didn't get hard enough, and—

Annie Lee. Oh, I guess you didn't boil it long enough.

Gil. Sure, we knew that, but we wanted to get to pullin' it. So Carrie and me, we—

Annie Lee. Gil, don't talk so loud! Pa thinks Lem has gone. He called bedtime on us so early tonight, that we decided to play a trick on him. You see (*pointing to the window and the shoes*), Lem said good night and went out with a whole lot of racket, took off his shoes, and—snuck back in again! (*She checks Gil's resounding laugh. He sees interesting possibilities in the shoes.*)

Gil. Well, if you-all are goin' to sit up much longer you better punch up the fire. I'm goin' to bed.

Lem. 'Spect we had better, Annie Lee. (*While they are poking the fire, Gil gets possession of the shoes, conceals them under his coat, and starts out with them.*)

Gil. Good night, you-all.

Annie Lee. Good night.

Lem. Good—(*She checks him by putting her hand over his mouth. He kisses it ardently. Gil, with the shoes behind him, chuckles and backs out of the room.*)

Lem (*they are seated together once more*). Gil made a lot of noise in here. Do you reckon your Pa heard?

Annie Lee. I hope not. (*But Pa's heavy footsteps are heard coming down the stairs.*)

Lem. Yes, he did, too!—Where are my shoes? (*A frantic search is made. Lem is about to leave without them when Pa, in his shirtsleeves with one suspender down—apparently having dressed in some haste—appears in the dooorway with the shoes in his hand. He has stumbled over them in coming down the stairs. Lem, as a last resort, dashes under the table, Annie Lee covering him.*)

Pa (*holding out the shoes*). Who left these here shoes on the staircase? These here ain't Gil's shoes! And what in thunder was you and him raisin' so much Cain about? Didn't I tell you-all to be quiet? Did Gil go to bed?

ANNIE LEE. Yes sir. . . . Gil went to bed. . . . Didn't you meet him just now? . . . I tried to get him to be quiet, but. . . .

PA. Well, whose shoes is these?

ANNIE LEE. Why, I guess they're . . . they're . . . they're. . . .

LEM (coming out from under the table). They're . . . they're mine! I thought Gil hid 'em under the table. . . . I was just lookin' under there.

PA. Well. What the Sam Hill does this mean? I called bed-time long ago. Do you know what time it is? It's time every-body was at home in bed where they belong. I thought you was gone, Lem. What you doin' back here? (GIL returns, grinning broadly.)

LEM. Well, you see . . . you see. . . . We hadn't quite fin-ished . . . when. . . .

PA. Hadn't quite finished! What the fire was you doin', then?

LEM. Yes, sir. You see, I was tryin' to tell Annie Lee—

PA. Well, why didn't you tell her and not take so dad-burn much time about it? (MA enters with her sewing in her hand.)

MA (going to ANNIE LEE). Now, Pa, don't be so hard on 'em. I knew all the time Lem hadn't gone.

GIL (appearing on the scene too). They was waitin' for me to bring 'em some candy. I think they've got a sweet-tooth.

LEM. Yes, sir. I was just about ready to go, when—(JACK enters, in his nightgown now.)

JACK (rubbing his eyes). Papa, get me a drink of water.

PA (pushing JACK in the direction of the waterbucket). Well, have you got anything more to say? If you haven't—(He throws the shoes dangerously near LEM's feet and turns away. LEM gets into the shoes as quickly as possible.)

LEM (in desperation now). Yes, I have got something else to say. I've been tryin' to say somethin' to Annie Lee ever since supper, but every time I get ready to say it somebody goes buttin' in. (MA looks accusingly at PA.) I wasn't aimin' to say it to any-body but Annie Lee, but . . . but. . . . Well, listen and look! All of you! (In spite of his determination to get it all said, LEM finds that the words still stick in his throat. He gulps, takes ANNIE

Lee *by the hand and makes a final effort.*) Annie Lee . . . I . . . do . . . love you. Will you marry me?

Annie Lee *(she looks to* Ma *for approval;* Ma, *beaming, nods her head, of course).* Un . . . huh. . . . *(Then he takes her in his arms and kisses her.* Ma *is radiant.* Jack *giggles.* Gil *pretends to be surprised.* Pa *says nothing, but grunts and starts out to take up his interrupted sleep. But upon second thought he turns for the final word.)*

Pa. Well! That bein' the case, you better come around in the mornin' and . . . slop the hogs!

Curtain

THE RETURN OF BUCK GAVIN

The Tragedy of a Mountain Outlaw

BY

THOMAS WOLFE

A FIRST PLAY BY A NOTED NOVELIST

Thomas Wolfe, during those days of World War I in Chapel Hill, was the only male student of Professor Koch's first playwriting group. A member of the Junior Class, he took the course through the entire year, and at the end of it was thoroughly endeared to dramatic composition.

Since Wolfe was a "big man" on the campus, he spread his energies in many directions; and in spite of his devotion to playwriting, he gave but little time to the plays he put together. "I was a boy of eighteen when I wrote those plays and I wrote each of them in a few hours, because I did not understand what heart-breaking and agonizing work writing is." Such was the statement he made after fame had claimed him. Wolfe thus did not think back with pride to his little mountain melodramas; indeed they *are* juvenilia. Nevertheless, even the earliest work of a genius has a certain fascination because, if for no other reason, of the one who wrote it. Wolfe needed not to have blushed. As the work of a busy undergraduate, the plays are remarkable efforts.

"The Return of Buck Gavin" was Thomas Wolfe's first published piece of creative literature—his first essay into the realm of the imagination. It was produced on the first bill of the Carolina Playmakers, March 15, 1919, with the author in the role of the hero. In a foreword to the play he wrote: "When the dramatic possibilities of this incident flashed upon me, I immediately started to work with a set of mountain characters, the principal being Buck Gavin, an outlaw. It is a fallacy of the young writer, I believe, to picture the dramatic as unusual and remote. It is therefore but natural that he should choose for the setting of his first effort a New York apartment house, the Barbary Coast of San Francisco, or some remote land made dramatic by all the perfumes of Arabia. . . . But the dramatic is not the unusual. It is happening daily in our lives. Some of us, perhaps, toil on a mountain farm, and when we relax from the stolidity of mind and allow ourselves thought, it is to think bitterly of the unvaried, monotonous grind of our existence. Here is material for drama in the true sense." This first stated credo, he followed in his mature years.

Other dramatic pieces written at Chapel Hill were "The Third Night" and "Payment Deferred," both of them melodramas of the hill folk like "The Return of Buck Gavin," and finally a ridiculous skit dashed off for the campus humor magazine, "The Streets of Durham, or Dirty Work at the Crossroads, a Tragedy in Three Muddy Acts, by Tommy Wolfe." Perhaps other unsigned dramatic bits of Wolfe remain buried in the files of the undergraduate publications of his student days. He wrote voluminously for them all.

Under George Pierce Baker, he continued his study of playwriting at Harvard. While many dramatic fragments of his Cambridge years exist in manuscript, his main plays were "The Mountains," a one act folk-play later extended to three acts in which a native mountain boy returns home a doctor and becomes engaged in an ancient feud, and "Welcome to Our City," a full-length drama of real-estate manoeuvres concerning a Negro district in a Southern city. The second play was given an elaborate production in Cambridge. *Mannerhouse,* a long play completed in New York in 1925 and produced at Yale in 1949, foreshadowed some of the moods and incidents of his novels.

Though Wolfe originally intended becoming a playwright, he turned to the novel form and, beginning with *Look Homeward, Angel* in 1929, made literary history.

He was born in Asheville October 3, 1900. His post-student years were spent for the most part in New York, where intermittently until 1930 he was an instructor in English at New York University. He died September 15, 1938, in Baltimore and is buried in Asheville. The Old Kentucky Home, his family's house, is now a literary shrine opened to the public.

THE CHARACTERS

BUCK GAVIN, *a mountain outlaw*
MARY GAVIN, *his sister*
THE SHERIFF

SCENE

The cabin home of Buck Gavin in a remote cove of the Carolina mountains.

TIME

About 1918. An afternoon in May.

The living and dining room of the log cabin home of BUCK
GAVIN.

The furnishings of the room are more pretentious than are
usually associated with mountain cabins. This is explained by
the fact that GAVIN is a mountain chief, the leader of a clan—
a kind of tribal leader, if you like. The interior is rude, but
comfortable, with not a little taste displayed in the arrangement.
A woman's presence is denoted by blue chintz curtains at the
windows and a covering of the same material on the table in
the center of the room. A shaded lamp, several weekly newspapers, and a knitting basket are on the table. At the left a
crackling wood-fire burns in a large stone fireplace. In the right
corner is a home-made cupboard. Skins are tacked to the wall
here and there. The garish lithographic display usually found
in mountain cabins is lacking here. Several hand-made, splint-
bottom chairs are grouped around the hearth. The outside door
is in the rear wall at the center, with small windows on either
side of it. In the right wall is another door, leading into the bedroom and thence into the kitchen shed. There is a rocker by the
table.

MARY GAVIN is seated in this rocker, knitting. She has a
face not old, but worn—not by toil, we should say, but careworn.
It is a good face—attractive, possessing a sensitiveness of feature
remarkable for a mountain woman. Although she is not more
than thirty-five years of age, her hair is even now streaked with
gray. As she knits, her back to the door, it opens softly, slowly.
A man steps quickly into the room and shuts the door as quietly
as it was opened. The man is BUCK GAVIN, master of the house,
a fugitive from justice, wanted on charges of illicit distilling
and murder. He has returned by stealth after being hunted for
six weeks.

BUCK GAVIN is a great, powerfully built fellow, aged forty
years, or thereabouts. He has a strong, heavily lined face, covered
by a beard of the Van Dyke type—although he would not call
it that. He has piercing black eyes and heavy black hair. In his
swift silent movements there is a suggestion of a veiled panther-
like power. This seems characteristic of him; he moves always
with the same decisiveness. He is dressed in a dark flannel shirt
and loose corduroy trousers stuffed into rough laced boots.

97

GAVIN (*stands quietly a moment surveying the scene; then he speaks casually, quietly*). Howdy, sis.

MARY (*springing from her chair and turning quickly*). Buck! Buck! My God! What air you doin' here? Why did you come back?

GAVIN (*simply*). I had to, sis.

MARY. But, my Lor', man, they've been lookin' fer you high an' low. There's nary a nook ner corner 'bout these hills they haven't scoured fer you.

GAVIN. Don't you reckon I know it? But I come, an' thar's an end to it. (*Speaking impatiently as she starts to interrupt him.*) Don't argue with me. I come . . . an' you know why, I'm thinkin'.

MARY (*sullenly*). Yeah. I calc'late I knowed why. (*Going to him.*) But 'twarn't no use, Buck, 'twarn't no use for you to risk yer neck after all's over.

GAVIN (*with quiet emphasis*). Thar's the rub. 'Tain't all over. There's one mo' leetle job to be done, an' I reckon I'll git to see that through . . . least-ways, I'd better. For they'd never o' caught me whar I was, an' I don't calc'late to come more'n two hundred miles jes' to be caught. I reckon they'll git me soon, anyway; they're so powerful smart.

MARY (*contemptuously and proudly*). Bah! They never could o' caught you in the ol' days, Buck, no matter how powerful smart they were. You'd allus fool 'em, Buck.

GAVIN. The ol' days is gone—the good ol' days—an' all that made 'em good. But now . . . now . . . well, I'm jes' not in the foolin' mood. (*Moving away from her.*) . . . He's gone . . . they got him, an' I'd ruther that it'd been me. I reckon you know it. . . . But they got him, damn 'em, an' now . . . now . . . (*Passionately.*) Aw, what's the use? (*Striding restlessly across the room.*) A lot I'd keer if they'd come now . . . only . . . only I want a leetle mo' time . . . jes' a leetle.

MARY. Buck! Buck! Perk up, man, you mustn't act this way. What's come over you?

GAVIN. Oh, don't worry 'bout me. . . . (*He speaks softly.*) Where'd you put him, Mary?

MARY. On the top o' big Smoky. You know he allus liked the

view up there . . . said kind o' jokin' that that was where he
wanted 'em to plant him.

GAVIN (almost in a whisper). I . . . rec'lect.

MARY. So the rest o' the boys built a kind o' box an' carried
him up there. 'Twarn't easy neither, for it's a good ten mile
from the Gap to the top o' the Smoky. But we all felt sort o'
like it was doin' the right thing by Jim. Allus was different, was
Jim, from the rest of us. He'd have them dreamy times when he
wanted to be left alone.

GAVIN (sits down at the table and gazes before him). He was
plumb foolish over the view from Smoky. Called it a leetle
bit o' God's country. Used to go up there an' stare off 'cross the
valleys till the sun got low an' everythin' was blurred an' hazy-
like. Didn't want to talk to no one when he got that-a-way. But
one time, when we was up there, he set a-lookin' out awhile an'
he turned to me an' says, says he, "Buck, this is shore purty.
We're powerful close to heaven, Buck. . . ." I reckon you done
the right thing to plant him there. . . . Good ol' Jim. It's 'bout
all we could do. But the best warn't good 'nough fer him.

MARY. On the box we carved out his name . . . jes' carved
"Jim." Somehow it seemed more nat'ral-like to have it "Jim"
than "James Preas." An' over the grave—at the head, I mean—
we struck a wooden cross that the boys made . . . an' on it we
carved "Jim Preas—He asked no favors from revenooers an' he
died with his boots off."

GAVIN (sharply). What's that 'bout his boots?

MARY. Oh, that's the funny part of it. He had his leetle joke
right to the end. You know he allus calc'lated he'd have his boots
off when he died. Well, when the Sheriff an' his dep'ties found
him, he was lyin' up agin' a rock with his boots off, with his gun
in one hand, an' grinnin' a funny leetle grin as if he was sayin',
"I had the last laugh, hey?"

GAVIN (quietly after a pause). How . . . how many did we git?

MARY. Three dep'ties.

GAVIN (with savage satisfaction). Good . . . good, damn 'em,
they had to pay. A lot o' good it does me, though. (He goes on
reminiscently.) I won't forgit the fight out there on the hill-
side, an' how they got him. He gives a funny leetle cough an'
crumples up an' quits pumpin' his gun. "Buck," he says, grin-

nin' that crooked grin of his'n, "Buck, my boy, I reckon they've settled my hash. . . . 'Tain't no use, big feller," says he when I starts to carry him, "They've got me, an' I'm done fer. You can't help me, so for God's sake, help yourself. Now git." So I left him jokin' an' grinnin' an' pumpin' lead at 'em. He was a great joker, was Jim. . . . (*They are both silent.*) Mary, I reckon I ought to git some flowers. Could you git 'em fer me?

MARY (*puzzled by the question*). Why, yeah, I reckon I could. I got some here picked fresh this mornin', but what on airth d'you want. . . . Buck, you can't be meanin' to go up there with 'em. Why, man alive, you cain't—they're searchin' high an' low fer you.

GAVIN (*doggedly*). No matter if they air—I'm goin'. That's what I come fer.

MARY. D'you mean to tell me, Buck Gavin, that you come all this way to risk your neck fer . . . fer . . . sech? . . .

GAVIN (*with quiet determination*). Yeah, I mean to tell you jes' that. That's what kep' pullin' me home; that's all I hanker to do an' after that's done let 'em come an' git me . . . an' to hell with 'em.

MARY. All right, Buck, I reckon you know. I'll git 'em.

GAVIN (*to himself*). With his boots off, hey? (*He sits down at the table.*) By cripes, that was like him, jes' like ol' Jim. Allus was a joker. (*He chuckles.*) I reckon that tickled him. Oh, Lord, that was a man fer you! (*He rises and strides across the room.*)

MARY (*returning with a large bunch of arbutus*). Reckon these'll do, Buck?

GAVIN. Guess so—too many, though. Here, le' me have 'em, I'll fix 'em. Say, how 'bout some vi'lets, got any? Jim was plumb daffy over 'em—the big blue uns. You know the kind, Mary?

MARY. I know where they's a sight of 'em. I'll go git 'em. 'Twon't take long. (*She goes out.*)

GAVIN (*sitting by the table, he speaks disjointedly as he arranged the flowers*). No, an' 'twon't take long fer you either, Gavin, my boy. . . . Your goose is 'bout cooked, I'm thinkin'. Fine way of cookin', too. Jim's was the right way after all. . . . Wish I'd stayed with him now. A purty sight I'll be with a noose 'round my gullet—first Gavin to be hung—a disgrace to the family. . . . They'll git me—they allus git us. We've fit 'em time an' time, an' they git us in the end. Lord, I reckon we'uns is all fools. . . . (*Holding the bunch of arbutus at arm's length.*) . . . There, that's purty now. (*Now the door opens slowly and a short, thick-set fellow steps into the room. The badge of an officer of the law can be seen under his coat. In his hand he holds a revolver. He is the* SHERIFF.)

THE SHERIFF (*smiling ironically*). Welcome home, Buck. (GAVIN *wheels swiftly, his hand moving to his hip pocket. He stops short on seeing the* SHERIFF's *gun.*)

GAVIN. Aw. . . . Hell. . . .

THE SHERIFF (*genially, highly pleased with himself*). Quite a surprise, eh? Knew you'd be back, my boy, so I jes' laid low fer you. You never had a chance.

GAVIN (*slowly*). Yeah, you got me, I reckon, Sheriff, but I ain't worryin' 'bout it. Fact is, I'm glad you come—only . . . only I wish to God you'd been a leetle later.

THE SHERIFF (*surprised*). Why?

GAVIN (*sullenly*). Aw . . . nothin'. Come on, let's be travelin'. My sister'll be back any minute now, an' I don't want her to see the kind o' company I've took up with.

THE SHERIFF (*in a high good humor*). Jes' as you say, Buck, jes' as you say. (*They start toward the door as* MARY *enters with a large bunch of violets. She sums up the situation at a glance.*)

MARY. Oh, Buck, Buck, why did you come? I told you. An' now they've got you. I knowed it! (*She sinks into a chair and buries her face in her hands.*)

GAVIN (*he speaks gently and clumsily tries to soothe her*). There, there, little sis, you mustn't carry on so. This is sartin' the best way out an' I'm not worr'in'—look at me. I'm glad, sis. What's in the game fer me now? My pal's gone an' there ain't no mo' fun in playin' it without him . . . . Tell the boys hello an' good-bye fer me, an' tell 'em I says—But you needn't t' mind. . . . As fer you . . . (*going to her*) . . . you needn't to worry 'bout nothin' no mo'. I've fixed things up fer you.

MARY. Oh Buck, you needn't o' been caught. You could've got away.

GAVIN (*with quiet emphasis*). It is the law. You cain't buck it. (*There is a pause. The* SHERIFF *stands with bowed head, his jesting spirit gone. Then* GAVIN *speaks awkwardly as he pre-*

pares to leave.) Well, I reckon that's about all, so I'll be a-goin'. Be good to yourself, sis. *(He notices the arbutus and the violets on the table and picks them up, muttering under his breath.)* I would've liked to 've took 'em up there, an' . . . an' . . . sort o' looked 'round. *(He looks at* MARY, *deeply moved.)* But . . . well, I reckon I cain't go now . . . but ol' Jim'll know . . . jes' the same. Sis,—you take 'em. *(He places the flowers in her lap.* MARY *does not raise her head. He pats her hair gently, clumsily, once or twice, then turns to go with the* SHERIFF. *At the door he turns and gives a last look around the room. His gaze rests finally on his sister. Then he goes out quietly.* MARY's *head is pillowed in her arms. The flowers are in her lap.)*

CURTAIN

QUARE MEDICINE

A Comedy of Folk Belief

BY

PAUL GREEN

Out nettle
In dock.
Dock shall have
A new smock.

—Old word charm

Two Short Plays by a Leading Dramatist

"Quare Medicine" and "The No 'Count Boy," which follows it, are representative of the folk-play at its best. Both are highly artistic achievements. During the time when many of the writers who had their literary beginnings in Proff Koch's playwriting classes were turning to other forms for expression, Paul Green stuck to the drama. In it he found himself at home. The dramatic mastery evinced in the two comedies reprinted in this volume serve as partial explanation. The stories they tell, and the themes they elaborate, are admirably suited to the possibilities as well as to the limitations of the short play.

"Quare Medicine" was especially written for the 1925 opening of the now famous Playmakers Theatre. It brings to mind an almost vanished creature—the patent-medicine vendor—who once walked the lanes of the countryside and, on Saturdays and Court Weeks, established himself before the rural courthouse to sell his concoctions. Paul Green recalls one such figure in and near Lillington during the first decade of the century; it is he, all unknowing, who served as the real-life model for Doctor Immanuel.

"The No 'Count Boy" probably could be labeled poetic fantasy, but it leaps from the usual conception of that type of drama. Though Negro dialect hints at realism, Paul Green has no such purpose in mind. His biographer says that the play is "too bubble-light to touch with any heavy finger of parable. This story of a seventeen-year-old Negro girl, her hard-working practical betrothed, and the wandering dreamy boy who almost enchants her with his tunes and tall tales, carries a suggestion of the yearning of all youth for faraway places, for escape from the commonplace." In 1925 a Dallas group used it to capture the Belasco Cup in the National Little Theatre Tournament.

"Quare Medicine" and "The No 'Count Boy" are two of the best known among Paul Green's more than thirty one-act plays.

The author, who is North Carolina's foremost dramatist and at present the dean of all North Carolina writers, was born near Lillington, Harnett County, March 17, 1894. After local schooling and Buie's Creek Academy, he went to the University of North Carolina but took time out midway to serve in World War

I. Returning in 1919, he registered for the playwriting classes only a year after their inaugural by Professor Koch. The young dramatist soon became the leading playwright of the group. Following his graduation he taught philosophy at the University for a while, but did not abandon the writing of plays. Shortly he was trying his hand at the full-length form, in which he also excelled. Most of the one-act plays are included in three volumes: *The Lord's Will and Other Carolina Plays* (1925), *Lonesome Road, Six Plays for the Negro Theatre* (1926), and *In the Valley and Other Carolina Plays* (1928). Most of them are written about the simple Negroes and the rural white people of his native countryside. His long plays are briefed in the Introduction to this volume.

Even though he is a master craftsman for the theatre, he is almost equally at home in philosophy, music, poetry, radio, television, motion pictures, the essay, the short story, and the novel—though always, first of all, he is a playwright.

His name was the first to be engraved on the Sir Walter Raleigh Award, given annually for outstanding work in imaginative literature by a North Carolinian. The citation was an unusual one, for always before, one book by a writer had been singled out for recognition in the various awards. Paul Green, on the other hand, was acclaimed for "the whole body of his literary achievement."

He lives today in Chapel Hill with Mrs. Green. Three daughters and a son are married and away from home. In Chapel Hill, Paul Green is continually writing new plays and revising his old ones.

THE CHARACTERS

OLD MAN JERNIGAN

HENRY JERNIGAN, *his son*

MATTIE JERNIGAN, *Henry's wife*

DOCTOR IMMANUEL, *a patent-medicine vendor*

SCENE

A farmhouse somewhere in the South

TIME

Several years ago at the close of a winter day.

The scene is the combined sitting-room and bedroom of the Jernigan house, with a fireplace to the left, a sewing-machine to the right and a table in the center of the room. The floor is carpeted with bright straw matting, and everything bristles with tidy primness. A door is at the center back and one at the left rear. The window at the right center, neatly curtained, shows a streak of somber autumn fields filling up with the blue dusk of a fading winter day. From another part of the house the voice of a woman can be heard shrilly singing "Rescue the perishing, care for the dying." The elder JERNIGAN, walking with a stick, comes carefully in at the rear door shivering with cold and carrying a mug-cup in his hand. Below a mass of white hair his face shines out like a ruddy autumn apple, and his whole person suggests the toughness and durability of a dried hickory root.

Halfway across the room he stops and listens to the singing.

JERNIGAN (sharply imitating). "Rescue the perishing, care for the dying!"

He moves over to the fire and sets his mug to warm; after which he takes a bottle from the mantel, pours out some medicine in a spoon and swallows it. He sits down and stretches his hands to the blaze with a grunt of satisfaction. In a moment he feels the cup and takes a long drink. The woman's voice calls from off the right.

VOICE. Father!
JERNIGAN (starting). Ah-hanh! What is it?
VOICE (nearer). Father—Fath-er!
JERNIGAN (moving towards the door at the left). What is it, Mattie?
VOICE. Supper's about ready. Where's Henry? (The singing begins again, fading towards the kitchen.)
JERNIGAN (calling futilely after her). He's feeding up and'll be here in a minute.

He listens a while and then reseats himself thoughtfully before the fire. Presently there is a heavy scraping of feet on the steps outside and HENRY JERNIGAN comes timidly in at the rear. He is a big awkward farmer of thirty or more, hesitating and shy. He takes his seat silently and wearily in a rocking-chair, being care-

107

ful not to touch the whitewashed hearth with his shoes. The old man looks at him closely.

JERNIGAN. Tired out, ain't you? Here, try some of this persimmon beer. I just drained the barrel.

HENRY *(in a slow, fumbling voice).* I don't want none of that, I believe.

JERNIGAN. Unh-hunh. *(They both lapse into silence, staring before them. Soon the elder JERNIGAN peers through the window at the winter sunset).* Going to be cold, Henry, cold. Robins been flying towards the south all day. *(HENRY says nothing.)* You're tireder than common, ain't you, Henry?

HENRY. Yeh. *(Lifelessly.)* Wore out, wore out.

JERNIGAN *(taking his bottle from the mantel).* Here, take this last dose of Doctor 'Manuel's tonic. *(HENRY shakes his head.)* Well, I will then. *(He pours out the last drop and swallows it.)* Doctor said he'd be by today. About night and he ain't here yet. You better get him to give you something, you better, Henry. You're looking thin, thin.

HENRY. He ain't no doctor, he's a humbug.

JERNIGAN. Lord help my life!

HENRY. Wonder that mess don't kill you—old branch water and chemicals he's mixed up, I betcha. *(He sighs heavily, listening to the song in the kitchen.)* That old man's crazy with his poetry and talking and medicine!

JERNIGAN. Hunh, not hardly. *(Solemnly.)* 'Tain't body tired what ails you, Henry, is it? *(After a moment he jerks his thumb in the direction of the song.)* Still singing, Henry. There it is.

HENRY. Yeh, I know.

JERNIGAN. Ah-hah, but folks will marry just the same. She's worse than ever, Henry. Good she is, religious good. Cooking and sewing and scrubbing and all fixed up for tonight. Look over there on the machine at what she's got finished for them there Hindoos or whatever they are. There's my coat I bought in Dunn five years back at old man Ransome Taylor's sale!

HENRY *(his eyes traveling heavily about the room.)* What's she got on for tonight?

JERNIGAN. Another one of them there meetings. Old Mis' Pate and her gang's coming here to sew for the heathen and them that's starving in the old world. (*Staring at him intently.*) This religious mess is going to kill Mattie off if you don't get up manhood enough to stop it. Sing and talk, sing and talk, Lord, I can't stand it no more.

HENRY. I—I can't—I ain't going to put my authority on nobody. She's her own boss.

JERNIGAN. Own boss! She's her own boss and our'n too. Well, if you're scared of her, all right. There ain't no help for it. (*He turns towards the fire, patting his foot forlornly on the floor.*) But, Henry, you ain't getting no fun out of living, and right now's the time you ought.—And as for me—I been wanting to talk —(*hitching up his chair*)—to you about this. Why the name of Old Scratch you don't up and put your foot down I can't see. (HENRY *says nothing.*) But you won't. (*Half to himself.*) He ain't got no backbone, lets everybody run over him. (*He reaches for his cup and drains down the last of his beer in an angry gulp.*) You didn't get that from your mammy nor from me, Henry. (*He mocks the singing in the kitchen.*) "Rescue the perishing—"

HENRY (*suddenly standing up*). I can't have no row with nobody, not with her anyhow, I tell you. (*At the door.*) I got to go part the cow and calf. (*He slams the door behind him and the old man jumps in astonishment.*)

JERNIGAN. Dinged if he didn't slam the door—hee, hee, hee. Good for you, Henry, good for you!

MATTIE, *a fair faced young woman, comes in from the left, singing and carrying a stone churn in her arms. Despite her housewifely certainty of action, there is an indefinite feminine frailty about her.*

MATTIE. What's good for Henry?

JERNIGAN (*hurrying in confusion to his chair*). Nothing, Mattie, nothing at all. (*She looks sharply at him a moment and then sets the churn by the hearth.*)

MATTIE. I'm putting the milk here to turn. I wish you'd look at it every now and then and stir it with the dasher.

JERNIGAN. All right, Mattie, all right.

MATTIE. And mind, don't you spill none of that old beer on the hearth.

JERNIGAN. I won't, Mattie, I won't.

MATTIE. What'd Henry go out for?

JERNIGAN. To get the calf away from the cow.

MATTIE (the words piling out). I bet he didn't wipe his feet when he come in. And did you? (Staring at the floor and following HENRY's trail.) No, he didn't—just look at the dirt, just look at it. (She hurries into the room at the left and returns with a broomsedge broom.) Here, sweep it up, Father. (She pushes the broom into his hand.) I've got to go back to my batter. (She sticks her head out the door at the rear and calls.) Henry—Hen—ry! Supper! (She turns back into the room and old JERNIGAN falls to sweeping.) Sweep it towards the hearth, towards the hearth, Father, and mind the milk, don't get it full of dust. (She goes out singing, beginning where she left off.)—"from sin and the grave—"

JERNIGAN (sweeping). Lord, Lord A'mighty, was ever mortal man so persecuted! (Leaning on his broom and musing.) There he is—(nodding his head to the right)—poor soul, not at peace in his own household, going about like a man with the mulligrubs, can't sleep, can't eat, worried, worried down to the ground. And there she is—(nodding to the left)—reading The Christian Herald and hearing about dirt and disease and famine over in Asia till she ain't fit to live with. Listen to her, listen to her, will you? What's to become of me, Old Master only knows. What, to come to this, to this in my old age and me—(thumping on his chest)— yeh, me, old and with a crippled leg from marching in Virginny! (He wipes his sleeve across his eyes and goes back to sweeping. Presently he stops and begins to muse again.) Puts me to sweeping, she does, and churning and getting up the eggs, and following old setting hens around. And she's had me at the washtub like an old woman, she has. Damn it! (His voice sags over the oath.) I ain't no woman. If Henry ain't got the grit to say something, I have. It's "Father do this, Father do that, Father—Father—Father!" But ding it all, she's a good girl. It's that drot'n old bell-cow of a Bella Pate and her gang what's got her worse'n she ever has been. I wish a storm would come up and blow the whole shooting-match of them women clean to Roosia or wherever it is. Then they'd get enough of them there heathen, I reckon. But they ain't got no right to interfere with me, not a bit. (He puts a hand into his pocket and holds up a small tin box in his left hand and a plug of tobacco in his right.) Here they come and set upon me about my tobacco. Chew chewing-gum, chewing-gum, they say, to save for the heathen and to protect my health. (*He rattles the tin box.*) And I've chewed that wad of stuff till I can't get rid of it in my sleep. Can't wear it out, can't by no means. I'm done of it, I am. Have to slip off and hide to chew my tobacco, and all in a land of freedom. (*He stands thinking, then goes to the door at the left and calls.*) Mattie, are you busy?

MATTIE. Yes, I've got my hands in the dough!

JERNIGAN. All right. (*He stealthily bites off a chew from his plug, drops his tin box back in his pocket and spits in the fire with grim happiness. Just as he is leaning to spit a second time, the door opens suddenly at the left rear, and* MATTIE *comes in with a cloth. Old* JERNIGAN *draws back, and begins sweeping in a flurry of embarrassment. He calls out testily.*) Thought you was busy. Ain't I doing all right?

MATTIE. Sweep it clean, Father. I forgot this cloth for the churn. (*She raises the lid from the churn and stirs the contents around with the dasher.*) It's all right and ready, lacking just a bit, for churning. Don't you let it slosh on anything while you're a-churning it. (*She wraps the cloth around the handle of the dasher. The old man is sweeping and watching her out of the corner of his eye. While she is bent over she sees something on the hearth that attracts her attention. She rises up to her height and with a sharp note in her voice turns upon him.*) Mr. Jernigan—

JERNIGAN. Nah, nah, Mattie.

MATTIE. Signs don't lie, and there's signs of it there on my hearth. (*Working around the room and watching him furtively.*) Right here in my front room! Ain't you got your mouth full of tobacco right this minute? (*He shakes his head.*) Yes, you have, yes, you have. (*She stands looking at him as he sweeps.*) Father, why don't you say something, can't you talk? (*He makes little movements of agony and finally chokes.*) Yes, yes, you are chewing right now. Spit it out, spit it out! Don't stand there and swallow that joice, it'll kill you. (*In desperation he runs to the fireplace and explodes into the fire, and stands coughing with a nauseated look on his face.*) I'll get you some water! (*She hurries out and reappears immediately with a glass of water and a battered wash-basin full of claying material.*) Here, drink it, and take this pan and rag and clay the hearth over. (*After drinking the water, he ruefully gets down on his knees and begins work. She goes to the machine.*) Hurry and get it done, I got supper nearly cooked. (*She sits down and begins sewing and singing "How firm a foundation—"*)

JERNIGAN (*indicating the garments*). Are they for the heathen?

MATTIE. They are that.

JERNIGAN (*timidly*). 'Course you know best, I reckon. But how you know they wear britches over there?

MATTIE (*staring at him in amazement*). Who ever heard of folks not wearing britches! You know they'd put 'em in jail for such, if they didn't.

JERNIGAN (*venturing*). I heard they don't wear nothing over there but a string around their waist to tell where the middle is.

MATTIE (*pedaling furiously*). You men don't care, of course, care 'bout nothing but your farming and your crops. Why, it's in *The Christian Herald* where the little children just go through the woods in big droves gnawing the bark off of the trees they're so hungry. We've decided to give up our breakfast and send the cost of it to them.

JERNIGAN. That's why you didn't eat breakfast this morning. Well—you et a whole lot more for dinner to make up for it, didn't you?

MATTIE (*sharply and with a nervous note in her voice as she gets suddenly up from the machine*). Father, take all this mess out when you get done—that old persimmon beer cup, and that old 'Manuel patent medicine bottle, and don't forget to carry the clay pan out—

She goes out at the left. Her song is heard rising in the distance. Old JERNIGAN *continues claying the hearth, muttering to himself.* HENRY *comes in at the rear.*

HENRY (*stretching his legs out carefully towards the fire*). What's the matter with the hearth now?

JERNIGAN (*setting the pan in the corner by the wood-box*). Nothing, nothing, Henry. She thought she saw a speck on it somewhere.

HENRY. You must 'a' been chewing tobacco again.

JERNIGAN. Well, why shouldn't I chew it?

HENRY. Yeh, yeh, I wish you could in peace.

JERNIGAN. You'd be better off if you'd go back to chewing.

HENRY. I know. But I promised her I'd quit and I have.

JERNIGAN. I used to chew it before it quit raining in Africa or wherever it is and before old Bella Pate brung her sanctified self around here, I did, and there was some joy in having a fire then, and some reason for having a fireplace too. (*Tapping on the andiron with his stick.*) That's what it's made for—to spit in.

HENRY (*timidly and somewhat hopefully*). Why don't you talk it out with Mattie? (*Earnestly.*) I wish you would.

JERNIGAN. Durned if I didn't come purty nigh telling her something a while ago. (*He catches* HENRY *by the arm.*) Now look-a here, Henry, you and me's got to do something. The thing for you to do is to walk down the road tonight and meet Mis' Pate and them folks and tell 'em they can't come up here to carry on no prayer-meeting and sewing business. Tell 'em to go somewheres else. Tell 'em to go to—hell!

HENRY (*shrinking away*). I can't do that, I can't. Lord, you're near about gone to cussing.

JERNIGAN. And tell 'em your wife ain't going to have nothing else to do with such.

HENRY (*quickly*). I tell you what, you do it.

JERNIGAN. I would in a minute, Henry, but you're the head of the house and you better, it's your place to. (HENRY *turns himself about before the fire.*)

HENRY. Maybe they won't come tonight, and before they meet another time maybe we can figure on something to do.

JERNIGAN. Hunh, they'll be here, all right.

HENRY (*staring off*). I hear say they's mad dogs about. One bit at Dick Ryall's child this evening.

JERNIGAN (*studying*). Well, that may break up the meeting, but I won't believe it till I see it, not me. Take more than mad dogs to stop religion. You stand up to Mattie, I tell you, put the britches on and wear 'em yourself. Lord, I can't understand you. Why you let her impose on me in my old age the way you do, I can't see. (*He turns away and sits down in his arm-chair.* MATTIE *comes in with a tin bucket in her hand.*)

MATTIE. I've got to go across the fields to Mis' Ragland's a bit —(*Suddenly stopping.*) Henry, go right back out that door and wipe off your feet.

HENRY (*mumbling*). I thought I cleaned my feet. (*He goes outside and is heard scraping his shoes on the edge of the porch.*)

MATTIE. Sweep it up, Father. (*He gets the broom and sweeps.*) I got to borrow some soda from Mis' Ragland and she wanted me to bring her a jar of jam.

HENRY (*coming back into the room*). I'll go over there for you, Mattie.

MATTIE. No, I'll go, and you-all go on and get your supper. I've put the biscuits in the stove, and they'll be ready by the time you wash and get to the table. Now Henry, don't let them biscuits burn. (*She goes out.*)

JERNIGAN (*scornfully*). Just look at her—didn't have a bit of business over there, just wants to go over see what old Nonie Ragland's got made up for the heathen. Henry, you got to lay the law down, I tell you.

HENRY. Yeh, yeh.

JERNIGAN. Now, I'm going to talk straight to you. Women is like mules and all dumb brutes, Henry, you got to break 'em before they'll work.

HENRY. Nah, nah, I can't do that. (*There is a knock on the porch.*)

JERNIGAN. Who can that be? (*Happily.*) That's my doctor, I betcha. (*The knock is repeated at the door.*)

HENRY (*raising his voice in sudden irritation*). Go on away! Go 'way!

JERNIGAN (*staring at him*). What—Come in, come in! (DOCTOR IMMANUEL *comes in.*) I knowed it was you, Doctor, I knowed it was you.

The DOCTOR *is a man of medium height, about fifty years old, dressed in a cheap threadbare dark suit, celluloid collar and dark tie. His coat hangs low and nearly to the knees, clerical-like. Despite his cheap dress there is an indefinite air of distinction about him; something scholarly, something forlorn in his pale clean-cut face and dark piercing eyes. He carries a well-worn medicine case in his hand. As he enters the door, he pulls off his derby hat, disclosing a huge mop of long black hair streaked with gray and resting like a bolster on his neck and shoulders.*

DOCTOR (*in a deep level voice*). Masters of this house, friends—

JERNIGAN (*pushing up a chair*). Come right in, come right in and make yourself at home.

The DOCTOR *lays his hat on the bed at the right and puts his case in a chair. He moves in a sort of dream-like mask-like manner, intent upon his business and paying little attention to the two men.*

DOCTOR (*his voice running in a level chant, half-singing as he opens his case*). What can I do for you tonight? What can I do for you tonight? (*He takes out bottle after bottle, shakes it, squints at it towards the light, and replaces it, chanting as he does so.*)

As you all know, wherever I go,
My name is Immanuel,
I treat you well, I make you well,
Sound as the sweet church bell.

(*He turns suddenly on old* JERNIGAN, *who starts back in surprise.*) Now what is it, brother? What can I do for you?

JERNIGAN (*fetching his bottle*). Another bottle. I just drunk the last.

HENRY (*growling*). Another bottle of stump water, dishwater, rainwater.

DOCTOR (*holding up the bottle*). Doctor Immanuel's Universal Remedy! Right it is and very fit. Distilled from secret weeds and herbs by mystic processes. Cures internal ailments, cuts, burns, bruises, is an antidote for poisons, can be taken internally or externally. For swelling in the joints, leg sores, sore throat, convulsions, dizziness, fits, and general disorders. (*The words roll from him in a flood. He turns towards old* JERNIGAN *and fixes him with his eyes, and suddenly sings out.*) What is your trouble, brother? Are you healed, better or— It's cold tonight, and ice on the pools in the lane.

JERNIGAN. In my knee, you remember, in my knee. (*He slaps his hand to it.*) I'm getting better, Doctor, slowly, slowly.

DOCTOR (*holding his hand up is assurance*). Slowly but surely, certainly, absolutely. Another bottle and you walk straight as any man.

As you all know, wherever I go,
My name is Immanuel,
I always make you well,
As any man will tell—

(His voice drops to a whisper and he hums under his breath, the while he is putting away the empty bottle and getting out another. He hands the bottle to old JERNIGAN.) The price is one and a quarter now, brother. Prices have gone up, prices are going up. The demand exceeds the supply. *(Again he chants.)*

I travel from morning till night
Curing and fixing things right.
From night until day
I'm on-a my way—

(He begins placing his other bottles back in his case.)

Seeking the saddened sight—

(Again he whirls upon the old man.) Is the knee all that troubles you? Have you other ills, diseases of the body or of the soul?

JERNIGAN *(shaking his head quickly)*. Nanh, nanh, I'm all right saving my knee.

DOCTOR *(picking up a small bottle and holding it lovingly before him)*. Now here is a remedy, *the* remedy, the heart and soul of the matter, the help for the world's evils. Down in Egypt, the country of darkness, it was discovered. Dug out of the tombs of the powers of evil. Hid away they had it, but my agent discovered it, sent it to me, here it is. *(Reading.)* Dr. Immanuel's Egyptian Tonic. *(Suddenly barking like an auctioneer, as* HENRY *jumps in his chair.)*

Two dollars a bottle, two dollars,
Going at two dollars,
Are you weak and heavy laden,
Sore distressed, sad distressed?
It will cleanse of evil passion,
Restore your bowels of compassion,
Accidents, diseases chronic—

(Suddenly shouting.)

The marvelous Egyptian Tonic.

(He sticks it out at old JERNIGAN.*)*

Two dollars once, two dollars twice—
Going at two—

JERNIGAN *(backing away from him as he fumbles in his pocket-book for his money).* Nanh, nanh, this bottle's enough, Here's your dollar and a quarter. *(The* DOCTOR *takes the money impersonally.)* Come up to the fire and warm yourself.

HENRY *(looking at old man* JERNIGAN *significantly).* Annh-hanh, what'd I tell you? *(The* DOCTOR *closes his case and goes to the bed for his hat.* HENRY *calls to him bitterly.)* You better look out down in that creek for mad dogs.

DOCTOR *(turning back quickly but with dignity).* Mad dogs?

HENRY. Yeh, dogs that are mad. Mad dogs. One of 'em bite you and you'll be madder'n you are now.

JERNIGAN. Yeh, you get bit and you'll foam at the mouth and gnaw bedposts and cut up terrible like Sarah Williams done before she died. Yes, you will, Doctor. She run out in the yard and screamed, and they tried to ketch her but she tore off and lay down by the hedgerow and died biting her legs and arms and barking like a dog.

DOCTOR *(quickly taking a tiny package from his case).* Doctor Immanuel's Mad Stone, good for all bites and poisons. Bring it near the afflicted spot and it seizes upon it—*(clapping it to the top of his hand)*—and sucks out the poison. Five dollars apiece, five dollars. *(Gazing at it fondly.)* This mysterious stone was taken from a bewitched deer, killed by the old prophet of the Cape Fear. *(Barking again.)* Five dollars apiece, five dollars, going at five dollars. *(He stops and holds the stone out towards old* JER-NIGAN.*)*

JERNIGAN. Nanh, nanh, I ain't run mad.

DOCTOR. Five dollars—five dollars once, five dollars twice—five dollars— *(Suddenly he stops and stares at* HENRY *as if perceiving something remarkable and strange about him. He mechanically wraps up the stone and drops it back in the case, never taking his eyes from the young man. He moves towards him and walks obliquely around him. Old JERNIGAN watches him with open mouth. As the DOCTOR approaches, HENRY turns and follows him suspiciously with his eyes.)*

HENRY. Here, here, what you up to? *(The DOCTOR continues to stalk him. He draws back dramatically and points a sharp finger at HENRY.)*

DOCTOR *(grotesquely).* Trouble!

JERNIGAN *(jumping and giggling nervously).* Trouble, hee-hee!

HENRY *(staring at him).* Trouble?

DOCTOR *(his words beginning to pour out in a roll).* I see upon that brow suffering. My name is Immanuel. I am needed, needed here and now. *(Looking at him in anguish.)* You are weak and heavy laden. Tell me, speak forth your heart. I am come that ye might have rest from your suffering. Speak forth, thou unbeliever.

HENRY. Here, here, I ain't going to have no monkey shines. *(With a touch of entreaty in his voice.)* Stop it now.

DOCTOR *(shaking his head mournfully).* I must help you. I feel the call of pain. Speak forth your heart.

HENRY *(turning towards old JERNIGAN).* What's he up to no-how?

JERNIGAN. Now, now, you needn't ask me. *(There is a long silence while the DOCTOR stares fixedly at HENRY.)*

HENRY *(looking anxiously about the room and presently bursting out).* I tell you to stop looking at me thataway!

DOCTOR. Trouble, trouble, suffering in the countenance of that face! *(Imploringly.)* Speak, speak, I have remedy for suffering. I can help and aid thee. *(He clasps his hands and waits. HENRY stirs uneasily in his chair and old JERNIGAN teeters nervously on his feet, beating his thighs with the back of his hands. At last old JERNIGAN explodes.)*

JERNIGAN. Well, you are in trouble, Henry!—In a way you're in the deepest sort of trouble. *(Muttering.)* Me too, and me too.

DOCTOR *(triumphantly).* Ah—hah! Speak, speak.

HENRY *(half in wrath and half in perplexed fear).* Well, what in the name of Old Scratch you want?

DOCTOR. Speak forth the evil that is possessing thee.

HENRY *(twisting about).* You tell him, Pa, if there's any evil to be told.

JERNIGAN. Him and me's been seeing a right smart of worry lately. We was talking about it before you come.

DOCTOR. I know it, I perceive it.

JERNIGAN (*going on haltingly*). As the Scripture puts it, he's married to a wife. (*He stops.*)

DOCTOR. One had his land, one had his yoke of oxen, another had his wife and could not come. As set forth in the gospel according to Luke.

JERNIGAN (*eagerly*).That's it, Doctor, his wife's took possession of everything here.

HENRY. Now, now.

JERNIGAN. Well, she has. And that there doctor can help you, I done told you he could. (*He steps nimbly out into the room and sweeps it with his arms.*) Look a' there, will you? Look at that there hearth. Clean as a sheet. And the floor and everything. A speck of dirt got no home here and we ain't neither. (*Pointing to the sewing-machine.*) And look over there at that there sewing. My good coat and britches gone for good, all for the heathen over the water.

HENRY. You might stop trying to tell everything.

JERNIGAN. Well, you tell it then.

HENRY. Go on then and say what you wish.

JERNIGAN. All right and I will as sure as you're born. That's just it, Doctor, she's plumb took with religion and sweeping and talking.

DOCTOR. Where is the lady of the house?

JERNIGAN. Off, off.

DOCTOR. A common case, a common case. The man must stand up and be the master. The Scripture tells as much.

JERNIGAN (*jubilantly*). There you are, Henry, there you are. (*Jerking his thumb at* HENRY.) But he won't, he won't, not him. He sets like a wedge in the rain and takes it every bit. Big as a house he is and ain't got no backbone in him more'n a sack.

DOCTOR. Timid? Afraid? Lacking in manly courage?

HENRY (*wrathfully*). Go on and have it your way!

DOCTOR. Doctor Immanuel will provide. He can cure.

JERNIGAN. You cure 'em both and I'll pay. Fix it so as I can chew my tobacco in peace and here's a five dollar bill for you. (*He pulls out his pocketbook.*)

DOCTOR. I shall cure them, I must cure them, I *will* cure them. Amen!

JERNIGAN. Do that and this here's your'n. (*He flaps a bill in his hands. The* DOCTOR *begins to pace up and down the room, pushing back his hair and mumbling to himself.*)

DOCTOR (*snapping*). When will the lady of this house return?

HENRY. She just stepped across the field. But you needn't be planning none of your mess. I ain't going to take no part in it.

DOCTOR. Mess! Mess! (*He resumes his walk.*)

JERNIGAN (*becoming excited*). I dunno what you going to do, Doctor, but I just betcha you do it. (*Gleefully.*) I bet he does, Henry. Yeh, she'll be right back.

DOCTOR. No sooner said than done. (*Whirling upon* HENRY.) I can cure you both. I can bring peace and order into this distracted home. I can make a man of might out of you. I can make you a mighty man in Israel, both in deed and in word. I can bring back humility and love to the erring woman's heart. Yea. (*Lifting up his voice.*) I can prepare a proper helpmeet for you in your distress. (*Thundering and glaring at* HENRY.) But—but —have you faith in my powers?

HENRY. I dunno— I dunno—Hah, crazy!

JERNIGAN (*ecstatically*). Try to raise up your faith, Henry. (*Grinding his hands in excitement.*) Hurry up, Henry, hurry up, she's going to be back in a minute.

HENRY (*shaking his head weakly*). I'm scared of all this business. How I know he won't kill me or something or hurt her.

DOCTOR. Kill! Hurt! (*His jaw falling open in amazement.*) Alas, young man, your words are wild, wild and full of poison to my kindly heart. (*His tone suddenly changes to anger.*) Take your own benighted way then. I offer you peace, you choose strife. So be it. (JERNIGAN *grasps* HENRY's *arm in supplication.*)

JERNIGAN. Henry, Henry, try it, try it, boy!

DOCTOR (*raising a warning hand*). But listen. Before I depart over the creek—(*to himself*)—a mule there swelled with the colic— Behold salvation is at hand and you refuse it.

JERNIGAN. Are you crazy, Henry? There he is now going off.

HENRY (*beginning to show an unwilling interest under the* DOCTOR's *spell*). Well—

DOCTOR (*picking up his hat*). I shall say no more.

JERNIGAN. Henry, Henry, don't let him go off like that there! *(The* DOCTOR *picks up his case and moves toward the door.)*

HENRY. Well, if you're sure you won't hurt me nor her, I might—

DOCTOR *(apparently no longer interested in him).* Well, goodnight and may you endure your punishment as befits a sufferer so blind. *(He grasps the door knob.)*

JERNIGAN. Henry, Henry!

HENRY. Are you sure you won't hurt me?

DOCTOR. Faith! Have you faith?

HENRY *(standing up with sudden decision).* Well, I'll try it then, by God! Where's your medicine? Bring it on. *(With an amazingly agile bound the* DOCTOR *springs back into the room.)*

DOCTOR. Saved! Saved! *(He opens his case and searches in its depths. Extracting two tiny bottles, he holds them up in his hands.* HENRY *sits down again watching him with open mouth.)* Ah, here they are, Doctor Immanuel's Cure for the Unhappy Soul. The one is red, the other gray. The red is for the rich blood of manhood. Drink it and you become masterful, fearless, a tamer of the weaker sex. They will bow down to you, worship you, feed upon your words of wisdom as upon honey-dew. Let the woman drink the gray and the man the red. He becomes the lord of his house and his goods. She becomes the meek and lowly helpmeet. There she sits by the fire silent, gentle and sweet. There he sits her master, her lord.

JERNIGAN *(his eyes shining).* Listen at him, Henry, listen at him talk!

DOCTOR *(lifting up the red vial).* I remember, I remember. I see in the past. It is a night of storm. The moon is sick and pale and wasting in the west.

The pale moon doth rain,
The red moon doth blow,
It bringeth water in its beak.
The white moon doth neither rain nor snow.

I rise up in my dreams. Doctor Immanuel comes forth from his couch at the midnight hour, for now it is the time to seek for the cure of unhappy souls. Silently I go through the forest towards the appointed place. The rain and the wind they comfort me on my journey. I go forth alone in the forest under the watchful heavens. The signs are right in the sky, it is the time of the bull, and the bull means life and more abundant life. (*He waves his hands before his face and treads up and down the room acting out his journey.* HENRY *and old* JERNIGAN *stare at him as if mesmerized.*) I go by the elder bush in the pathless swamp, I touch the sorrel tree, and place my hand upon the bark of the smooth bay tree. I mount the hill and taste of the sweet sassafras and a bit of the bitter pine, and I, Doctor Immanuel, as the cocks begin to crow, come to the place of the silent old man and he waits for me. He has had his dream. Together we go towards the east, he with his dried sticks of the bloody mulberry and I with six of the nameless bush I shall not name. We come where the strong young man died for love and his rich red blood ran into the ground. There we set the pot and build the fire. (*His voice takes on a hypnotic monotone and he moves back and forth in the room with the queer unreal steps of an automaton.*) And into the pot Doctor Immanuel casts his one and two and three. And likewise the silent one casts his one and two and three which shall not be named till time is done. The bottles are brought forth and filled. The silent old one to his home again which none but two can find. And Doctor Immanuel forth into the world to heal the distressed. (*His voice dies away and he hums to himself.*)

HENRY (*breaking from the spell*). Ain't he crazy right?

DOCTOR (*picking up the gray vial and throwing up his hand*). And hark! (*He stands with his hand uplifted, and they wait. Presently he goes on.*) It is night, a night of peace. The farmer sleeps his toil away, and the stock rests in the stall. The seeds wait in the earth, in the warm ground. The poor bird sits in the hedgerow and the snake goes not forth to prey. And now the old moon sleeps in the new moon's arms, hanging in the heavens above the three dark pines. (*Again he falls to striding up and down the floor.*) Doctor Immanuel is forth from his couch again. The signs are right. The virgin walks in the sky. He comes to the three dark pines and waits in prayer. And the three maids of the deep swamp minister unto him, they minister unto him. Out of the darkness they come with song and with dancing, their heads hanging low and their rings shining and their garments flashing silver and the flames of gold. (*He turns and stares at* HENRY *who watches him groggily.*) From the mud of the turtle and the scaly snake they come, rising out of the deep night time, out of the mire and the swampy slime, where the owl and the bat and the fever are. They rise, bringing the cure, the gray cure, the draught of humility, of peace. (*He stares at the gray vial and stands lost in thought. Presently he turns, his voice humming.*) Drink the red and be filled with life and power; drink the gray, become the meek and gentle of the earth. Doctor Immanuel has said his say! (*He begins walking back and forth across the room.* HENRY *and old* JERNIGAN *stare at him as if fascinated. Far off a woman's voice is heard singing. It draws nearer, and* MATTIE *passes around the house singing "Rescue the Perishing," and goes into the kitchen.*)

HENRY (*swallowing hard*). Here, there's something quare!

JERNIGAN. He's going to cure you, Henry. He is! Sink your trust in him, Henry!

DOCTOR. Come, drink the drink! (*He closes his case and sets the two bottles on top of it.*) Call the lady of the house. She shall have the gray.

HENRY (*starting from his dream, sidling up to the bottles, and staring at them suspiciously*). Might be something in it, might not. (*A queer unreal smile breaks over his face and he comes up to the* DOCTOR *and looks at him intently.*) All right, dinged if I don't do it. Dinged if I don't! (MATTIE's *sharp insistent voice is heard in the kitchen.*)

MATTIE. Father! Fath—er-r! Henry! Hen-ry!

JERNIGAN. Drink it, swallow it down, Henry! Can't be no worse than—(*he turns and mocks* MATTIE)—Father! Henry! and—(*sing-ing*)—"Rescue the perishing—" Go on, Henry. (HENRY *picks up the red vial, uncorks it and smells it and sets it down, then takes up the gray one and does likewise.*)

HENRY (*vacuously*). Why it don't smell like nothing a-tall.

DOCTOR (*stopping in his walk and looking at him piercingly*). Bid the lady of the house come in.

HENRY (*throwing his head about and beating himself as if trying to fight off the* DOCTOR's *influence*). You call her, Pa. (*The door flies open at the left and* MATTIE *springs in with a pan of burnt biscuits in her hands.*)

Mattie (*in a shrill nervous voice*). Look what you've done, both of you. I told you not to let the biscuits burn. (Jernigan *looks at* Henry *and* Henry *looks at him.*)

Jernigan (*finally*). I thought Henry was seeing after them biscuits.

Henry (*fumbling*). I didn't even think of 'em, Mattie.

Mattie. I know, I know. That's just the way it is. That's just the way it is. That's always the way it is.

Doctor. Madam, lady of the house!

Mattie (*starting back*). Oh, I didn't see you, Doctor 'Manuel. Put some wood on the fire, Father. When did you come, Doctor 'Manuel?

Doctor. Madam, when you appeared in the door we were in the midst of a most momentous question.

Mattie. What in the world is all this to-do about? You'll have to tell it quick, I've got to hurry and get supper. We are sewing here tonight—(*with a weary, defiant look towards* Henry *and* Jernigan)—sewing for the heathen.

Doctor. Madam, after tonight you will not bother about the heathen. You have enough trouble in your own household. We are solving that momentous question.

Mattie. What in the world is all this to-do about, I ask you?

Doctor (*with high dignity*). Madam, behold the two bottles there. The one is red, the other gray. The red is for your husband, the gray for you.

Mattie. Needn't think I'll drink any of your crazy mess.

Doctor. The husband will drink the red and take charge of his household. You will drink the gray and obey him in what he says hereafter.

Mattie. The Lord help my life! (*Turning to* Henry.) Have you gone out of your head same as him, to be taking on to such stuff?

Henry (*timidly*). Try and drink at little bit, Mattie. It won't hurt you! He says it's good for you.

Mattie. The dog's foot!

Henry (*with a hint of determination in his voice*). He's done said if I drink that stuff you won't know me for another man. (*Decisively.*) And I've said I'll drink it.

DOCTOR. He's going to drink his and you're going to drink yours.

MATTIE. That I'm not. I've never heard of such. Henry Jernigan, you must be crazy to fool with him.

HENRY. Yes, I'm going to do it. I'm plumb tired of such a mess of things. I'm going to change it or die a-trying. (*With a lunge he grabs one of the bottles and throws the contents down his throat.*)

MATTIE. Henry, it'll poison you! (HENRY *stands tasting his lips. A foolish smile breaks over his face.*)

HENRY. Why it ain't no more'n—(*His eyes suddenly narrow and he walks back and forth across the room. The* DOCTOR *moves around as if unconcerned. Suddenly* HENRY *springs into the air with a yell. Old* JERNIGAN *starts back and falls over a chair.*)

JERNIGAN. Lord, Lord a-mercy!

MATTIE (*running up to* HENRY). Henry, honey, what is it?

HENRY (*tearing wildly around the room and shrieking*). I'm pizened, pizened! Help, water, I'm afire inside. (*He doubles over in pain.* MATTIE *pursues him, wringing her hands. All the while the* DOCTOR *walks ecstatically and yet unconcerned around the room, carrying on his automaton-like actions and his monologue.*)

DOCTOR (*chanting*).

As you all know, wherever I go,
My name is Immanuel,
I treat you well, I make you well,
As sound as the sweet church bell,
Down the road I travel,
Going in rain or shine,
Healing the sick and afflicted,
No medicine like unto mine.
This I tell who comes like Immanuel.

HENRY (*falling into a chair and slobbering heavily at the mouth as he gasps*). Pizened! Pizened! Help, water! (MATTIE *throws her arms around his neck.*)

MATTIE. Run, Father, run and bring the bucket of water. (*The old man shoots into the kitchen and back like a streak. All the while* MATTIE *is crooning over* HENRY *and rubbing his face and forehead feverishly.)* Oh, darling, honey. What can I do? *(She breaks into wild sobs.)*

JERNIGAN. Here, here, drink some water, Henry. *(HENRY springs out of his chair, knocking MATTIE from him. He souses his head in the bucket and drinks, spits out great mouthfuls of water on the floor and empties the bucket over his head. Then he stamps the bucket to pieces, shrieking and yelling.)*

MATTIE. Run for the doctor, run for the doctor!

DOCTOR. I am Doctor Immanuel at your service, madam. *(MAT-TIE turns and glares at him a moment and slaps him in the face. HENRY snatches up the broom and begins chasing the DOCTOR around the room and beating him. The DOCTOR makes an effort to get his case and hat as he is pursued, calling out.)* This is wrong, wrong! *(He opens the door and flees into the night. HENRY falls into a chair and rocks back and forth, groaning and moaning. MATTIE comes sobbing up to him.)*

HENRY *(whirling and seizing MATTIE by the throat).* Who are you? I know—Mattie. You sew for the heathen and worry your husband's life out about dirt. Now in the grave they'll be plenty of dirt. And you sing, and you sing; and you talk and you talk. *(He grabs the remaining bottle and uncorks it.)* Drink this here bottle of stuff.

MATTIE *(clenching her teeth and fighting back).* I won't, I won't! It'll poison me, it'll kill me!

HENRY *(pulling open her mouth and pouring the contents in).* Nunh—unh, I reckon it won't! *(She swallows and coughs and strangles, then drops to the floor crying. HENRY strides about the room kicking the furniture to pieces and throwing out his shoulders and shouting.)* I'm a new man, a man of might, a he-man in Israel! *(Turning upon MATTIE.)* And you have drunk the drink. You're going to be humble down, a helpmeet. *(He drops back in his chair in a dying posture.)*

MATTIE. Oh, Henry, Henry, baby!

HENRY. When I'm gone, take care of Pa. Let him live in peace. Let him have his tobacco and spit in the fire. *(MATTIE crawls on her knees before him and lays her head in his lap, weeping.)*

MATTIE. Get the doctor, Father. Hitch up and go for the doctor. *(Old JERNIGAN starts for the door, HENRY jumps up and snatches him back.)*

HENRY. You ain't, you ain't. Let me die in peace. (*There is the sound of a medley of voices outside, women gabbling in excitement. MATTIE climbs up to her feet and runs to the door.*) MATTIE. Is that you, Mis' Bella? Come here, come here quick. Henry's poisoned and he's a-dying. (*The gabble and excitement outside increase. A voice replies from the yard.*)

VOICE. I'm coming, Mattie, I'm coming! (*She is heard coming up on the steps. HENRY gets up from his chair and begins to bark like a dog, blubbering and growling.*)

HENRY (*shrieking again*). I been bit by a mad dog! (*He barks.*)

VOICE. Lord a-mercy, he's run mad! (*A low murmur of horror rises from the women outside, followed by shrieks and then the sound of running feet. HENRY rushes out of the door barking and pursuing them.*)

MATTIE (*looking at old JERNIGAN through her tears*). He ain't been bit by any mad dog!

JERNIGAN (*stuttering with excitement*). Maybe that's the way the pizen works. The doctor said he got it a quare way in the middle of the night and a storm on and a' old man helping him.

MATTIE. He's crazy. (*Wringing her hands.*) Why'd you let him give Henry that stuff? The mess I took wa'n't nothing, weak as water! (*She goes to the door calling piteously.*) Henry! Henry! (*Old JERNIGAN comes up to the bottle she has dropped and looks at it.*)

JERNIGAN (*with a shout*). He's took the wrong medicine, Mattie! He took that there gray stuff and you took the red!

MATTIE (*at the door*). Henry! Henry! (*HENRY comes back on the porch and gives a farewell bark. MATTIE runs out and throws her arms around him. He flings her from him and strides into the room. His shoes are covered with mud. He goes to the fireplace and stamps it off on the hearth.*)

JERNIGAN (*running up to him excitedly*). Here, here, you took that gray stuff. Look, look!

HENRY (*waving him off*). It don't make no difference. 'Twa'n't nothing but water. (*MATTIE comes in and stares at him as he casually cleans his boot on the hearth.*)

MATTIE (*whimpering*). What's happened, Henry? You seem—

HENRY. I been cured, that's what. The medicine done it. (*He gets up, looks around the room, goes over to the machine, gathers up the clothes for the heathen, picks out a coat and trousers and throws them at the old man.)* Here, there's your Ransome Taylor coat and your britches. The heathen ain't going to get 'em. *(He wipes his shoes with the other garments and then calmly goes to his chair and sits down.* Mattie *has been looking on a moment and then with a glad cry of comprehension falls on her knees by him and lays her head sobbing in his lap.)*

Jernigan *(dropping in his chair thunderstruck).* Well, I be durned if I ever seed the beat! *(He thinks a moment and then bursts out in a low musical chuckle. His mouth spreads into a grin that breaks over his face in a thousand wrinkles. He cuts a caper on the floor, stopping now and then trying to comprehend what has happened.* Henry *sits solemnly stroking* Mattie's *head. The door is cracked open at the rear and* Doctor Immanuel *pokes his head in.)*

Doctor. Masters of this house—

Henry *(turning and snarling).* Hanh—Scat! *(He barks and the* Doctor *slams the door. After a moment* Henry *calls old* Jernigan.) Pa, go and tell him to come in and get his hat and case. *(*Mattie's *sobs gradually die away.)* Yeh, I know, poor child. I did scare you, didn't I? *(Only a whimper from* Mattie *and a hugging of* Henry's *knees answer him.)*

Jernigan *(at the door).* Come on in, Doctor, and get your stuff. He ain't going to hurt you. *(The* Doctor *comes gravely in and gets his case and hat.)*

Henry. Pa, give him that five dollars.

Jernigan *(his sides shaking with enjoyment).* Here, here it is. You done it, Doc, same as you said you would.

Henry. You needn't come back. I don't need you! *(He lifts his head with decision written on his face.)* Let me have a look at the plug of tobacco, pa.

Doctor *(at the door).* Remember that I am always at your service. Peace abide with you and this house always. I am on my way now to another patient, a mule sick at brother Gaskin's house.

Henry. That's all right, Doctor. You needn't bother about us. We ain't going to need you no more. Are we, Mattie? *(*Mattie *shakes her head.)*

Doctor *(going out).*

As you all know, wherever I go,
My name is Immanuel.
(*He closes the door and his chant dies away in the night.*)
HENRY. I said, Pa, I'd like a look at that tobacco.
MATTIE (*raising her head*). Don't you spit on—
HENRY (*crushing her back on the floor*). Nanh, nanh, I tell
you I been cured, I'm boss. At first I was scared to death. Then
when I'd started it come over me all of a suddent like a wave
of joy, and I felt my own strength. (*Breaking into a loud roaring
laugh.*) Hooray! Hooray! I'm another man. I'm cured, I'm boss.
Gimme that tobacco.

The old man hands it to him eagerly. HENRY *bites off an
enormous chew and hands the plug back. Old* JERNIGAN *hesitates
a moment and then also bites off a mouthful. A look of deep con-
tent comes over him. He snuggles into his chair and chews.*
HENRY *chews. They look across at each other.* HENRY *signifies
to the old man with a motion of his hand that he spit first. Old*
JERNIGAN *with signs refuses.* HENRY *spits profusely and loud in
the direction of the fire. Old* JERNIGAN *does likewise.*

JERNIGAN (*eyeing* HENRY *slyly as he rolls his tobacco sweetly
in his mouth*). Hee-hee! (MATTIE *sits hugging* HENRY's *knees.*)
HENRY (*nodding happily and wisely*). Unh-hunh-yeh. (*They
sit saying nothing. Presently* HENRY *looks over at the old man
and laughs suddenly and deeply.*)
JERNIGAN. What?
HENRY. I run them there women right into the mudhole out
there—up to their waist.
JERNIGAN (*beating his thigh gleefully*). Hee-hee! Hee-hee!
HENRY. I sure did. (*They lapse into silence. By this time* MAT-
TIE *has somewhat raised her head and is staring contemplatively
by* HENRY's *shin into the fire.*)
JERNIGAN (*shivering a bit and stirring the fire*). Going to be
cold, Henry, cold.
HENRY. Yeh.
JERNIGAN. Robins been flying towards the south all day.

They both lean towards the fire and spit.

CURTAIN

THE NO 'COUNT BOY

A Play of Folk Imagination

BY

PAUL GREEN

She hug me and she kiss me,
   She helt my hand and cried,
She said I was the sweetest thing
   That ever lived or died.
She hug me and she kiss me—
   Oh, heaven the touch of her hand!
She said I was the purtiest thing
   In the shape of mortal man.

—Negro song

THE CHARACTERS

PHEELIE

ENOS, *her beau*

THE No 'COUNT BOY

AN OLD NEGRO WOMAN

SCENE

Before a farmhouse somewhere in the South.

TIME

Several years ago.

The scene is the small yard immediately before a Negro cabin. There is a lilac tree in the yard with a bench under it. PHEELIE, *a neat Negro girl of seventeen, is sitting on this bench looking through a book. She is dressed in her best frock, white shoes and stockings. It is a late Saturday afternoon in summer. Presently there is the sound of an approaching buggy in the lane off at the left and a voice calls "Whoa!"* PHEELIE *listens a moment, and then gives her head a toss and goes on fingering the leaves of her book.* ENOS *comes in at the left and stands watching her. He is a short stocky Negro of twenty or more, dressed in a faded gray suit and black felt hat. His celluloid collar and scarlet tie shine out brilliantly against the black of his face.*

ENOS (*in a drawling voice that now and then drops into a stammer*). Well, Pheelie, here I is.

PHEELIE (*looking up casually*). I see you is, and you's 'bout an hour early.

ENOS. But ain't you all dressed up to go?

PHEELIE. I's dressed up, but I ain't ready to go.

ENOS (*dubiously*). Well, suh, now—I–I—

PHEELIE. I just put on these here clothes 'cause it was so hot in the house with my work duds on. (*He takes off his hat and discloses his naturally kinky hair combed back in a straight pompadour. He waits for her to notice it, but she keeps looking straight before her.*) Set down and rest yourself. (*Somewhat ill at ease he sits down in the rocking-chair and watches her.*)

ENOS. I drapped by a little early hoping—a—mebbe you'd like to take a small drive before church begun.

PHEELIE (*in the same cold voice*). Thanky, I don't believe I wants to take any drive. (*She becomes absorbed in her book.*)

ENOS (*picking at the lining of his hat*). And I thought we might stop by Buie's Creek and get some ice cream. (*He watches her narrowly.*)

PHEELIE (*after a moment*). That'd be nice, I reckon, but I don't want no ice cream neither. (*She is silent again. He pulls nervously at his fingers, making the joints pop.*) And I'd be much obliged if you'd quit popping your finger joints.

ENOS (*jerking his hands apart and running his fingers over his greased hair.*) 'Scuse me, Pheelie. (*Somewhat timidly, but with a hidden touch of spirit.*) You—you don't seem glad to see me much.

133

PHEELIE. You didn't have no date to come over here an hour before time.

ENOS (worried). I knows it. But what's the matter with you? You ain't mad at me, is you?

PHEELIE. No, I ain't mad.

ENOS. Seems like you'd rather look at that old book than talk to me.

PHEELIE. Maybe I had. (He feels his tie, twirls his hat, and spits softly through his teeth off to one side.)

ENOS. What sort of book is it, Pheelie?

PHEELIE. What difference do it make to you? You ain't interested in no book.

ENOS. 'Spect that's right. But you sure seems more took with it than anything I ever seed you have before.

PHEELIE. It's a fine picture book.

ENOS. Where'd you get it?

PHEELIE. This morning I was up to Mis' Ella's helping her hoe out the garden, and she told me a whole heap about the places she and Mr. Jack went when they was married. And she give me this book that showed a passel of things.

ENOS. Hunh, they had money to travel with and enjoy theirselves.

PHEELIE. She said one place they went to was some sort of Falls or something like that, where the water poured over in a great river and made a racket same as the world was busting up.

ENOS. That ain't nothing—mostly talk, I bet a dollar.

PHEELIE (closing the book with a bang). That's what you always says. You don't care a straw about going off and seeing things.

ENOS (sharply). Ain't I done told you, honey-bunch, we ain't going to have no money to be traipsing round the world, not yet nohow.

PHEELIE. Don't you honey me no more, I tells you.

ENOS (amazed). What'n the name of Old Scratch ails you? Ain't I got a right to honey you, and you engaged to me?

PHEELIE. Engaged to you! It's you engaged to me.

ENOS. Aw right, I's engaged to you then, and you knows mighty drot'n well I's glad to be too. They ain't no put-on with me.

PHEELIE. I reckon you is glad. But mess with me and you won't be engaged to nothing.

ENOS (*pleadingly*). Now, Pheelie, you better throw that book in the fire and come on and let's go for a drive. It's stirred you all up. Come on, I's got a mess of news to tell you.

PHEELIE. I ain't going on no drive. And I'm about decided not to go with you to no meeting tonight neither.

ENOS (*alarmed*). Lord, don't talk like that. Here I's been waiting all the week for this Saturday night, and you ain't going back on me, is you?

PHEELIE (*softening*). But, Enos, you's so samey, allus satisfied with what you has. You just gets my goat.

ENOS (*humbly*). If you means I ain't took with no wild ideas or such about trips way off yonder to see folks making fools of theirselves, then I is samey. But you listen here, child, they ain't no miracles and such off there like what you thinks. Once I spent a good five dollars going on a 'scursion to Wilmington, and they weren't a thing to see, not half as much as they is on this here farm.

PHEELIE. You got to have eyes to see things. Some folks is naturally born blind.

ENOS (*placatingly*). Well, maybe when we's married we'll take a little trip to Raleigh or Durham and see the street cars and big buildings.

PHEELIE. But I wants to go further, clean to the mountains, and right on then, maybe.

ENOS. By craps, you must think I got a can of money buried somewhere.

PHEELIE. I don't neither. Us could hobo, or walk part the way, just fool along.

ENOS (*laughing*). Hobo! Us'd hobo right into some white man's jail, that's what. And they ain't nothing to that walking business. We'd be a pretty sight with our feet blistered and somebody's bulldog tearing plugs out'n—well, you knows what.

PHEELIE (*ignoring his reply*). Setting there looking through that book I got plumb sick and tired of you and all this farming and sweating and getting nowhere—sick of everything. And just looking at "old lazy Lawrence" dancing over the fields made me want to puke.

ENOS (*eyeing her*). Honey child, the last time I was here you said you'd like working in the fields with me and keeping the house and such.

PHEELIE. I will, Enos, I reckons I will. But that there book set me wanting to go off and get away.

ENOS (*moving his chair over to her*). Listen to me. I knows I ain't fitten to breathe on you, but I's going to do my best by you. And what you reckon? Mr. Pearson done told me today that he's having the lumber sawed to build our house. September she'll be done, then you'n me can have business—can see the preacher.

PHEELIE. Mr. Pearson's good to you all right.

ENOS. Ain't he! That's a man what is a man. And it ain't all for me he's building that house. He likes you and says he'll be glad to have you on his place.

PHEELIE (*with signs of interest*). What kind of house is it—just a shack with a stick-and-dirt chimney?

ENOS (*jubilantly*). Now I was just a-hoping you'd ask that. No, suh, it ain't no cowshed you could throw a dog through the cracks—nunh-unh. It's going to be a nice frame house with wide porch, and it'll be ceiled. And listen here, it's going to have wallpaper. And, honey, Mr. Pearson said he wanted you to come up a-Monday and help choose the pattern. (*He looks at her delightedly.*)

PHEELIE (*her face brightening somewhat*). Oh, that's so nice of you and him! (*She bows her head.*)

ENOS. What's the matter now?

PHEELIE (*looking up with tears in her eyes*). You's too good to me, Enos, and I hadn't ought to always be so unsatisfied.

ENOS. Sure, never mind now. (*He puts his arm around her.*)

PHEELIE (*letting her hand rest on his hair*). Granny's alive! You done spent money to git your hair straightened.

ENOS (*with a kind of shamed joy*). Yeh, yeh, I has. But it was to celebrate a little.

PHEELIE. That's throwing away a dollar and a half. In a little bit it'll be kinky again.

ENOS. 'Course it will, but I thought you'd like it while it lasts.

PHEELIE (*laughing*). You sure is a proud nigger. (*She kisses*

him quickly and stands away from him.) Nunh-unh, I ain't goin'
to do it no more. (*He drops reluctantly back into his seat, and she
sits again on the bench.*)

ENOS (*after a moment*). You want to take that little drive now?

PHEELIE. I might, I guess.

ENOS (*slapping himself*). Hot dog, then let's go, honey!

PHEELIE (*brightly*). Let me shut up the house and we'll be
ready. Muh and Pap and all the kids is over to the ice cream
supper at Uncle Haywood's before preaching. (*She starts up.*)

ENOS (*standing up*). All right, honey babe. I sure likes to see
you jollied up. And I's got another surprise for you too.

PHEELIE (*stopping*). You has?

ENOS (*mysteriously*). Unh-hunh. But I'll tell you a little later.

PHEELIE. Naw, suh, tell me now—please.

ENOS (*anxious to tell it*). In course I can't stand out against
you. Well, we ain't going to drive behind no flop-eared mule
this time.

PHEELIE. We ain't! (*She starts towards the left to look out.*)

ENOS. Naw, suh. I's driving Egypt today.

PHEELIE. Mr. Pearson's fine horse!

ENOS (*grinning*). Yeh, yeh, sure is. I worked hard all the week
and this morning he come to me and asked me if I didn't want
Egypt to haul you with tonight.

PHEELIE (*looking off*). There he is. Ain't that fine, and is he
safe?

ENOS. Safe! Safe as a cellar. But, Lord, he can burn the wind!

PHEELIE. Goody-good. Now come help me shut the house.

ENOS (*as they go off at the left rear*). Mr. Pearson knows I
ain't going to beat his stock and bellows 'em like some the nig-
gers. I tells you, sugar lump, if we stays with him and do right,
some these days we going to have money to take them there trips
you wants to. (*They have hardly disappeared when a slender Negro youth of sixteen or seventeen, barefooted and raggedly dressed
in an old pair of overalls, shirt and torn straw hat, comes in at
the right front and stands staring after them. He is whittling a
green walking-stick. In a moment he pulls out a small mouth organ
and begins playing a whirling jig.* ENOS *looks back around the
corner.*) Who's that playing to beat the band? (*He and* PHEELIE
come back into the yard. PHEELIE *stares at the boy in delighted*

astonishment. Suddenly he winds up on a high note. As he beats
the harp against his thigh, he bursts into a loud joyous laugh.)

Pheelie. Lord, you can play. Who is you?

Enos *(with a touch of authority in his voice)*. What you want
here? I ain't never seed you before.

Boy *(in a clear childish voice, as he looks at* Pheelie*)*. You
ain't?

Enos. Naw, I ain't. What you mean walking up in people's
yards and acting like you was home?

Boy. I thought I might get me a drink from the well there.

Pheelie. Help yourself. *(He draws water from the well at the*
right and drinks like a little horse. Enos *and* Pheelie *watch*
him.)

Enos *(in a low voice)*. I bet he's some boy run away from home.
Maybe a tramp, I dunno.

Pheelie. That boy a tramp! Hunh, he ain't no such.

Enos. I bet you on it. Looks 'spicious to me.

Boy *(returning from the well and wiping his mouth with his*
sleeve). I thought I might get a bite to eat here maybe. *(He looks*
from one to the other, a lurking smile in his eyes.)

Pheelie *(uncertainly)*. You might.

Enos. Like as not the lady wants to know where you come
from and what your business is before she begins to feed you.

Boy *(looking at* Pheelie*)*. Would you?

Pheelie. Yeh. What's your name?

Boy *(laughing and blowing out a whiff of music)*. Mostly I
ain't got no name. *(Beating the harp in his hand and scratching*
his leg with his toe.) 'Way, 'way back down there—*(pointing indef-*
initely behind him)—where I come from some of 'em calls me
Pete, but mostly they calls me the No 'Count Boy.

Enos. Why they call you that for?

Boy *(laughing again)*. 'Cause I don't like to work in the fields.

Enos. Unh-hunh, unh-hunh, I s'picioned it.

Boy, S'picioned what?

Enos. Aw, nothing. Anyhow that's a good name for you, I bet.
Whose boy is you and where'd you come from 'way back down
there as you calls it?

Boy *(quickly)*. Cuts no wool whose boy I is. As for where I
come from, I can't tell you, bo, 'cause I dunno hardly. *(Hesitat-*

ing and pointing off to the right.) You see where the sky come down to earth—'way, 'way yonder?

Enos. Yeh, I sees it.

Boy *(grinning to himself).* Well, I come from miles and miles beyond it. *(A kind of awe creeping into his words.)* Lord, Lord, how far has I come?

Pheelie. You been all that distance by yourself?

Boy. Sure has. And what's more I walked it every jump. *(Again he draws the harp across his lips in a breath of music, all the while watching them with bright eyes.)*

Enos. Where you going?

Boy. Just going.

Pheelie. You mean you ain't got no special place in mind—you just hoboing along?

Boy. That's it, I reckon.

Enos. How does you get your rations—beg for it?

Boy. I pays for it when I can get 'em. Times I goes hungry.

Enos *(looking at him keenly).* You ain't got no money, has you?

Boy *(cunningly).* That's all right. I pays for it just the same. *(He stops and looks at* Pheelie *with big eyes.)* You's purty as a pink, ain't you?

Pheelie *(turning away her head).* Why you ask that?

Enos *(sharply).* You needn't be thinking you'll get your supper on soft talk, horse-cake.

Boy *(still looking at* Pheelie*).* What's your name?

Pheelie. My name's Ophelia, but they calls me Pheelie.

Boy *(staring at her admiringly and cracking his palm against his thigh).* Dawg-gone! Just like me for the world. I's named one thing and they calls me another.

Enos *(with a hint of uneasiness).* Here, I 'spects you better be going on up the road. Me'n Miss Pheelie's just ready to go out for our afternoon drive, and we don't want to be bothered with nobody's no 'count boy.

Boy *(his face falling).* I hates to hinder you, Miss Pheelie, but can't I get nothing to eat—a 'tater or anything?

Pheelie. I 'spect I could give you a snack in your hand right quick.

Boy. No sooner said'n done. I hopes. And I pays you for it too.

Enos (*almost sarcastically*). Got your pockets full of silver and gold, apt as not.

Boy. Naw, suh, I got something better'n new money. Here she is. (*Holding up his harp.*) I plays you a piece or two pieces or three, and you gives me a bite and what you pleases. (*In mock seriousness he pulls off his hat and addresses them.*) Ladies and ge'men, the first piece I renders is called "The Dark-eyed Woman." It's music 'bout a woman what had three little boys, and they took sick and died one June night whilst the mocking-birds was singing. And always after that they said she had a dark shadow in her dark eyes. (*He clears his throat, spits once or twice and lays the harp gently to his lips. Closing his eyes, he begins to play. Enos stirs about him as the notes flood from the Boy's mouth, and now and then he looks questioningly at Pheelie's averted face. The Boy's nostrils quiver, and he makes a sobbing sound in his throat. Tears begin to pour down his cheeks. After a moment he winds up with a flourish.*)

Enos (*gruffly*). Lord Jesus, that rascal can blow!

Boy (*looking at Pheelie as he wipes his eyes*). I hope you don't mind. Every time I blows that piece I cries. (*Pheelie glances up with moist eyes.*)

Pheelie. I sure don't mind. Where you learn that?

Boy. It's a made piece.

Enos. Who made it?

Boy. Me.

Enos (*ironically*). Hunh, you might!

Boy (*his face troubled*). You believes I made it, don't you, Miss Pheelie?

Pheelie. That I do.

Boy (*his face clearing*). All right then. And I'll play you another piece for that snack of grub.

Pheelie. That one's enough to pay.

Enos. You sure you didn't get no rations down the road?

Boy. Not nary a chaw.

Pheelie. Ain't you had nothing all day?

Boy. Nothing but some branch water and a little bitsy bird I killed with a rock and fried. (*His face takes on a sober look, and tears again glisten in his eyes.*)

ENOS (*looking at him in astonishment*). You sure is a queer fellow.

BOY (*staring up at the sky*). That little bird was singing so sweet and ruffling his breast in the wind, and I picked up a rock and just throwed devilish like, never thought I'd hit him. But that's the way it is—when you thinks you won't, you does, and I kilt him.

PHEELIE. And then you et him?

BOY (*wiping his eyes on his sleeves*). I was so hungry then, and I built a speck of fire and baked him. (*Wretchedly.*) Weren't it better for me to eat him than for maggots to get at him?

PHEELIE. 'Twas that.

BOY (*mournfully*). But I sure felt bad about that little bird. I can't get his tune out'n my head. He sot on that limb and would give a long call and then a short one—(*imitating on his harmonica*)—just like that.

ENOS. You're a mighty big fellow to be crying over a bird, seems like to me.

PHEELIE. Enos, you quit that making fun.

BOY. When I come through the creek back there, a good-god was pecking in a high dead tree, and he turned his head sideways and whickered at me. I heared him say he going to ha'nt me for killing that bird.

ENOS. I swear! (PHEELIE *gives* ENOS *a cutting look, and he stops his laughing.*)

BOY. I've hearn't that them good-gods is old women turned to birds 'cause they was wicked. And you see they's still got on little old red caps.

PHEELIE. They won't hurt you.

ENOS. Pshaw, they ain't nothing but great big sapsuckers.

BOY. How you know? Just the same this un scolded me for throwing that rock. I could tell it in his talk and the way he looked at me.

PHEELIE. You didn't mean to do it nohow, and you was hungry too. Now play us some more.

BOY. I 'spect maybe then it's all right. I 'spect so. Now I plays you my other piece to pay you plenty for my eatings.

PHEELIE. 'Tain't that, 'tain't that. We likes to hear you. I'll feed you for nothing.

BOY. Well, listen to this, folkses, this moan song. (*He again pulls off his hat and makes his stage bow.*) Ladies and gentlemen, this is a talking piece I's going to render. It's 'titled "The Coffin Song," and tells about a nice girl what went away from home all dressed out in white and died, and they sont her body back to her Muh and Pap. This here's the Coast-Line coming down the track on a dark and rainy night with her coffin on board. (*He closes his eyes and begins blowing the choo-kerr-choo of a starting train. He intersperses his blowing with short speeches.*) The rain is beating on the window panes and everybody is mournful. (*The choo-kerr-chooing takes on a sobbing note, and the speed of the train increases.*) The old man and the woman is at the station waiting for their daughter's body, her they loved so well, oh, her they loved so well. "Don't cry, honey, she gone to heaven," the old man say, Lord, Lord, the old man say. Then he hear that coffin-blow. (*A long mournful wail of the engine's whistle follows, swallowed up in the growing speed of the locomotive. He opens his eyes and begins to chant his bits of dialogue.*) Now she's balling the jack 'cross the river trestle. (*He quivers and sings with the straining timbers of the bridge.*) Here she is passing by the gravel-pit. How she goes by, how she goes by! Like a great black horse, a great black horse! And now she's blowing for the crossing. (*The whistle moans again.*) Her Muh and Pap's on the platform at the station and they feel their hearts in their mouths at the crying of that train, Lord, Lord, the crying of that train! (*Again he gives the coffin-blow, long and heartbreaking.*) The train she slow up. (*The choo-kerr-chooing slowly stops.*) They takes out the coffin and flowers and puts her in a hearse, and they all drives off slow, slow, like this. (*He plays a sort of dead march and stalks back and forth across the yard.*) Then the next day they takes her to the graveyard, the lonesome graveyard. And the preacher preach—shout hallelujah—the preacher preach and the people sing, shouting glory to the lamb. And then they begin to throw dirt in on her. (*He imitates the thump, thump of clods falling on the coffin.*) Then the father and mother and sisters and brothers all cry out loud. Her Pap cries like this. (*He gives forth a long deep groan.*) And the sisters and brothers like this. (*A medley of weeping sounds.*) And the mother cry like this. (*A high piercing shriek.*) And then they roach up the grave and the preacher make prayer—"Lord, Lord Jesus, have mercy upon us!" Then they all go off and they ain't nothing left 'cepting a crow in a high scraggly pine a-saying:—(*He mingles his music with a raucous h-a-r-r-c-k, h-a-r-r-c-k.*) Then after that when night come, dark and rainy night, the last and leastest thing is a small wind in the bushes like this. (*A trembling flute-like note rises, bubbles and disappears. He beats the harp against his hand and looks uncertainly at* ENOS *and* PHEELIE, *the tears wetting his cheeks.*)

ENOS (*presently*). I can't deny you got the world beat handling that baby, but what'n the name of God makes you cry so much?

BOY (*watching* PHEELIE'S *bowed head*). When I plays that piece I feel so lonesome like I can't help crying, I always cries.

ENOS. I's seed folks cry when their people died, but Lord, I never seed no such cry-baby as you.

BOY. You's hard-hearted. Look at Miss Pheelie, she's crying.

ENOS. Help my life! What ails you, Pheelie?

PHEELIE (*hurriedly drying her eyes*). Don't make no fun of me, Enos. I just had the blues again.

ENOS (*patting his hat anxiously*). Here, don't you get to feeling that a-way no more, honey. Let's go on with our drive.

BOY. You calls her honey!

ENOS. That I do. She's my girl, that's what. And listen to me —I don't want no no 'count fellow come piddling by with a harp and wild talk to get her upset.

BOY (*unhappily*). I didn't know you was her man. I—I thought she was too purty and like a angel for that. (PHEELIE *looks at him tearfully and he gazes back warmly.*)

ENOS (*angrily*). Look out, nigger, mind what you's up to!

PHEELIE. Enos, you quit talking to that boy like that.

ENOS (*coming up to her and catching her by the arm*). Come on now and let that fellow go on where he's started.

PHEELIE (*springing up*). Turn me a-loose. He's going to stay right here if he wants to and eat and sleep to boot.

ENOS (*hesitating a moment and then flaring out, his timidity and slowness gone*). The hell you say! (*He turns suddenly towards the boy and points off to the left.*) You see 'way, 'way yonder in the west where the sun is setting in the tops of them long-straw pines?

BOY (*questioningly*). Yeh, yeh, I sees it.

ENOS (*moving towards him*). Well, I wants you to get in that road this minute and start there.

PHEELIE (*putting herself quickly before him*). He ain't, I tell you.

BOY (*emboldened by* PHEELIE's *protection*). You means you wants to run me off before I gets any rations?

ENOS. I don't care whether you gets any rations or not. I wants you to leave here before you gets Pheelie all tore up with your foolish notions. (*Snapping.*) You better git from here.

BOY (*swinging his stick before him and smiling with weak grimness*). Ah—hah—I ain't going. (ENOS *makes another step towards him. The* BOY *jumps back.*) Don't you come towards me. I'll split your head open with this here stick. (ENOS *stops and eyes him cautiously. The* BOY *holds his stick in trembling readiness.*)

PHEELIE (*getting between them*). I tells you, Enos Atkins, you ain't going to harm nary a hair of this boy's head. You do and I'll scratch your eyes out apt as not.

ENOS. God a'mighty! Done hyp'otized with him already, is you? (*In a wheedling tone.*) Now, boy, can't you see how it is with me? We was just ready to go off to church, and here you pops up and sets yourself in betwixt us. (*He feels in his pockets and pulls out a dollar.*) Here take this dollar and go on. You can buy enough grub with it to last you a week.

BOY (*breaking into a loud derisive laugh*). Ain't he a sight trying to hire me off from his girl!

ENOS. Them there laughs is likely going to be tacks in your coffin. (*The* BOY *closes his eyes in merriment. With a quick movement* ENOS *snatches his stick from him.*) Now see if you don't hit the grit up that road. (*He puts out his arm and pushes* PHEELIE *back. Egypt is heard off at the left pawing the ground and shaking his bridle.*) Whoa, Egypt!

BOY (*half whimpering*). Don't hit me with that stick.

ENOS. I ain't going to hit you if you lights a rag out'n here this minute. Scat, or I'll wring your neck. Make yourself sca'ce, nigger!

PHEELIE. Let him alone, let him alone, I tells you!

BOY. You better go tend to your horse, bo. I hear him trying to get loose.

ENOS *(looking appealingly at* PHEELIE*).* Egypt's getting restless, Pheelie. You about ready to be driving now? *(He steps to the left and calls.)* Whoa! whoa there, Egypt! *(Turning back.)* Come on, Pheelie, and let's go.

PHEELIE *(shaking her head determinedly).* I ain't going on no drive with you, and that's my last say.

ENOS. Oh, hell fire! *(He lowers his stick. At the left he turns and speaks.)* You just wait here, while I fix my horse, you little pole-cat, and I'll fix you. *(He hurries out.)*

BOY *(turning boldly back into the yard).* Hunh, that nigger ain't nothing but bluff.

PHEELIE. And he ain't going to make you leave neither. You stay right with him.

BOY. He thinks you's getting to liking me, that's what he thinks. *(He falls to staring at her intently.)*

PHEELIE. Why you look at me like that?

BOY *(shyly).* How old is you?

PHEELIE. Seventeen.

BOY *(joyously).* Is? Then we's just the same age. Can't—can't I call you Pheelie?

PHEELIE *(looking at the ground).* Yeh, yeh, you can.

BOY. I feels just like I knowed you all my life, and I ain't never seed nobody like you in all my progueings, nobody—and I's traveled a heap too.

PHEELIE. And you's seed a monstrous lot where you traveled, ain't you? Yeh, you has, I bet.

BOY. I has that—Lord, Lord!

PHEELIE *(dropping into the rocking-chair).* Has you seed any big rivers and waters and such?

BOY. Rivers! Lord, yeh!

PHEELIE. Has you been by a place where a great river pours over a steep hill roaring like the judgment day?

BOY *(dropping on his knees and marking in the dirt as he ponders).* I dunno—yeh-yeh, that river was two miles wide and you had to stop your ears in a mile of it.

PHEELIE. Go on, go on, tell me some more. Has you been in any big towns?

BOY. Has I? I's been in towns that had streets so long they wasn't no coming to the end of 'em.

PHEELIE. Was they many people there?

BOY. People! People! (*He rolls over on the ground at the remembrance of it and then sits up.*) All kinds and sizes. People running, people walking, some wearing diamont dresses and gold shoes. Rich, my, my, how rich! Ortymobiles as big as that house with horns that jar like a earthquake and boiler busting all at once.

PHEELIE (*a little dubiously*). Aw—

BOY. Hit's so. And street cars running with nothing pulling or pushing 'em. And buildings so high that the moon brushes the top. High! Lord, Lord, how high! And people hauling money with trains, big train loads where they keeps it in a big house with a school breaking of folks to guard it.

PHEELIE. I been looking at pictures in this book, but nothing fine as that. (*She brings the book and shows it to him.*)

BOY (*somewhat disturbed*). Yeh, I's got a book like that. (*He begins picking his teeth meditatively with a straw.*) It was give to me by a peddling man. (*Smiling wisely.*) But that was before I went out traveling for myself. Lord, Lord, compared to what I seed in New York that book ain't nothing.

PHEELIE. New York! You been there?

BOY. That I has. She's a long ways yonder too, maybe two hundred miles, who knows. But Pheelie, that's the place to go, everything easy, people good to you, nothing to do but eat ice cream and maybe now and then drink lemonade—and see people, people! Worse'n the fair at Dunn. Never seed such a mess of people. (*ENOS is heard quieting his horse.*)

PHEELIE. How'd you travel so far and pay your way? Must take a lot of money.

BOY. I walked, that's how, bum my way. And when I gets hungry I plays my harp.

PHEELIE. Where you sleep?

BOY. You don't know nothing about traveling, does you? I sleeps on the warm ground. Come sunset, I stops in a hollow and breaks down bushes and rakes up pinestraw and sleeps like a log. And in the morning I wakes and sees the dew on everything and hears the birds singing, and I lies there a while and practice on my harp. Then I's off down the road breathing the fine air and feeling just as happy as I can.

PHEELIE (*vehemently*). I done told Enos we could do like that. I sure has told him time and again.

BOY. Would you like to live that a-way?

PHEELIE. Unh-hunh, yeh, oh, yeh, I would.

BOY (*earnestly*). Why can't you, Pheelie?

PHEELIE (*twisting her hands nervously*). I dunno—I wants to—I do wants to go and keep on going.

BOY (*leaning quickly forward*). Pheelie, Pheelie, come on with me and go tramping through the world. You can leave that bench-leg Enos behind.

PHEELIE (*turning impulsively towards him and then dropping her head*). I can't do it, I's afraid to. (ENOS *slips in at the left rear and watches them.*)

BOY. I tell you we would have the best time going. Come on and go with me.

PHEELIE (*hesitating*). I—might do it—I's half tempted to do it.

BOY (*catching her hand*). I tells you what—how about me waiting out in the woods there till dark comes down and then you can put on a old dress and join me?

PHEELIE (*pulling her hand unwillingly from him*). That'd be fine—fine, but wouldn't folks raise cain?

BOY. Let 'em. What you'n me care? We'll be splashing in the rain and shouting in the sun. And we'll step along together, and I'll hold your pretty little hand and you'll hold mine, and I'll teach you to sing songs. I knows a bushel of purty ones. And then I'll learn you how to blow my harp. And we'll slip down the roads at sunrise and sunset, singing and blowing the finest tunes they is. Please'm say you'll go with me.

PHEELIE (*with shining eyes*). You has the purtiest talk of any man or boy I ever seed, and oh, I wish—wish— (*With sudden abandon.*) Yeh, yeh, I will—I will, I'll go. (*Ecstatically he touches her arm and looks straight into her eyes.*)

BOY (*cooingly*). Birdie mine, birdie mine. (*He stands up and bends over her chair.*)

PHEELIE (*her face alight as she leans her head against him*). Oh, it makes my head swim to think of all we's going to see and hear. (*He timidly puts his arm over her shoulder.* ENOS *throws his stick behind him, springs forward and snatches the* BOY *away from* PHEELIE.)

ENOS. Here, you low-down rascal, trying to steal my girl, is you? Oh, yeh, I been hearing what you said. (*His nostrils dilating.*) And I's going give you a kick in the seat of your britches that'll send you where you's gwine.

BOY (*retreating behind* PHEELIE). I ain't trying to steal her neither. She don't care nothing for you and wants to go on with me.

ENOS. That's a lie, you little ficey fool, and you better look out before I gives you the lock-jaw.

BOY. She much as said she don't love you, now then.

ENOS. You didn't say that, did you, Pheelie?

PHEELIE. I dunno whether I loves you or not.

ENOS (*turning savagely upon the* BOY). Damn your soul, I got a notion to ham-string you. (*He makes a movement towards the* BOY, *who darts over to the left, sees his walking-stick, and seizes it.*) You just come here rolling off your lies by the yard and tear up everything! Why don't you leave? Want me to bring out a feather bed and wash your feet and sing to you and fan you and put you to sleep, does you? (*Jumping forward.*) I'll put you to sleep!

BOY (*falling quickly behind* PHEELIE *and drawing his stick*). You make another move at me and I'll scrush your skull.

PHEELIE (*crying out*). Enos, stop that, stop that!

ENOS (*sarcastically*). Yeh, and who's you to order me—you lost every ray of sense you ever had! Wouldn't you be a purty fool running off with this here woods-colt and sleeping in the jambs of fences and old hog beds and scratching fleas like a mangy hound! (*His voice rising high in wrath.*) That you would. And in winter weather you'd have your shirt-tail friz to you hard as iron. You'd be a sight for sore eyes!

PHEELIE. Shut up.—Boy, I wouldn't let him call me no woods-colt.

BOY (*weakly*). Don't you call me that.

ENOS (*taking off his coat*). Call you that! I ain't started yet. I's going to twist off both your ears and make you eat 'em without no salt. Hell, you ain't got no more backbone than a ground puppy.

BOY (*trembling and clinging to his stick*). Pheelie, Pheelie, don't let him get at me!

PHEELIE. Don't you hurt that boy, I tells you again.

ENOS (*laughing brutally*). Hurt him! I's going to crucify him. (*He begins circling* PHEELIE. *The* BOY *keeps on the opposite side.* ENOS *reaches out and pulls* PHEELIE *behind him.*) Now, my little son of a gun, where is you?

BOY (*in desperation raising his stick*). Don't you come near me. (ENOS *makes a dart at him. The* BOY *starts to flee, but as* ENOS *clutches him, he turns and brings his stick awkwardly down on his head.* ENOS *staggers and falls to his knees.*)

PHEELIE (*looking on in amazement and then screaming*). Lord, you's kilt Enos! (*She stands in uncertainty, and then runs and holds him to her.*)

BOY (*in a scared voice as he drops his stick*). Mercy, what's I going to do? Is—is you hurt, Enos? (ENOS *groans.*)

PHEELIE. Get out'n here, you, you. You's murdered my husband. Enos, Enos, honey baby, is you hurt bad? (*He groans again and she helps him to a chair.*)

ENOS (*twisting his head from side to side*). Hurt? Nothing but a little crack. That lizard ain't strong enough to kill a flea with a sledge hammer. (*He suddenly whirls around and runs his tongue out, snarling at the* BOY.) Ya-a-a-h! (*The* BOY *bounds backwards and, tripping over the bench, falls sprawling on the ground.*) See there, blowing my breath on him throws him into fits. (*The* BOY *lies stretched out still.*)

PHEELIE. Oh, my Lordy, you—I believes he's dead or something!

ENOS (*trying to hide his fear*). Sure nothing but the breath knocked out'n him.

PHEELIE (*shrilly, as she bends above the* BOY). He's hurt, I tell you. Poor boy. (*Turning towards* ENOS). What if you's kilt him?

ENOS (*rubbing his own head*). Shut up, he ain't hurt bad.

PHEELIE. You hateful mule-beating rascal, he is hurt. (*Moaning over him.*) Oh, my sweet honey-boy!

BOY (*sitting up*). Jesus, that fall jarred the wind out'n my stomach. (*Suddenly getting to his feet and eyeing* ENOS *fearfully.*) Don't let that man make at me.

PHEELIE. I don't reckon he will. You given him a dose to last for a while.

ENOS (*standing up*). A dose! Hunh, he can't faze me with no little tap on the skull. (*He begins rolling up his sleeves. There is a hail off at the right front.*) And now I rolls up my sleeves for the hog-killing.

PHEELIE. You all stop that rowing now. Yonder comes somebody. (*The* BOY *reaches down and gets his harp out of the dirt.*)

ENOS. Who is that? Some old woman in a steer cart.

BOY (*looking up hastily*). Lord Jesus, that's—who's that! Hide me, people, hide me quick so's she can't get to me. (*He looks around him in terror.*) Where must I go?

PHEELIE. Why you scared of her?

BOY. Pheelie, put me somewhere, cover me quick!

PHEELIE. Drop down on your knees, she's coming up the path. Better get behind the house maybe.

BOY (*on his all-fours*). And if she asks for me, don't you tell her.

PHEELIE. We'll tell her we ain't seed hair nor hide of you. But why you so tore up? (*He crawls rapidly off at the left rear around the house.*) Now, Enos, you keep your mouth shut. They's something up—that boy afraid so.

ENOS. They is something up, and my suspicions is coming to the top.

OLD WOMAN (*calling off the right front*). Heigho!

PHEELIE. Heigho! (*A stout old Negress, dressed in rough working clothes, comes in at the right. She carries a long heavy switch in her hand with which she cuts at the ground as she talks.*)

OLD WOMAN. How you all come on?

PHEELIE. Well as common, and how does you?

OLD WOMAN. Well, I thanky. I's looking my boy—seen anything of him?

PHEELIE (*slowly*). What sort of boy?

OLD WOMAN. Lord, take me all day to given you a picture of him. He's just the no'countest fellow ever was born. He goes round playing a harp, and he's not just right in his head. He talks wild about being off and traveling everywhere, and he ain't never been out'n Harnett County. Got all that mess out'n picture books and such. (*A delighted grin begins to pass over* ENOS' *face.* PHEELIE *looks dejectedly at the ground.*)

PHEELIE (*in a choked voice*). I ain't seed him nowhere.

OLD WOMAN (*watching her closely*). I whipped him the other day 'cause he's so sorry, and he run off. And when I catches him this time I's going to cure him for good and all. You say you ain't seed him?

PHEELIE (looking up). Naw'm.

OLD WOMAN (eyeing her). That's queer, I thought I seed somebody like him standing here in the yard. Last house down the road said he passed there a hour ago, and they ain't no road to turn off.

PHEELIE (persistently). Naw'm, I ain't seed him. (Unseen to PHEELIE, ENOS makes a signal to the WOMAN that the BOY is behind the house.) Maybe he went by when we weren't looking. (The WOMAN darts around the house and is heard crying out.)

OLD WOMAN. Ah—hah—here you is, here you is!

PHEELIE. How'd she find out he's there? (There is the sound of blows followed by loud crying.)

ENOS. Listen at him cry, the baby!

PHEELIE (who has started towards the rear). Quit your laughing. (She chokes with sobs.) You set her on him, that's what you done. And I'll help him out, she shan't beat him so. (She meets the OLD WOMAN coming in leading the BOY by the collar. He is crying like a child.)

OLD WOMAN (yelling at him). Dry up! (He stops his sobbing and looks off ashamed.) Now ain't you a mess to be running off and leaving me all the cotton to chop! (Looking around her.) Well, we's got to be moving and I's going to give you a beating what is a beating when you gets home.

ENOS. Where you live?

OLD WOMAN. Down near Dukes.

ENOS. Oh-ho, I thought maybe from your boy's talk you was from New York or the moon or somewhere.

OLD WOMAN. I be bound he's been lying to you. He can't tell the truth. The devil must a-got him in the dark of the moon. (She brings the switch across his legs. He shouts with pain.) Step on now! (He struggles against her and holds back.)

BOY. Pheelie, Pheelie, help me, can't you?

PHEELIE (raising a face filled with wrath). Help you! That I won't. (Coming up to him and glaring in his face.) You dirty stinking rascal, why you fool me so?

OLD WOMAN (giving him another cut). You put a move on you or I'll frail the stuffing out'n you. (They move off towards *the right front, he looking back and holding out his hands to* PHEELIE.)

BOY. Pheelie, don't turn against me so, Pheelie! *(They go out.)*

ENOS *(going up to Pheelie).* Honey, don't—don't be mad now. See, if it hadn't been for me, apt as not you'd-a-let that little fool got you into going off with him. (PHEELIE *bursts into wild sobs. He pulls her head against his breast, but she shakes herself free from him. The loud voice of the* OLD WOMAN *is heard outside.)*

OLD WOMAN. You get in that cart or I'll Pheelie you!

PHEELIE. I don't want— I ain't never going to speak to you again! Oh, he's done gone! *(She runs to the right and calls down the road.)* Heigh boy! Boy!

BOY *(his voice coming back high and faint).* Pheelie-ee-ee!

PHEELIE *falls on the bench, sobbing in uncontrollable grief.* ENOS *stands looking at her with a wry smile while he gingerly rubs his bruised head. After a moment he goes over to her and puts his arms around her. They are still around her when the curtain falls.*

CURTAIN

CA'LINE

A Country Comedy

BY

BERNICE KELLY HARRIS

A Comedy Based on Fact

Though best known as the author of seven widely read novels, Bernice Kelly Harris, like so many North Carolina writers, began with short plays when she started out on her serious work as a creative artist. She was born in rural Wake County in 1893. After attending Meredith College in Raleigh, she taught in the public schools. In 1919 she was a member of Professor Koch's first summer-school playwriting class. She had always had a yen to write, and the encouragement received at Chapel Hill set her on a career she is still pursuing.

After her marriage she settled down in the small town of Seaboard in Northampton County and, as the years passed, experimented further with dramatic composition. The one act plays were written for local production with no thought of publication. Nevertheless, their excellence was soon recognized by the "experts" from the University who visited the county drama festivals, and many of her plays were imported to Chapel Hill for a more statewide audience. Shortly after the success of her novel *Purslane* in 1939, seven of the many one-acters were issued in book form as *Folk Plays of Eastern Carolina.*

"Ca'line," which won the Community Drama Contest at Chapel Hill in 1932, was the first effort of her mature years. The central figure was based on an actual person Mrs. Harris had known, and the main thread of the action came from fact. Ca'line's changed attitude after living in the County Home is no fiction. This illiterate person, wrote Koch in his introduction to *Folk Plays of Eastern Carolina,* "was a picturesque character, headstrong, none too truthful, given to exaggeration, blunt, but witty, industrious, and well-meaning according to her light. It is a source of regret that her quaint sayings, her apt names for people and things have not been recorded. One day when Lam walked in where she was seated on the floor cutting a nightgown out of flannel, he asked her what she was making. Quick as a flash, she said, 'A circis (circus) jacket' (a short close-fitting homemade coat). Many women would have blushed and hesitated at a reply."

Perhaps a bit of the background of the real Ca'line will help the reader in his enjoyment of the comedy. The real Ca'line was a Wake County woman who, without a home of her own, worked from house to house in the community (Bernice Kelly Harris's native Mt. Moriah) until the families became tired of her coarse manners and she was told to "move on." It was always a dreadful day when the departure became mandatory, for Ca'line mightily dreaded landing in the poorhouse. After her first visit there, however, the stigma vanished.

Ca'line is one of Mrs. Harris's favorite fellow creatures. Years after her debut in the one act play, Ca'line appeared briefly in *Purslane* and then became the dominant character, as Kalline, in a later novel, *Wild Cherry Tree Road.**

Mrs. Harris's novels, for a considerable part, are extensions of the sort of material used in "Ca'line." *Purslane* won the Mayflower Society Cup in 1939 for the published work of "outstanding excellence" by a North Carolinian. Her other novels, all dealing with the folk of Wake and Northampton Counties, are *Portulaca* (1941), *Sweet Beulah Land* (1943), *Sage Quarter* (1945), *Janey Jeems* (1946), *Hearthstones* (1948), and *Wild Cherry Tree Road* (1951). In their totality, along with her plays and short stories and other writings, they present the details and varieties of a certain age and a geographical section, but their common humanity extends them beyond the regional.

Today Mrs. Harris lives in Seaboard, busily at work on other books of her people. She hopes eventually to return to the drama, where she met her first success.

---

*Cf. the short biography *Bernice Kelly Harris: Storyteller of Eastern Carolina* (University of North Carolina Library, 1955) by Richard Walser.

THE CHARACTERS

ELLA BANKS, *Charlie's second wife*
VEOLA BANKS, *Charlie's daughter*
CHARLIE BANKS
LAM WILDER, *Charlie's brother-in-law by his first wife*
CA'LINE
PREACHER YOUNG
JOHNSON AND OTHER NEIGHBORS

SCENE

The "front-room" of Charlie Banks's farmhouse in eastern Carolina.

TIME

Late afternoon of a raw, cold day in February, 1920.

156

The "front-room" of Charlie Banks's farmhouse. The "front-room" is a term applied to the best room, before the farmhouse turned city, with its parlor and separate "company room." It had to serve as a place to entertain Sunday guests and "to sleep the preacher in." In it were the bed dressed up with its pillow-shams, the enlarged pictures, the family album, the stereoscope, the washstand, and the organ. The door at the left leads to the kitchen; the door at the right, to the front porch. In the rear, center, is a fireplace with a mantel displaying a collection of vases, statuettes, and portraits. To the right of the fireplace is a window with neat white scrim curtains. A washstand, with a porcelain bowl, is midway of right wall. In the left corner is an old-fashioned oak bed un-made, showing the mattress. At the foot of the bed is a small table holding a "rayo" lamp. A rocking chair is at right side of the fireplace, and another at the left.

When the curtain rises, ELLA is on her knees at the fireplace, "claying" the hearth from a rusty clay-kettle. She is a short, fat brunette of about fifty. She wears a soiled housedress and a greasy apron. Her hair is dishevelled. She is a loud, fast speaker—very decided and sure of herself. VEOLA enters from the kitchen, left, carrying a white pitcher, several clean towels thrown across her arm, and two rugs under her arm. She drops the rugs as she hurries to washstand with the pitcher and towels. She is a robust country girl, a senior at the county high school where she has developed nonchalance and a hint of sophistication. She wears a cheap, gaudy jersey—the twin of a "two-for-six-ninety-eight."

ELLA (at the hearth). Veola, shut to that cold door.

VEOLA. All right, in a minute. (She places the towels on the rack.)

ELLA. I 'bout got this hearth clayed. How does it do? (She sits back on her knees, surveying her work.)

VEOLA. It looks all right, Miss Ella. They'll spit on it again anyway.

ELLA. I reckon they will. Wish you'd pour me out some water there in the bowl, Veola.

VEOLA (pouring water from the pitcher). Here you are.

ELLA (rising). I'm sure glad you come this week end, Veola. Hadn't been for you I'd never got cleaned up in this world.

157

VEOLA (*going to shut the door*). It was clean enough—(*lowering her voice*)— for who's coming here.

ELLA (*washing her hands*). Some flowers would just set things off. Wish't I had some flowers.

VEOLA (*spreading the rugs*). I wouldn't bother.

ELLA (*turning from the washstand*). I tell you. Go yonder in mine and your papa's room and bring me here them pink paper roses.

VEOLA. Those things!

ELLA (*drying her hands on the towel*). Yeh, I think they're pretty.

VEOLA (*shrugging her shoulder with "Umph! Umph!" goes out right, returning with the gaudy pink roses*). Here!

ELLA. Now you look there in that bottom draw' and get out some clean sheets and pillow-cases. (ELLA *arranges the flowers in a vase on the mantel, while* VEOLA *moves clean linen from the drawer to a chair.*) And le's get Ca'line's and Lam's bed made up. They'll be here sure. (VEOLA *begins very ungraciously making the bed.*)

VEOLA. What have they got to stay here all night for? Why don't they go on to Uncle Lam's?

ELLA (*challengingly—to* VEOLA's *back*). You don't think much of me and your papa plannin' this weddin', do you, Veola?

VEOLA (*at the bed*). No, I don't—to tell it like it is—it's ridiculous. Ca'line getting married! To Uncle Lam anyhow!

ELLA. 'Tain't no more ridiculous than Lam a-livin' with her last winter when she was cookin' and keepin' house for him. (*She crosses to the washstand.*) It's right for Lam to have Ca'line, and I'm goin' to see he does it.

VEOLA. I don't reckon Uncle Lam's the only one that ever turned her out.

ELLA (*she has been blowing her breath into the lamp chimney and is now polishing it with a towel*). Yeh, but he made her such fair promises. I heard Lam tell Ca'line with my own ears that he'd keep her as long as she lived, and bury her when she died. And that's all the poor soul has ever wanted—all she's ever asked for—just to be kep' out'n the poorhouse in her old age. Bad as she's always hated the thought of goin' to the poorhouse, I'd rather seen her laid in her coffin than to been took there, I had.

VEOLA. Well, since she's there now, you better let her stay there.

ELLA (*her voice rising*). She ought not to be there! Veola, hain't you got no heart? Ca'line's lived hard! She's told me many a time how she's mauled cord-wood in the snow till her feet would get so cold-hurt they'd near 'bout rot off. She's followed the mule and plow reg'lar as a man. She's ditched, she's chopped, she's cleaned manure out'n stables—they ain't nothin' she ain't done! And the poor soul's never had nothin', nothin' but her vittles, and them begrudged to her—and her few cheap rags folks was mint to give her—and nowheres to keep them but in a cracker box—and her little snuff. Smart as she's been all her life, for Lam to pack her off to the poorhouse! It's pitiful! It's pitiful! (*Wiping her eyes with her apron as she goes to the washstand with the towel.*)

VEOLA. If she has lived hard that's no reason for forcing Uncle Lam into this marriage. I don't know what he's thinking about to let folks influence him—

ELLA (*her voice is still rather tearful*). Lam is willin'. He said she suited him. He wouldn't turned her out last winter if hadn't been for that bigity Lela comin' in, and runnin' Ca'line off, and then leavin' her pa right there by hisself. (*She goes to window and looks out.*)

VEOLA. Cousin Lela offered to stay with him.

ELLA (*turning*). Yeh, she offered till she run Ca'line off to the poorhouse, and then she went right on back to her clerkin'—and her pa there with no help neither. I can't help it if she is your kinfolks, Veola, I—(VEOLA *turns quickly and is about to interrupt.*) Now I didn't work up this here marriage because Ca'line happens to be kin to me. Lam r'ally needs somebody. (*Still looking out of the window.*)

VEOLA. I'd have to laugh if Uncle Lam changed his mind—after all your plans and preparations.

ELLA (*triumphantly*). Him and Charlie's a-steppin' up on the porch right now. He ain't goin' to back out.

VEOLA (*hurrying out, left*). Well, if he wants to let folks make a fool of him, it's up to him!

ELLA (*following her to the door*). Set the 'possum in the stove, Veola—to brown. I'll be out there in a minute. (CHARLIE *and*

LAM *enter from the porch.* CHARLIE *is tall and dark and ugly. His hair is black and his mustache red. He wears a white, collarless shirt, dark suit—soiled and baggy—and a wide-brimmed felt hat. He is about sixty-five. He speaks in deep, booming tones.* LAM *is a neatly dressed man of seventy, with grayish hair and mustache. He wears gold-rimmed spectacles. One arm is stiff at the elbow. He has a rather high-pitched voice and a quick, jerky manner of speaking.)*

LAM. Good evenin', Ella.

ELLA. Heigho, Lam, heigho. Set down. (*Indicating chair.*)

CHARLIE. You women folks drawed off any 'simmon beer since dinner?

ELLA (*starting toward the kitchen*). No, but I'll bring you in some.

CHARLIE. Wait! We'll go to the barrel soon's Lam gets warm. Have you a seat, Lam, here in the corner and thaw out.

LAM (*sitting*). I been chilly all day.

ELLA (*hovering over him*). You ain't sick?

CHARLIE (*slapping* LAM *on the back*). Oh, he'll be all right soon as he gets somebody to keep his back warm o' nights. (*A boisterous laugh.*)

ELLA (*laughing too*). Ca'line'll do that. She covers up head and ears when she gets in bed. (*Teasingly, as she leaves.*) Lam, yours and Ca'line's bed's done fixed.

CHARLIE. You just as well pile on 'bout sixteen quilts.

LAM. There won't be no sixteen quilts on top o' me! It'll be like I say—'bout quilts and everything else at my house.

CHARLIE (*laughing heartily*). That's the idea! Rule the roost! Break 'em in young! (*He goes over to the kitchen door to get the collar which* ELLA *has gotten for him.*)

LAM (*fidgeting and shaking his foot nervously*). Young, the dog's foot! That's what I need—somebody *young* and able to look after me.

CHARLIE (*motions* ELLA *out of the room. He can handle* LAM). The young'uns ain't a-huntin' that job. Ca'line's the woman for you, Lam.

LAM. I don't know. If I hadn't jumped into this here so quick—

CHARLIE. Come on, man, you've forgot them fancy hoecakes you been a-makin'.

Lam. No, I ain't forgot them neither.

Charlie. They was ragged-lookin' customers. And Ca'line sure can cook—

Lam. After a fashion. Charlie, you ain't done spoke to the preacher?

Charlie. Yes, I have. Everything's all fixed. He'll be here in short.

Lam. I'm fit to back out. If Ca'line wa'n't such a *ugly* white woman.

Charlie. Yeah, but any woman makes a sight o' difference in a kitchen, even if she ain't got no pretty face.

Lam. Pretty! Ca'line's right down . . . hard favored. You know it.

Charlie. Oh, come on, man. You said she suited you all right last winter, and you've sure lived hard since she left.

Lam (*thinking, stops rocking and shaking his foot*). Yeah, I been through somethin' this winter, for a fact.

Charlie (*sits, straddling a chair*). Layin' aside all foolishness, Lam, Ca'line will make you a good woman. She's smart as a briar, and she'll wait on you, and make things easier than it's been since you was left by yourself.

Lam (*rocking and shaking his foot*). I might o' found somebody else if you and Ella hadn't been in such a swidget to get me tied to Ca'line.

Charlie. You won't find nobody to fit the bill just like her, though. And, like I told you, she won't cost you five dollar a year —outside her rations.

Lam (*stops rocking at the word "cost"*). There's somethin' in that, of course.

Charlie. Everything in it. (*Moving nearer to* Lam, *he lowers his voice.*) You take me. I've had two good women, but the second one (*looks toward the kitchen*) sure will spend if she gets her hands on it. Ca'line won't. She won't spend.

Lam. Ain't no woman goin' to spend up what I've got.

Charlie. Ca'line's savin'. You know it. You know it's so.

Lam. Yeah, she's savin'. If it just wa'n't for her cranky ways.

Charlie. Yeah, she's got her ways, but all you got to do is jes' be firm and pos'tive with her. The women folks gives way to her too much, but you take me, I wouldn't have a speck of trouble with Ca'line.

LAM. I won't have none. She'll do like I say.

CHARLIE. If she ever tries to get high with you, just threaten to send her back to the poorhouse. That'll quieten her down.

LAM. I aim to keep her 'umble all right.

CHARLIE. That won't be hard. She's learnt her lesson up yonder, and she'll be too thankful to get back down here to God's country!

LAM (rising and going to the door). I don't reckon Johnson will have no trouble 'bout gettin' Ca'line out'n the poorhouse. I had to fix up some papers to get her in.

CHARLIE. No, I reckon not. Johnson might o' had car trouble. His ti'es was old.

LAM. I wish they'd come on. I despise to wait.

CHARLIE (joining LAM at the door). You can bet your bottom dollar it ain't Ca'line's fault they're late. She's a-r'arin' to get here, I know, poor thing.

LAM. How near time is it?

CHARLIE. Oh, Johnson will get her here all right. Set down. Johnson ever tell you 'bout the time he took Ca'line to the poorhouse—that cold, rainy day?

LAM (returning to his chair). He said she cried to come back.

CHARLIE. Un-hunh! He said she raised the rafters! Cried near 'bout a quart. And she begged and she pled for Johnson to bring her back and not leave her up there with all them curi's strangers. It got next to Ella. Johnson cries every time he tells it. And dog if my eyes ain't a-gettin' watery.

LAM (getting his handkerchief). She thinks somethin' o' old Mount Zion Cemetery. (He blows his nose.)

CHARLIE. She does that. And Lam, I reckon the good Lord had a hand in this here, for they ain't nobody but Him knows what a hard road poor Ca'line's had to travel. And what was it the Sunday School lesson said last Sunday about the sparrows? Well, I reckon—

ELLA (entering, crosses hastily to the front door). A car's a-comin'. I think it's the Johnsons!

CHARLIE (hurrying to the door after her). Yeah, that's Johnson's Ford. They're turnin' in. Lam, they're here!

ELLA. That's Ca'line on the front seat. Le's go out. *(She leaves.)*

CHARLIE. Ain't you goin' out, Lam?

LAM. No, I'll set here. I near 'bout got a chill.

CA'LINE *(outside).* Whyn't you light some lamps? It's as dark as pitch out here!

CHARLIE. That's her—that's Ca'line!

LAM. It's her, all right.

Enter CA'LINE, *low, thin, and stooped from much hard work. Her face is wrinkled. Her wispy gray hair is drawn to a tight little knot at the back of her head. She wears a black sateen dress, plainly made—her "Sunday best" for eight years. Her wraps are an old cheap coat from Lord-knows-whose-wardrobe, a "fascinator," a worn sweater, and "circis" jacket. She wears a black straw hat at one side of which is a bunch of faded violets. Altogether she is an odd, quaint figure, though she has a native neatness that has survived the peculiarly hard circumstances of her life. She speaks in a high, shrill voice.*

CHARLIE. Howd'y', Ca'line.

CA'LINE. Git out o' my way, Charlie Banks; I'm near 'bout frozen. Let me have that corner, Lam. Git up! *(LAM crosses to the left of fireplace,* CHARLIE *is in front of it,* CA'LINE *is seated in the warm corner, and* ELLA *is standing with* CA'LINE's *battered old suitcase.)*

CHARLIE. How you makin' it, Ca'line?

CA'LINE. I ain't much. My feet's near 'bout froze off.

ELLA. I'll take your wrops, Ca'line.

CA'LINE *(rising).* Take this 'ere, Ella! Here, Charlie Banks, you take this here. *(She removes her hat and peels off her wraps.)* And this here, and this here, and this here, and I'll jes' keep on my circis jacket till I git warm. *(CHARLIE starts towards the bed with the wraps.)* Hold on here! I want my box. I'm a-goin' to have me a dip o' my snuff. I'm near 'bout perished. *(She searches the pockets of her coat.)*

ELLA. I believe I'd wait just a little, Ca'line.

CA'LINE. Naw, I ain't. Lord! Where's my bresh? Well, 'tain't no matter, I can lip it. *(She "lips" it.)*

CHARLIE (*starting toward the kitchen*). Le's go hunt that beer barrel, Lam. Want some beer, Ca'line? (*They go out.*)

CA'LINE. Naw, I don't. I'd take a cocy-coly.

ELLA (*crossing to the bed with the suitcase*). You're lookin' good, Ca'line. (CA'LINE *moves her chair very close to the fire. She pulls her dress above her knees, revealing white hose and high-topped shoes.*)

CA'LINE. I'm a-cold. I'm a-gwine to warm my knees.

ELLA. How come you all so late?

CA'LINE. I wa'n't thar when the Johnsons come after me. I and Bet was at the market, and I had a fraction a-walkin' back.

ELLA. Walkin'? Ain't it about two mile to Raleigh?

CA'LINE. Yeah, hit's every bit o' two mile, Ella.

ELLA. I didn't know they'd let the in-mates out like that—that far 'specially.

CA'LINE. We c'n go where'bouts we please if we tell the boss man. He don't care. He's jes' as good and kind as he c'n be. Bet, she's been a-gwine to the market every week. This here was my fu'st trip, and I made me twenty-five cent. (*She takes it out of her stocking to show.*)

ELLA (*sitting*). How'd you make it?

CA'LINE. I ast the men on the wagons for it. Bet, she makes about fifty cent a week that-a-way.

ELLA. Who is that "Bet" you talkin' about?

CA'LINE. Why, Ella, Bet is Bud Peeler's own sister. Bud's Ekie and his wife comes to see Bet 'bout every month and brings her some 'taters, and some purserves, and some cracklin's, and some freshlets when they kill hogs.

ELLA. Sure 'nough?

CA'LINE. They sure do. I eat so many cracklin's last week I spewed all night long.

ELLA (*leaning forward, eagerly*). You missed our Native Herb pills then, didn't you?

CA'LINE. Lord, Ella, they've got nu'ses and doctors that gives you medicine a sight better'n Native Yerbs, and they waits on you like you was they own kinfolks.

ELLA (*indifferently*). They do?

CA'LINE. They sure do. And hit don't cost us a cent. The doctor

come in to see Bet t'other night when she didn't have nary thing
but the cholery marbus.

ELLA. Good gracious, that's bad enough!

CA'LINE. 'Twon't as bad as I've had hit a many a time when
I use' to stay out here in the country, and not nary drap o'
medicine to take neither. Bet jes' eat too much fresh shoat—
that'll all ailed her.

ELLA (*eagerly*). You don't get nothin' fittin' to eat up there.

CA'LINE (*excited*). Lord have mercy, Ella! They cook enough
vittles for a log-rollin'. If you don't get a-plenty, hit's your own
fault. Hit's sure put on the table.

ELLA. You all have it to cook.

CA'LINE. Lord no, Ella! They got cooks! (*Drawls.*) Course sometimes we help shell the peas, and peel the I'sh 'taters, and wash
the cabbages if we're mint to. We don't have to do it though.
I ain't done nary thing this week but set down to my vittles when
I was called to hit.

ELLA (*rising*). Well, you're warmed through now. Come on in
yonder and put on another dress. I made you one out o' that
old wu'sted one o' mine you use' to beg me for. Want you to see
it.

CA'LINE. I got a silk dress thar in that 'ar suitcase. Bet give it
to me. Bud's wife give it to her.

ELLA (*resentfully*). Well, come on—put that on. Come on.

CA'LINE. You got a good fire in thar?

ELLA. No, but it won't take you long to change.

CA'LINE. Well, ain't you got a woodpile out yander?

ELLA. You forget the wood has to be cut and toted in, Ca'line.

CA'LINE. They keep it hot up yander, I can tell you—the rooms,
and the halls, and the water closets, and even to the porches is
het up.

ELLA. Well, it ain't goin' to take you long to change. Come
on. It's time to get ready.

CA'LINE (*getting up and starting off*). I got to get me a
swallow o' warter. I'm near 'bout perished.

ELLA (*trying to intercept her*). Wait! I'll bring you a dipper.

CA'LINE (*elbowing her away*). Take care! I'm gwine draw me
a bucket o' fresh. (*She goes out.* ELLA *now opens the suitcase to*

examine its contents. VEOLA *enters with a copy of* Home and Fireside, *sits and reads.*)

ELLA (*holding up a dress*). Well, look here, it's silk!

VEOLA. Umph! Some class. Where's Ca'line gone?

ELLA. She went after a drink o' water. I declare Ca'line's like a bird out'n a cage when she gets out here in the country. She ain't satisfied nowheres else.

CA'LINE (*outside*). Drat take such a mess!

ELLA (*hastening to door*). What's to matter, Ca'line?

CA'LINE (*entering hurriedly*). My Lord! I'm wet to the hide! That nasty stinkin' well-chain slipped out'n my hand. I tried to ketch the bucket, and doggoned if the whole business didn't spill right on my front parts. Everything I got's wet and cold!

ELLA. Take off that wet dress. Quick! (ELLA *turns to the suitcase and gets out some dry linen.*)

CA'LINE (*hugging the fire*). Them's bad 'rangements anyhow— drawin' water with a old rusty chain. Up yander you don't have nothin' to do but turn a spicket, and you c'n get warter hot or cold—all you do want.

ELLA (*coming to fire with the linen on her arm*). Humph. All town water tastes hot to me.

CA'LINE. Up yander the warter's as cold as ice.

ELLA. Maybe so. I ain't never tasted none at the poorhouse.

CA'LINE (*excited, angry*). Ella, that ain't what they call hit! Hit's the County Home. That's what the town folks calls hit. Ain't hit the County Home, gal?

VEOLA. Sure.

CA'LINE. Ella don't keep up, does she, gal—way off down here ten mile from nowhere.

ELLA. Shucks! You come on, Ca'line. If you ain't ready when the preacher comes, Lam ain't goin' to mess with you.

CA'LINE. Le' me strip right here by this here fire. Hit's cold in yander I know. I done washed my neck and years good this mornin' afore I went to the market, and I changed my underwear las' Sad'd'y, and I ain't a-gwine to do no more washin' till hit turns warmer. Gi' me here that dress, gal. (*She unpins the skirt revealing a gray outing petticoat as the skirt falls to the floor.*)

ELLA. You can't dress in here—I hear the menfolks. That's them a-comin' in!

CA'LINE. I ain't nothin' but a woman if it 'tis.

ELLA. Veola, take that valise on in yonder. (VEOLA *starts out, left, with the suitcase;* ELLA *follows her, with the linen.*) Here take these things too. (CHARLIE *enters with a pitcher of beer and a glass.* LAM *is with him.*)

CHARLIE. Get ready, Ca'line. The preacher's a-comin'.

CA'LINE. I don't care nothin' 'bout no preacher. (ELLA *rushes to* CA'LINE, *frantically pulling up the skirt at* CA'LINE's *feet.*)

ELLA. Ca'line, ain't you got no manners? (*Then, pinning the skirt up around* CA'LINE.) I can't get her away from this fire. (CA'LINE *turns first her "hind parts" and then her front to the fire, twisting all the while.* ELLA *is having a "fraction" pinning on the skirt.*)

CA'LINE. Naw, fer time I git het up in front, my hind parts is a-freezin'. I tell you, folkses, this here's a cold house. You all had oughter git you some little hot-box concerns like they got up yander. I can't call hit, but Bet she can. They jes' stand up agin' the wall, and the whole house is het up all day and all night, and not nary stick o' wood to cut and tote neither.

LAM. Humph! Hot houses ain't healthy!

CA'LINE. What'd you say, Lam?

LAM. I say hot houses ain't healthy. That's what I said.

CA'LINE. I ain't had nary bad cold since I been up yander— not nary one.

ELLA (*pushing* CA'LINE *toward the kitchen door*). No more o' your gab, Ca'line. You got to get ready.

CA'LINE (*going*). I ain't got to do nothin' but die, and I ain't gwine to do that till I get good and ready.

CHARLIE (*offering* LAM *beer*). Better take another little sip, Lam. You didn't drink much at the barrel.

LAM. I got to save room for the 'possum.

CHARLIE. Ella didn't think 'twas just proper to have 'possum at the supper tonight, but good as I knowed you loved 'possum—

LAM (*sitting*). There ain't nothin' eats better to me.

CHARLIE. Now here's this beer when you feel like it—right on the table. Help yourself.

LAM. 'Simmon beer's somethin' fittin' all right.

CHARLIE. You can take you a jugful home in the mornin' if you want to—for you and the madam.

LAM. Well, I don't care if I do. (*Enter* CA'LINE, *half dressed. She has slipped on an old silk dress; her hair is hanging around her shoulders.*)

CA'LINE. Gi' me here a lamp, Charlie Banks. I can't see by that'un in yander. 'Tain't no more'n a lightnin' bug. (*She goes at once to the fireplace.*)

CHARLIE. This-un's a "rayo." She'll light you up.

CA'LINE. Gi' me some matches, Lam.

LAM. Here. (CA'LINE *is holding lamp and chimney awkwardly in one hand. The match flickers out.*)

CA'LINE. Hain't you got no matches, nor nothin'?

CHARLIE. Here, Ca'line, here's matches. Let me light it for you.

CA'LINE (*elbowing* CHARLIE *away*). Git out o' my way; I'll light it myself. (*She strikes several matches, screaming out as she burns her finger.*) Drat take sech a mess! (CHARLIE *watches her.*)

CHARLIE. Why don't you bob your hair, Ca'line? All the flappers is a-bobbin'. Ain't the style got to the poorhouse yet? (*Because of a burned finger, or from exasperation,* CA'LINE *drops the lamp on the floor, breaking the chimney. She stoops, and throws broken pieces into the fire.*)

CA'LINE. My Lord! Ain't this here a mess? Charlie Banks, you ought to get you some 'lectric lights like they got up yander. Then you wouldn't have no lamp chimbleys to be forever lastin' a-breakin'—Lord, have mercy! I've stuck a piece o' glass in my thumb. Here, Charlie Banks, git hit out! (CHARLIE *takes out his knife, and begins probing for the glass.*) All you got to do there is jes' press a little knob on the wall, and the whole room's as light as daytime. And when you gits ready fer bed, you don't have to blow out no lights—jes' press that little knob, that's all. Bet, she learnt me how.

CHARLIE. I'm a-gittin' it out. Hurt much?

CA'LINE. Yeah, hit hurts. Them doctors and nu'ses up yander can git glass or splinters out and don't hurt you nary bit. They knows how to take holt.

LAM. And we taxpayers got to pay them doctors and nu'ses. They ain't nothin' but humbugs. I ain't never had no doctors myself.

CA'LINE. What'd you say, Lam?

LAM. I said doctors is humbugs.

CA'LINE. Country folks don't know nothin' 'bout doctors. Law', they can split you wide open and take out and put in a piece nowadays.

LAM. 'Tain't no use to get doctors in *your* head—you was always tough as a light'ood knot.

CHARLIE. Look! Here 'tis. Here's your splinter o' glass. Send for me, Dr. Charles Banks, when you need a doctor, Ca'line.

CA'LINE. Now you have to paint cucumber on this here to keep the pizen out.

ELLA (*rushing in*). Ca'line! What in the world! Come on back and do up your hair. The preacher's drove up! He's a-comin' in. Come on out right now. What'll he think? (*She pushes* CA'LINE *out left.*)

CA'LINE. I want you to paint this here, Ella.

ELLA. Go to the door, Charlie. (CHARLIE *goes to the door to admit* PREACHER YOUNG. *He is a young man, well-dressed and conventional.*)

CHARLIE. Dog if Ca'line ain't learnt to put on airs! (*At the door.*) Come in, come in to the fire, Brother Young.

PREACHER YOUNG. How's Brother Banks this time?

CHARLIE. I'm makin' out. How are you?

PREACHER YOUNG. Very well, thank you. And Brother Wilder. How are you?

LAM. First rate. How you?

PREACHER YOUNG (*shaking hands all around*). All right, thanks. You took me by surprise. I didn't know you were contemplating marriage.

LAM. Well, I. . . .

CHARLIE. He was like myself, he sure needed somebody. Stand up to the fire, Brother Young.

PREACHER YOUNG (*removing his overcoat*). Fire does feel good today.

CHARLIE. Let me hang it up for you.

PREACHER YOUNG. No, thanks, Brother. I'll just lay it here on this chair. (*He looks at his watch.*) It's six o'clock. That was the hour, wasn't it?

CHARLIE. Yes, that's the hour.

PREACHER YOUNG. I hope I'm not rushing you unduly, but I've got an engagement, and I must hurry.

CHARLIE. Ain't you goin' to stay for the supper? The women's expectin' you.

PREACHER YOUNG. I wish I could. Sorry I have this engagement. If I had known earlier. . . .

CHARLIE. The women folks has got it smellin' good out 'bout the kitchen.

PREACHER YOUNG. I'm sure of that. I can't stay, though. Now, Brother Wilder, if you're ready, suppose we proceed.

LAM. Well, I'm ready. One time's as good as another.

CHARLIE. You want me to go tell 'em all to come in? We just ast two or three o' the neighbors—they wanted to come.

LAM. I told you not to ast anybody, Charlie.

CHARLIE. It was some o' Ella's doin's. Just homefolks anyhow. I'll tell 'em to come in.

PREACHER YOUNG. Suppose you do, Brother Banks. In here, you say?

CHARLIE. Yes sir, right in here.

PREACHER YOUNG. Have them come then, those who wish to witness the marriage. (CHARLIE starts out.)

PREACHER YOUNG. Wait! I mean all except Miss . . . er . . . the bride!

CHARLIE. Ca'line. Ca'line Davis is her name. Tell her to come too?

PREACHER YOUNG. In just a minute. Brother Wilder, you join her now, and tell the others to assemble here. Then you bring Miss . . . er . . . Davis on in. I'll stand just here. Is there any special direction or suggestion before you go?

LAM. Get it over with quick as you can.

PREACHER YOUNG (smiling). Brother Wilder seems a bit nervous for a man who's making his second trip to the altar.

CHARLIE. Oh, he'll steady down soon's the knot's tied.

PREACHER YOUNG. You have the license of course.

CHARLIE. Yes, sure. Here they are. (PREACHER YOUNG examines the license.)

PREACHER YOUNG. You and your wife can sign your names here as witnesses.

CHARLIE. I ain't much of a hand at writin'.

ELLA in her Sunday dress, several neighbors, and VEOLA tip

in and solemnly take their places. The faces register interested expectancy; ELLA's, *smug complacency. There is intense silence which deepens in intensity as the seconds tick off and the bride and groom fail to appear.* ELLA *and* CHARLIE *glance toward door, left. After three or four minutes of painful waiting,* ELLA *tips out and, after a short wait,* CHARLIE *too. They re-enter, presently, gently pushing* CA'LINE *before them.* PREACHER YOUNG *places them in formal positions, clears his throat and begins reading the marriage service from his book. The ritual is barely begun when* CA'LINE *interrupts.*

CA'LINE. Hold on here now. I ain't had my say out yet, and I'm a-gwine to—yes I am too, Ella.

ELLA. Hush, Ca'line.

CA'LINE. You hushed me in yander, but it's a-comin' out now. My mouth was made to talk, and I' a-gwine to talk.

PREACHER YOUNG. Was there something you wanted to know —a question?

CA'LINE. Yeah, I want to know—Oh! I'm a-gwine to talk, Ella, and 'tain't no use to be a-jabbin' me in the back. (*To the* PREACH-ER.) Can't I talk if I want to?

PREACHER YOUNG. Why certainly. You wanted to ask something?

CA'LINE. I done ast' it—in yander, but that Charlie pushed me in here and—

ELLA. Ca'line, what in the world will Mr. Young think o' you? He don't know you like we do.

CA'LINE. I don't care nothin' 'bout Young. If he eats me, he sure can't swallow me.

PREACHER YOUNG. Miss . . . er . . . Davis, can I help you?

CA'LINE. I got a good place up yander . . . electric lights, the house het up, good warter, and a-plenty somepin' t' eat. I want to live up *thar*.

ELLA (*to* CHARLIE). She ain't got a bit o' sense. Anybody might a-knowed it'd take her to make a mess of a weddin' or anything else. (*To* CA'LINE.) Straighten yourself 'round there, Ca'line, and get through. Mr. Young's in a hurry.

CA'LINE. I ain't a-keepin' him, sure thing. Lam, you ain't said where we's gwine to live.

LAM. You know where I live, Ca'line.

CA'LINE. And that means Ca'line will draw the warter, and cut and tote the wood, and wash the lamps, and feed the hogs, and milk the cow, and chop the garden, and cook three meals o' vittles everyday, and—

LAM. Course I'll help you out, Ca'line. I'll feed the hogs.

CA'LINE. This here thing's happened too quick. You didn't give me time to think—

LAM. And I'll milk the cow o' nights.

CA'LINE. Johnson, he jes' busted in thar where I and Bet was settin', and grabbed me up, and pushed me in his circis cart, and shut the door, and cranked up, and didn't hardly give me time to git my breath and—

LAM. I'll give you all the snuff you can dip and the butter-and-egg money.

CA'LINE. You ought not to o' busted in on me so sudden—

ELLA. You're too near married now to back out, Ca'line.

CA'LINE (rushes to the bed and puts on her coat). Naw, I ain't married neither. I got me a good place up yander and I'm a-gwine thar. (ELLA remonstrates with her.) Gi' me my hat, Ella. (She grabs her hat off the bed and claps it on.)

ELLA. Ca'line!

CA'LINE. Gi' me my jacket, gal.

ELLA. Oh, Ca'line, wait—listen just a minute—

CA'LINE. Git out'n my way, 'oman. Lord have mercy! Where 'bouts is my circis jacket? Oh, hit's in yander in the cold storage room. (She darts out of the room, left. ELLA is exasperated.)

PREACHER YOUNG (after an ominous silence). The marriage is . . . er . . . postponed, I suppose?

ELLA. I can't do nothin' with her. Charlie, see what you can do.

CHARLIE (going out after her). Well. But it looks like her head's set.

ELLA. I don't understand it. I never been so took back in my life.

LAM (going to the fireplace). Wait till she comes back. I'll 'tend to her. I'll tell her—(CA'LINE re-enters, followed by CHARLIE. She is carrying her "circis jacket," suitcase, and old clothes on her arm. She is finishing putting on her wraps.)

CHARLIE. Now, you look a-here, Ca'line—

CA'LINE. I ain't mad with you, Charlie. I jes' ain't a-gwine to freeze myself to death out here in the country, and draw warter, and cut and tote wood, and—

CHARLIE. You ought to thought about that sooner.

CA'LINE. I just sort o' forgot how common you all did live down here. Up yander hit's warm, a-plenty o' good warter, bright lights, good vittles, and there's Bet and Lucetty and Sudie and—

LAM. Ca'line, you can pile sixteen quilts on us and—

CA'LINE. If the house was het right, you wouldn't need no sixteen quilts, what I'm talkin' 'bout.

LAM. And you can burn all the lamps you please and eat ham meat, and I'll let it be like you say about everything and—

CA'LINE. Bet give me some ham meat the other night, and I spewed.

ELLA. Ca'line.

CHARLIE. This is all foolishness. Go on, Brother Young. She don't mean nothin' by all this gab. All right now, Ca'line. Square yourself 'round there. (CHARLIE *tries to urge her back into position before the* PREACHER. LAM *grabs at her arm.*)

PREACHER YOUNG. Very well, I'm ready.

CA'LINE. Here, you hold on! (*She begins to take something, tied in a handkerchief, from her stocking. All watch intently.*) This here's some o' Bet's hard knots. I'm 'bout to git hit. That's got hit. (*She produces a five-cent piece and hands it to the* PREACHER.) Here, take it.

PREACHER YOUNG (*puzzled*). What . . . er . . . shall I . . . do with this?

CA'LINE. You c'n have it. Here, Lam, this here's your five-cent. I ain't mad. And here's yourn, Charlie; you c'n divide with Johnson over thar. I ain't got no more, but I c'n make me some more soon's I git back up yander. The men on the wagons will give it to me. (PREACHER YOUNG *goes to the fireplace and takes up his overcoat.* LAM *looks on, drooping helplessly.*)

CHARLIE. You'll have to get married, Ca'line. Here's your license done paid for!

CA'LINE (*gaily*). You can have 'em, Charlie.

CHARLIE. Don't you never beg me no more to get you out'n the poorhouse.

ELLA. You see, Ca'line—

CA'LINE (*to* JOHNSON). Johnson, you gwine to take me back to Raleigh?

LAM. Ca'line!

JOHNSON. Oh, you're not going back tonight. . . .

CA'LINE. I sure am.

JOHNSON. Oh, no. Wait until tomorrow.

CA'LINE. Johnson, you brought me here; but if you don't want to take me back, I can sure walk.

JOHNSON. I'm not going to let you walk, of course.

CA'LINE. You better crank up your circis cart then.

JOHNSON. You spend the night here anyhow, Ca'line, and go back tomorrow.

CA'LINE (*starting out*). I'm a-gwine back tonight, and I'm a-gwine back *right now*.

LAM (*advancing as if to follow*). Ca'line!

CA'LINE. Come on, Johnson. John-son-n! (JOHNSON *starts.* CA'LINE *turns at the door.*) You'll see me 'round the market when you come to town. You can bring me 'long some 'taters, and purserves, and some cracklin's, and some freshlets next hog-killin'. I ain't mad. (*She goes out, singing triumphantly.*) I'm gone!

ELLA. Let her stay there. I ain't goin' to worry myself over her no more.

CHARLIE. Ca'line's gone off to the poorhouse and got the big-head!

ELLA. That's just about the size of it. (*All stand amazed.*)

CURTAIN

SEA PSALM

A Tragedy of Carolina Sea-Folk

BY

CHARLES EDWARD EATON

PROLOGUE

The sea is a mad Spirit,
Strange and inconstant
Like a wild old woman.
Her song is the eternal whispering of life and death.
People who live along the sturdy coast,
Close to the sea which has captured them,
Hear forever the rush of water on the sands,
And their spirits are lost
Within a labyrinth of lonely fears.
There is nothing—nothing but the constant tide,
The long, cold fingers of the tide.
The swirling of the water is a psalm
—Monotonous music
    Of a thousand lost souls.

Produced 1934 by the Carolina Playmakers

A FISHERFOLK PLAY BY A POET

"The idea for the plot of 'Sea Psalm' was taken from a story told me by a friend who lives on the coast of North Carolina." So wrote Charles Edward Eaton at the time the play was originally produced. "When I first heard this story, I was struck with its dramatic possibilities. I could see the play take form in my mind, and I immediately began to seriously consider dramatizing this rather fantastic story of the people of the North Carolina coast. The plot, then, was drawn from a folktale, here and there supplemented by incidents of my own invention. The characters of 'Sea Psalm' have been drawn from actual observation and experience. From time to time, I have visited this part of the coast of which I write, and have had the opportunity of observing these coast people and learning something of their customs and traditions. The characters, of course, have been to some degree elaborated for dramatic purposes. As you will notice, Johnny, the dead lover of Cecelia, is really the chief character of the play. The memory of him colors and dominates the lives of the rest of the characters. Around his ghostly presence the action of the play revolves.

"I do not think it would be unwise to make an explanation concerning the folk superstitions which are a basic part of my play. Many of these simple people who live along the coast have a great reverence and awe for the sea. Quite naturally, they have in years past come to regard this vast, strange body as the home of spirits and phantoms which come up out of the surf at night. Other superstitions, such as a firm belief in dreams and ill omens, I have endeavored to weave into the story at intervals.

" 'Sea Psalm' is a play of mood. It is meant to be like the sea itself—strange, brooding, and enigmatic. The effectiveness of the play depends upon how well the eerie atmosphere and sea mood is created. The prologue is intended to help create poetically the feeling of the play."

Though the work of a well-known poet, "Sea Psalm" was written at the age of eighteen when, as an undergraduate, Charles Edward Eaton was a student of Professor Koch. Eaton was born in 1916 in Winston-Salem. There he began composing poems, plays, and short stories—a "three-fold interest" continued at

Chapel Hill, Princeton, and Harvard. After several years of teaching in Puerto Rico and at the University of Missouri, he served as Vice-Consul at the American Embassy in Rio de Janeiro during the war years. Then he returned home and was instructor of creative writing at the University of North Carolina from 1946 to 1952. Since 1952 he has lived in Woodbury, Connecticut, where he devotes his entire time to poetry and fiction.

Of the "three-fold interest," poetry has so far been the dominant segment, at least judging from production. When *The Bright Plain* was published in 1942 by the University of North Carolina Press, the book received high critical praise. It was followed in 1951 by another volume of poetry, *The Shadow of the Swimmer*, which won the Ridgely Torrence Memorial Award of the Poetry Society of America. *The Greenhouse in the Garden* is his latest book. The critic Manly Johnson wrote that Eaton's poems "turn on paradox—the paradox that one must die in order to have life. . . . The first paradox, the duality of life and death, sorrow and happiness, is cosmic and man is passive in its sway; the second, the leap, is both acceptance of the inevitable and revolt against it. . . ." The germ of the theme of his mature poetry may be found in his early play "Sea Psalm." Cecelia must die in order to realize happiness; her sea-folk kin do not find it overly difficult to accept the inevitable.

THE CHARACTERS

JENNIE MASON, *a spinster*

KATE MASON, *her sister, also a spinster*

CECELIA MASON, *their orphan niece*

JED MILLER, *a storekeeper*

SCENE

The combined sitting room and dining room of the Mason cottage on the North Carolina coast, in the vicinity of the Cape Fear River.

TIME

A stormy night of early fall.

The room is simply, but not uncomfortably, furnished. On the left is a smoke-blackened fireplace with a wood fire burning in it. On the mantel there are an old clock, two old-fashioned candlesticks and a few odds and ends. On the floor nearby is a box of small logs. In the center of the room is a table covered with a blue cloth. On the table an oil lamp is burning. There are three straight chairs in the room, one standing near the table, the other two against the wall on the right, and two rocking chairs by the fireplace. Also standing against the right wall is a small table covered with a checkered oil cloth. The dishes are on this table. In the rear wall there is a window curtained with a blue print. There are several rag rugs on the floor. The door leading outside is in the rear wall to the right. A door leading into the other part of the cottage is on the left. Behind the entrance door there are, on the wall, nails upon which to hang coats.

It is a stormy night, and the sea is wild. The wind is blowing around the house. Lightning and thunder are intermittent. The sound of the surf is heard throughout the play.

JENNIE and KATE are sitting around the fireplace, talking. JENNIE, the elder of the two, whose knitting needles and yarn repose in her lap, is knitting a wool shawl for the long, cold winter that is coming. She is about fifty years old, tall and rather slender. Her hair is nearly grey; her eyes are brown. She wears a long, black dress and a short coat. She is not very happy looking. Life has not been easy, and she is a trifle disgruntled. KATE, a woman of about forty-five years, is lower and plumper than her sister. She has kind eyes and a sweet smile. Her light brown hair is greying. She wears a long, brown dress. Sewing basket in hand, she enjoys sitting by the fire gossiping. She has become used to the monotony of life by the sea, and does not consider it a burden.

JENNIE. Kate, I'm worried 'bout 'Celia. She sure has been a-actin' strange today. Stranger'n usual.

KATE. Yes, Jennie, she does 'pear a little upset. Maybe it's jes' the rainy weather.

JENNIE (*sighing*). No, Kate, it ain't jes' the weather. There's somethin' a-worryin' her. (*She stops rocking for a moment, then*

179

continues.) She won't eat nothin' and half the time she walks around sort o' dazed-like.

KATE. Seems like she ain't been exactly right since pore Johnny died last year. It sure was a pity. Him a-gettin' killed so sudden-like, an' her a-lovin' him so.

JENNIE. He was sure a purty lad, too. As big an' strong as they come, an' the best young fisherman in these parts. 'Celia sure set a lot o' store on marryin' him.

KATE. Looks like them two was jes' made for each other. She loved him better'n anyone on earth, better'n God almost.

JENNIE. Maybe that's why he's a-lyin' in a watery grave right now. Let a-body set too much store on somethin', and it ain't long 'fore bad luck takes it away.

KATE. Don't seem like more'n yesterday Johnny was a-settin' here a-laughin' an' a-talkin'. It's sort o' hard to get used to not seein' him around.

JENNIE. Ain't it funny how you remember little things when a-body's gone. Jes' like when I was a-makin' a apple pie the other day. Didn't seem right not to set a piece on the shelf for Johnny. He always had sech a likin' for apple pie.

They are silent for a moment. They are thinking about Johnny, who is still a living and dear memory in their minds and hearts. The wind howls mournfully outside and the sound of the surf is a constant sobbing. KATE shivers and pokes up the fire.

KATE *(shivering and rubbing her shoulders).* Jes' listen to that wind, Jennie. *(She rises and pokes up the fire; then after a moment she resumes her seat.)* Sounds so mournful an' sad-like. It's a bad storm a-brewin'. God help those out on the sea tonight.

JENNIE. Yes, God help 'em, Kate. It's a wild night—jes' like it was when pore Johnny was lost.

KATE. I'll never forget that night, Jennie. Looked like the devil was a-whippin' up the waves an' we was all doomed. Then mornin' come, an' they come an' told us about Johnny. *(She shakes her head solemnly.)* I won't never forget that.

JENNIE. Ain't it pitiful they never found his body. I reckon he's a-floatin' out thar in the sea now, pore lad, with nobody to give him a decent burial. An' nothin' but the wind a-sighin' for him in the night.

The wind sobs past the door like a lost soul in the night. The surf moans in an undertone. It is very weird and strange. The window-shutter and the door rattle faintly, as if someone is outside wanting to come in.

KATE (*standing up with fright and glancing fearfully in the direction of the door*). What was that? Sounded like someone at the door a-tryin' to get in.

JENNIE. Wasn't nothin' but the wind a-rattlin' the door, I reckon.

KATE (*relaxing somewhat*). Yes, I reckon it was jes' the wind. Did sound sort o' quare, though. It sure is bad to be a-havin' sech a storm tonight. 'Celia's sure to take on about it.

JENNIE. Yes, a storm always does sort o' set her off. An' she's liable to do anything when she gets one o' her quare notions.

KATE. She told me this mornin' she was a-dreamin' about Johnny all last night, jes' like she's been a-doin' every night since he died. Only last night, she seen Johnny out thar in the surf an' he was a-callin' an' callin' to her.

JENNIE (*shaking her head while repeating an old folk-saying*).

"Dreamed last night an' morning told
Will come to pass 'fore the day's old."

That's a bad sign, Kate. It sure is.

KATE. It's more'n jes' dreams an' signs that's worryin' me. I'm 'fraid 'Celia's been a-hearin' some o' the tales old Ma Anders has been tellin' about the spirits o' the sea a-takin' Johnny away 'stead of him gettin' drownded.

JENNIE (*scornfully*). Has that old card been a-tellin' some more o' her fish tales? Looks like she's forever a-tryin' to stir up trouble, a-babblin' about spells and sech.

KATE. An' Taisie Fulton told me she's been sayin' that, every since Johnny got killed. She lows she hears the spirits a-moanin' over the sea on stormy nights, a-callin' out like lost souls, an' lurin' men to their death.

JENNIE. Law', it ain't right to be a-believin' in sech things, Kate. An' old Ma Anders is a-sinnin' 'fore her Jesus every time she tells such tales. Wouldn't surprise me a bit, though, if she ain't got 'Celia to believin' them stories.

KATE. Yes, Jennie. You can't never tell what 'Celia is a-thinkin'. Jes' last week I was settin' here peelin' potatoes, an' she was standin' at the window a-watchin' the tide. Said she didn't reckon there was anything left for her, since the sea had tuk her Johnny. I felt like cryin', but all I could do was jes' set thar, and peel potatoes. (*Outside there is a flash of lightning, and then a mighty peal of thunder.* JENNIE *and* KATE *jump with fright.*)

JENNIE. Land sakes! That sure was a awful streak o' lightning.

KATE (*glancing around timorously*). Sounded mighty close to me. (*She pauses.*) This storm sure does make me feel uneasy. Jes' like somethin' was a-hangin' over us and a-waitin' to happen.

JENNIE. It is a powerful bad storm, but it'll blow over after a while, I reckon.

KATE (*calmer, now that it has ceased thundering*). I reckon 'Celia's a-settin' in her room a-pinin'. Seems like her heart's so full o' sorrow, she can't get it out. An' she keeps a-gettin' thinner'n paler every day. (*She pauses; then continues tearfully.*) Looks like she'll be gone to Jesus 'fore another spring comes around.

JENNIE. It sure is a pity. I wish she'd get to likin' some o' the young men around here. Might get her mind off her sorrow. Wouldn't have no trouble at all a-makin' up to 'em.

KATE (*proudly*). Well, I reckon not! There's Jed Miller. He'd marry her tomorrow, if she'd give him a chance.

JENNIE (*nodding her head approvingly*). Jed's a good man, too, Kate. Ain't as purty to look at as some, but he's steady an' a good provider.

KATE (*shyly*). Jennie, I do believe you're plum' crazy over Jed yourself. You're always so special friendly to him.

JENNIE (*blushing guiltily*). Hush your mouth, Kate. I stopped eyein' the men folks long ago. I'm a-gettin' too old.

KATE (*teasingly*). It ain't never too late, Jennie. Jed sent word he's goin' to drop in tonight. Hadn't you better put on your Sunday dress?

Just as KATE *finishes her last speech, the door opens, and* CECELIA *quietly comes in.* KATE *is so interested in her bantering conversation with* JENNIE *that she does not notice* CECELIA. JENNIE *motions to her to be quiet;* KATE *then turns and sees* CECELIA. *They are silent for a moment while they both look at her.* CECELIA *is a timid, nervous girl, with pretty hair pushed back from her pale face—one that is illumined by sad, gentle eyes. She is wearing a blue dress and a sweater. She is very restless, and has a habit of running her fingers through her hair, so that it frequently has a dishevelled appearance. Her poetic wistfulness and grace give her an almost supernatural appearance. She stands for a moment gazing listlessly about.*

JENNIE (*ending the discussion abruptly*). Come in, 'Celia, an' set by the fire. Where you been a-keepin' yourself all this time? (CECELIA *walks over to the chair by the table and sits down.*)

CECELIA. Oh, I've jes' been a-settin' in my room, Aunt Jennie, a-watchin' the sea, till it got too dark to see anything. The wind's jes' a-blowin' the water up on the beach. It sure is an awful storm.

KATE (*as she rises and crosses to the back of the table*). You shouldn't be a-settin' in your room a-moonin' so much, 'Celia. It ain't good for the brain.

CECELIA. I reckon not, Aunt Kate. But it ain't much else to do but jes' set an' think.

JENNIE. Law', 'Celia, you a-talkin' like that as young as you are. Only them as is old an' bent like me'n Kate sets around and moons.

KATE (*a little offended at being classed with the "halt and lame," moving around to the right of the table*). Yes, old, Jennie, but not bent. I'm a up'n comin' woman for my years. (*Turning to* CECELIA.) Ain't I, 'Celia?

CECELIA (*listlessly*). Yes, I reckon so, Aunt Kate.

JENNIE (*consolingly*). Don't get riled, Kate. I was only sayin' that for fun, so as to show 'Celia she's doin' wrong to always be a-dwellin' on the past. (*She turns to* CECELIA.) You've got to forget, child, same way as everybody else forgets.

CECELIA (*brokenly*). Forget, yes, that's what I must do, forget like it was all a dream. (*She sobs.*) An' maybe it was, maybe it was. (*She pauses.*) An' how can I forget, with Johnny a-comin' to me in my dreams every night, an' all through the day, too?

(The wind blows loudly past the house, and there is a rumbling of thunder as the storm increases. CECELIA glances nervously about, and runs her fingers through her hair.)

KATE *(sitting down in the chair at the right end of the table).* Law', 'Celia, it ain't all that bad. You only make things worse by a-thinkin' about 'em. *(She suddenly remembers.)* I forgot to tell you Jed Miller sent word he's a-aimin' to drop in tonight. *(CECELIA does not seem to hear. KATE repeats her speech in a louder tone.)* I say Jed Miller is a-aimin' to come to see you tonight.

CECELIA *(aroused from dreaming of her lover).* Oh he is? I ain't seen Jed in a long time.

JENNIE. It ain't his fault, though. He'd be here every night if he had a chance.

KATE. He sure is a good, steady man, too. Seems like he's a-gettin' shy o' you, 'cause you don't pay him no mind.

CECELIA. It ain't that I don't like Jed. He's a good man, but somehow he jes' ain't for me. *(Sadly.)* I had one man an' he was all I was a-wantin'. But the sea tuk him away. *(KATE rises and starts toward the door, leading into the other part of the house.)*

KATE *(speaking while crossing to the door).* Well, it ain't for us to say who you're to have. But Jed's a powerful good man. *(At the door, turning back to CECELIA.)* He may be a-jumpin' the broom with one o' them Jamieson gals some o' these days. Reckon I'd better get me a shawl. *(To herself, as she opens the door and goes out.)* It's gettin' sort o' cold in here.

JENNIE. Are you warm enough with jes' that light sweater on, 'Celia?

CECELIA. Yes, Aunt Jennie, plenty warm. *(JENNIE gets up, goes to the center table, and puts her knitting on the table.)*

JENNIE. Well, I reckon I've been a-knittin' enough for tonight. Gets sort o' tiresome after a while. *(She notices that the fire is low.)* Guess I'd better put on another log. *(She takes a small log from the box and tosses it on the fire. Outside are heard the thunder and the constant moaning of the surf. Somewhere off in the distance a bell buoy is clanging faintly.)*

CECELIA *(nervously).* Listen, Aunt Jennie! Listen! It's jes' like the night—*(She doesn't finish, but goes quickly to the window and peers out. She continues rather disconnectedly.)* I knew it would be like this. The sea tuk him away, an' now it'll come again. But it don't matter. He's thar. He's thar. (*She turns to* AUNT JENNIE, *who stands in amazement before the fireplace.*) Don't you hear, Aunt Jennie? The sea's cryin', cryin', cryin'. Sounds jes' like it was Johnny, a-sobbin' for me. An' he's cryin', cryin', cryin' in the night. (*She says these last words in a monotone. A rather loud knock is heard at the front door. There is a stamping of feet. The sudden noise has the effect of breaking the tension.*)

JENNIE. Land sakes, 'Celia! Quit a-takin' on so. You plum' scared the liver out o' me. (*She crosses the room in order to open the door.*) Things jes' a-happenin' like a house afire. Sounds like somebody a-tryin' to knock down the door. (*She opens the door rather crossly. A gust of wind blows in, and the lamplight flickers.*)

JED (*speaking from outside*). Howdy do, Miss Jennie. Howdy do.

JENNIE (*recognizing the newcomer*). Howdy, Jed. Come right in. Come right in. I know it ain't no fun a-standin' out thar in the storm.

JED (*talking as he enters*). Thank you, Miss Jennie. I thought I'd jes' stop by on my way home, and see how you-all are a-gettin' along.

JED *is now in the room. He is wearing a rain cap and a muddy-looking yellow oilskin. When he takes these off, we discover that he is a tall, heavily built, rather awkward man with a shock of unruly red hair. His plump, round face expresses naiveté and a childish good humor. He is obviously not the type of man who would appeal to a young girl's fancy. He is wearing a lumber jacket, corduroy pants, and heavy shoes.*

JENNIE. I sure am glad you did, Jed. I sure am.

JED. Howdy, Miss 'Celia. I sure am glad to see you. I hope you're feelin' peart as a cricket tonight.

CECELIA (*turning from the window*). Howdy, Jed. I'm feelin' tol'able.

JENNIE (*taking hold of* JED'S *oilskin coat*). Let me rid you o' this, Jed. (*As* JED *slips out of the oilskin, some raindrops fall from it onto the floor.*)

JED (laughing). Looks like I brung the storm in with me, a-wettin' your floor like that, Miss Jennie.

JENNIE. Pshaw, Jed. A little water won't hurt nothin'. (JENNIE hangs the oilskin on a nail on the wall. Then she takes a broom out of the corner and vigorously sweeps up the water on the floor. CECELIA in the meanwhile has remained standing at the window, gazing out toward the sea. She is calm now. Listlessness has in some measure replaced her agitation.)

CECELIA (indicating a rocking chair by the fire). Have a chair, Jed, an' set a spell.

JED (sitting down). Thank you, Miss 'Celia. I believe I will.

JENNIE (still sweeping). It sure is a bad night out. Ain't it, Jed?

JED. It is that, Miss Jennie. The surf's jes' a-pilin' up on the beach. Looks like Old Nick's a-ridin' the wind tonight. (At this moment KATE re-enters. A black wool shawl is wrapped around her shoulders.)

KATE. Howdy, Jed. How're you a-feelin' tonight?

JED (rising). Howdy, Miss Kate. I'm a-feelin' fit as a fiddle, thank you.

KATE. I thought somebody was a-comin' in. I heard such a rumpus.

JED (laughing uproariously). Guess that was jes' my big feet. Can't seem to move around much without raising a clatter.

KATE (laughing). Don't matter if you do have big feet, Jed. Jes' so they get you thar and back is all that counts.

JED. I reckon you're right. (He offers KATE his chair.) Here —have this rocker, Miss Kate. I'll get one o' them chairs agin the wall. (JED gets one of the chairs, places it between KATE and the table, and sits down. KATE sits down in the rocker.)

KATE. Thank you, Jed. (JENNIE puts the broom in the corner and resumes her seat.)

JENNIE. How's your folks, Jed?

JED. All purty good, Ma'am, 'cept the old man. He's sort o' down in the mouth. Gout's a-givin' him right smart trouble.

KATE (sympathetically). Ain't that a shame! It's the rainy weather we've been a-havin', I reckon. Seems like damp weather does make gout seem a lot worser.

JENNIE. Rain don't help nobody feel no better. I can tell you that. (Turning to JED.) Jed, how's your store a-gettin' along?

JED. I'm doin' purty good, Miss Jennie. Sellin' more washin' soap an' cigarettes than anything else. Orter have a purty good trade 'fore long.

JENNIE. I'm glad you're a-doin' so well, Jed.

JED (turning to CECELIA). You ain't been up to my store in a long time, Miss 'Celia. Been a-savin' you some purty blue cloth, if'n you'd jes' come an' get it. Thought maybe you'd like to make a new dress.

CECELIA. Thanks, Jed. But you better sell that cloth. Don't reckon I'll be a-needin' any new clothes for a long time.

JED. I won't be a-needin' to sell it, Miss 'Celia. I been a-aimin' for you to have that cloth for a long time. You'll take it, won't you?

CECELIA. Yes, Jed, since you've set your heart on it.

JED (smiling). Well, ain't that nice? You always look so purty in blue, Miss 'Celia.

JENNIE. It's plum' nice o' you to be a-doin' that for 'Celia, Jed. She'll be proud to wear the dress, I know.

KATE. I reckon when 'Celia gets that new dress on, she won't stand second to nobody.

JED. Law', no, Miss Kate. Seems like Miss 'Celia looks better'n the other gals jes' in her everyday clothes.

CECELIA (blushing slightly). I guess you're jes' a-flatterin' me, Jed. Reckon blue does set me off a bit, though.

JENNIE (rising and yawning). Kate, I reckon we'd better be seein' if everything is all right in the back o' the house. (She smiles and winks at KATE.) These young folks won't be a-needin' us any more. (KATE rises, nodding her head significantly.)

KATE. I reckon not.

JENNIE. Good night, Jed.

JED. Good night, Miss Jennie.

KATE. Good night, Jed. An' don't be a-waitin' so long to come to see us the next time.

JED. Thank you, Miss Kate. I won't. (JENNIE and KATE go out, and when the door closes behind them, JED turns to CECELIA, who walks slowly back from the window to her chair, left of the table.) Gee, Miss 'Celia. (Admiringly.) You sure look purty as pink tonight. I jes' been a-settin' here a-watchin' you. (CECELIA sits down in her chair.)

CECELIA. Thanks, Jed. Ain't had nobody to tell me that in a long time. (*She is reminiscent.*) Johnny used to always say I loved purty talk better'n a cat loves milk.

JED. I reckon all the women-folks likes to be told how purty they are once in a while. (JED *sits down.*)

CECELIA. But I ain't got no right to be a-wantin' to hear purty talk. I ain't got no right to be wantin' nothin'. He was all I was a-wantin'. An' the sea tuk him, an' there ain't nothin' else.

JED (*trying to sympathize*). You got plenty o' friends around here, Miss 'Celia.

CECELIA (*bitterly*). I ain't a-wantin' any friends. All I'm a-wantin' is Johnny.

JED (*kindly*). Law', Miss 'Celia. Don't do no good to be a-pinin' after them that's dead an' gone.

CECELIA. But he ain't gone. Seems like he's a-settin' thar now—jes' like he used to—a-laughin' an' cuttin' a splurge. An' me jes' a-settin' here a-laughin' fit to kill. (*She points to a rocker by the fire. She seems to see him there as a ghost. For a moment the past year is swept away, and Johnny is with her again. Quite often during the past year she has had hallucinations such as this one. Then reality rushes back upon her in all its inevitability.*) But, no, it ain't Johnny. It can't be. An' yet it seems so real. (*Sorrowfully.*) It was jes' another dream, I reckon. (*During this weird and ghostly soliloquy* JED *has been watching* CECELIA *with amazement and fear. He is obviously disturbed by* CECELIA's *apparition of her lover. He feels very uncomfortable in this eerie atmosphere. There is a flash of lightning, and then a terrific peal of thunder.* CECELIA *and* JED *jump nervously.*)

JED (*laughing nervously*). That was sure some lightning! Come so sudden-like it almost had me skeered for a moment.

CECELIA (*nervously*). It sure is one awful storm. I wish it would let up. Seems like it's only gettin' worser, though. (*They wait expectantly for another flash of lightning but it does not come, and the thunder rolls off into the distance. They become calmer, and* JED *tries to turn the conversation to a more pleasant subject.*)

JED. Miss 'Celia, Dora Jamieson's havin' a little gatherin' over at her house Friday night. (*He hesitates.*) I . . . I was a-thinkin' maybe you'd like to come along with me.

CECELIA. I reckon not, Jed. I ain't goin' out much these days.

JED (pleading). Aw, jes' this once, Miss 'Celia. Besides, it'll do you good. You'll go, won't you?

CECELIA. Reckon I won't this time, Jed. Seems like it ain't no fun goin' places no more.

JED. What's the matter, Miss 'Celia? Don't you like parties like you used to?

CECELIA. Oh, I don't know, Jed. I reckon it's somethin' gone out o' me—somethin' gone out o' here. (She indicates her heart.)

JED (insisting). But you hadn't orter stay at home all o' the time, Miss 'Celia. It only makes things worser.

CECELIA. You don't understan', Jed. (She continues sadly in a far-away tone.) You ain't never lost somebody you loved better'n anyone else in the world. It's like bein' dead an' still livin'. An' nothin' matters but the awful loneliness.

JED (sympathetically). Law', Miss 'Celia. I sure do hate to hear you a-talkin' that way. I wish you would go. It'd do you a sight o' good.

CECELIA. I reckon I can't this time, Jed.

JED. I'm powerful sorry. Maybe we can go some other time.

CECELIA. Maybe so, Jed.

JED (glancing at the clock on the mantel). It's gettin' sort o' late. I'd better be a-moseyin' along home. (JED rises to go.)

CECELIA (with little enthusiasm). Don't be in no hurry, Jed.

JED. I'd better be a-goin', Miss 'Celia. It's a right smart piece home. An' it ain't goin' to be easy walkin' in sech a storm. (He suddenly remembers his raincoat and cap, and walks over to the wall to get them. He laughs as he slips into his oilskin.) I nearly plum' forgot my old storm breaker. Wouldn't I've been a crazy galoot a-piddlin' along in the storm without a stitch o' coverin' on? (CECELIA gets up, takes JED's cap off the nail and gives it to him.)

CECELIA. Here's your cap, Jed.

JED (putting on the cap). Thanks. An' good night, Miss 'Celia. I'll be a-seein' you sometime soon.

CECELIA (relievedly). Good night, Jed. (JED goes out the door with a noisy scuffling of feet. A gust of wind blows into the room as he passes through the door. As the door closes behind him, CECELIA runs to the window and looks out into the night. Out there in the lonely darkness is the spirit of her lover. She

wants desperately to be with him. She cries out.) Johnny! Johnny!
*(There is no answering cry. Only the sound of the waves and
the howling of the wind. She stands at the window a moment
silently; then she hears footsteps and quickly takes a seat by the
fire.* Jennie *re-enters.)*

Jennie. I thought Jed was a-leavin'. I heard the door bangin'.
He didn't stay long, did he?

Cecelia. No, Aunt Jennie. I reckon he got tired o' settin'.
Where's Aunt Kate?

Jennie. She went to bed. I thought I'd better wait up for you.
(She sits down in her rocking chair.) I guess we'll jes' set up a
while longer. The tireder you get, the better you sleep anyhow.
*(They sit silently for a moment, gazing into the fire. The only
sounds are the ceaseless roaring of the surf, and the howling of
the wind.)*

Cecelia *(starting up nervously as the wind moans).* Jes' listen,
Aunt Jennie. Sounds like someone cryin'. It makes me feel so
quare.

Jennie. It ain't nothin' but the wind, child. An' the wind
don't hurt nobody.

Cecelia *(continuing).* Jes' listen to the waves. Won't never
let up beatin'. Seems like we'll always be jes' a-settin' here a-
listenin' to the surf years 'n years 'n years.

Jennie. It does sort o' get on your nerves. But I don't let it
worry me much.

Cecelia. But there won't never be nothin' else, Aunt Jennie.
But the waves a-comin' in and the waves a-goin' out. Sort o'
makes you feel far away from the rest o' the world. Jes' like
we belong to the sea, and can't never get away. *(The wind
howls again, and* Cecelia *nervously taps on the table with her
hand.)*

Jennie. God made the sea for our good, 'Celia.

Cecelia *(bitterly).* But it ain't good, Aunt Jennie. It's mean
and evil, an' full o' bad spirits—jes' like old Ma Anders said.

Jennie *(rather sternly).* 'Celia, you're plum' out o' your head.
A-believin' all them tales Ma Anders been a-tellin' you. She's
more'n half crazy herself.

Cecelia *(insisting, in a low, intense voice).* No, she ain't,
Aunt Jennie. She's old 'n dried-up 'n quare, but she ain't crazy.

I can see her a-settin' in her hut right now. " 'Celia," she says
to me, "the sea tuk three o' my sons, an' my old man, an' it'll
be a-takin' me, too, some day. (*Slowly rising and becoming more
and more excited.*) The sea's full o' bad spirits that're a-waitin'
an' a-hungerin' for the souls o' men." (*Wildly.*) An' she's right,
too. They tuk my Johnny, them spirits. (*She pauses a moment.
The intense wave of emotion leaves her body, and she continues
resignedly.*) An' they'll take me, too. An' it'll be all of us they'll
be a-takin' in the end.

JENNIE. Quit a-talkin' so foolish, 'Celia. Lord knows what
you'll be a-sayin' next.

CECELIA (*disregarding her aunt, and talking on as if to herself,
still intensely*). Seems like it wouldn't matter much if the sea
did take me. Johnny'd be thar. (*Her voice breaks with her sorrow.*) Maybe it wouldn't be so lonesome-like. (*She sits down
and runs her fingers through her hair, wearily.*) An' maybe
there'd be a little peace an' a little rest at last.

JENNIE (*in a kindly voice*). 'Celia, child, you have to be for-
gettin' Johnny. It won't do no good to pine. He's gone an' he
won't never come back.

CECELIA. Yes, he's gone. But he ain't so far away I can't find
him. Me a-lovin' him like I do. (*Talking as if thinking out loud.*)
An' it's a long time he's been a-waitin'. An' thar won't be no
rest till I find him. No rest anywheres. (*During the last few
minutes the storm has been approaching a crescendo. The thunder has become almost deafening. It seems as though the heavens
have burst loose. A bell buoy is clanging somewhere on the sea.
Suddenly there is heard above the storm a faint, mournful cry
—like the ghostly wailing of a man left to die in the storm. CECE-
LIA and JENNIE are horrified. CECELIA whispers fearfully as
another crash of thunder is heard.*) What was that? What was
that, Aunt Jennie? Sounded jes' like someone cryin' out thar in
the storm.

JENNIE (*whispering in an awed tone*). I guess it was jes' the
wind. But it did sound quare. Sort o' sad an' mournful. Jes' like
somebody a-wailin' for the dead. (*The cry comes again. This
time it is more distinct. It begins quaveringly, and then passes
into a long wail which chills the heart. CECELIA jumps up trembling with excitement, runs to the window, and looks out into*

the darkness. The ominous roaring of the surf and the crashing of thunder are unceasing.)

CECELIA *(wildly).* Thar it is again, Aunt Jennie! Thar it is again! It's someone a-callin'. I know it is.

JENNIE *(rising in excitement, an expression of terror on her face).* Set down, child! It ain't nothin' but the wind a-howlin'. *(The cry comes louder and more quickly now. It is strange, wild, and ghostly. The storm has reached a terrifying height. There is a constant crashing of thunder. The waves lash madly on the beach and make a menacing roar.)*

CECELIA *(hysterically).* It ain't the wind. I know it ain't. It's Johnny! I hear him a-cryin'! He's out thar in the surf! An' he's a-callin' me! *(The cry comes weirdly wailing again.* CECELIA *is caught in its irresistible spell. Her face is drawn and deathly pale. She turns from the window frantically.)* Don't you hear, Aunt Jennie? It's Johnny! It's Johnny! He's callin' me an' I've got to go! I've got to go to him! (*CECELIA starts toward the door. The terrible cry continues amid the storm. It is drawing* CECELIA *to the sea and destruction.* JENNIE *stands dumbfounded and powerless to restrain her.)*

JENNIE *(stretching out her arms imploringly).* Wait, 'Celia! It's jes' the wind. Wait, wait, child! It'll be your death.

CECELIA *(moving swiftly to the door as the cry comes again insistently).* He's callin' me, callin' me out thar in the surf! An' I've got to go. It's me he's wantin', and I've got to go! God knows he's been waitin' long enough! *(She opens the door and rushes madly out into the storm. A roaring wind blows through the open door. There is lightning and thunder.* CECELIA's *voice is heard from the outside calling.)* Johnny! Johnny! I'm comin'! I'm comin'! *(The awful cry is now triumphant. It is luring her onward to the sea.* JENNIE *recovers her sense and rushes frantically after her.)*

JENNIE *(despairingly calling as she runs across the room).* Come back, child! *(Opening the door violently, amid a great gust of wind and rain.)* Come back! It'll be your death! *(There is no answer—only the cry calling mockingly above the roar of the surf and thunder.* JENNIE *pauses for a moment on the threshold, starts to run out into the storm, but realizes the futility of such an action. With her arms uplifted in terror, she turns*

slowly and walks unsteadily back to the center of the room.)
She's gone—gone into the sea! *(Almost swooning.)* She'll never
live a minute in the surf. God have mercy on her! God have
mercy on her!

*The cry is still heard faintly calling above the thunder and
the surf.*

CURTAIN

THE BEADED BUCKLE

A Comedy of Village Aristocracy

BY

FRANCES GRAY PATTON

A SMALL-TOWN COMEDY BY A WRITER OF FICTION

"The Beaded Buckle" is quite unlike the other plays in this volume. In fact, it can hardly be considered a folk-play at all; for it deals with a segment of society somewhat apart from the farmers, Indians, mountain people, and Negroes portrayed by the rest of the dramatists. Finesse and sophistication, which are characteristic of Mrs. Patton's principals, have little to do with the more elemental folk of the hills and plains. Mrs. Agnes Miller, accused of stealing a beaded buckle from a local clothing store, is a figure straight out of drawing-room comedy, and her method of handling the delicate situation is quite beyond the artifices of her fellow North Carolinians in the other plays.

Professor Koch wrote that, in this intimate glimpse of present-day small-town aristocracy, the author had withheld the actual name of the town where the action occurs, as well as the real name of the heroine—"for obvious reasons"—but that at the time the play was written, the real Mrs. Agnes Miller still flourished as the leader of the "smart set" of her "Glendale" and still fascinated all who knew her with her irresistible charm. Still in "Glendale," too, were Louise, and the University son Joe, and old Herb Shine, and the sniveling clerk Leona King. Of Agnes Miller, Mrs. Patton says, "Her soft, beguiling voice is very sweet, and I am still under her spell."

Those who are familiar with Mrs. Patton's later writings will notice a similarity between them and "The Beaded Buckle," even though this play came from her pen at the age of eighteen. All of her work displays an ingratiatingly urbane quality which is peculiarly Mrs. Patton's. The "village aristocracy" and the upper middle-class patricians are objects of a gentle satire which may not be obvious at first contact. The reader of "The Beaded Buckle" must pause for a moment upon finishing the play before he is assured of the playwright's intention. Underlying the comedy is a rather sober protest.

Frances Gray was born on March 19, 1906, in Raleigh, where her father was a newspaperman. "My first literary production of any length," she tells us, "was a play in seven acts which I wrote at the age of eleven. It was all in rhymed couplets. . . . I produced the play, with the aid of the neighborhood children, in the backyard on Blount Street. We charged a nickel a head and took in five dollars which was split between the Red Cross and the War Camp Community Service." She continued to write plays, poems, and stories in high school and at Duke, which she attended for a year, and later at Chapel Hill. After a fling as an actress with a stock company in Cincinnati, she was married in 1927 to Dr. Lewis Patton, then and now a professor of English at Duke.

Writing activity waned as her three children started coming along, and it was not till 1944 that she found herself back into the swing of things. Her short stories in the *New Yorker* and other magazines were immediately recognized as the work of a meticulous craftsman. In them not only the situation, but each sentence was carefully planned to convey in an exact way the not so humdrum lives of seemingly ordinary people.

A first collection of stories, *The Finer Things of Life,* was published in 1951 and won both the Christopher Award and the Sir Walter Raleigh Award. *Good Morning, Miss Dove,* a novel of a fictitious schoolteacher who had appeared in several of the short stories, was issued in 1954 and won wide approval. It was a choice of the Book-of-the-Month Club. A second volume of short stories came out in 1955, *A Piece of Luck.* Like Thomas Wolfe and Bernice Kelly Harris, Frances Gray Patton found her way from university playwriting to successful fiction.

THE CHARACTERS

Mrs. Agnes Miller, *a charming widow*

Joseph Conroy Miller, *her son, a University student*

Mrs. Louise Bailey, *a neighbor*

Mrs. Berkeley, *a gossip*

Herb Shine, *proprietor of the "Metropolitan Store"*

Leona King, *his clerk*

SCENE

Mrs. Miller's living room, Glendale, North Carolina.

TIME

The present. An afternoon in May.

The scene is the living room of Mrs. Agnes Miller. *A door and window in the rear wall look out upon the village street. The room is furnished to conform to* Mrs. Miller's *aristocratic taste: old portraits on the wall, a vase of fresh roses from her garden on the small table at left; a large sofa, a whatnot and several chairs of Colonial design—family heirlooms, evidently. The telephone is on the table at the left. Beside the table is a large chair in which* Joe Miller *is seated, reading a popular magazine and smoking a collegiate-looking little pipe. He is a well-built, handsome youth hardly out of his teens.*

Mrs. Louise Bailey *enters hurriedly. She is a woman of forty-five, inconspicuously but a bit carelessly dressed in a dark blue voile. Her manner and appearance suggest her generous outlook on life. She has evidently come on an important errand.*

Louise *(calling).* Agnes, oh Agnes! *(She sees* Joe *who has risen.)* Hello, Joe, what are you doing at home?

Joe *(goes to greet her).* How're you, Miss Louise, mighty glad to see you. I just hopped off for the week end. I don't know where mother is. But sit down and wait; she'll be in pretty soon, I reckon.

Louise *(sitting in* Joe's *chair).* Yes, I will stay, Joe. I've got something very important to tell your mother. I suppose she's still at Sadie's tea.

Joe *(drawing up a chair for himself).* Well, I wish she'd come on home. Seems like a year since I've seen her.

Louise *(laughing).* It hasn't been quite a year since the Easter holidays, but I know Agnes will be glad to see you. How'd you leave the Hill?

Joe. Oh, quite as I found it. Very pleasant, but slightly monotonous.

Louise. Chapel Hill isn't exciting, but it's a mighty sweet old place. . . . Studying hard?

Joe. Yes'm, I'm keeping my nose to the grindstone. You know I entered the law school this quarter.

Louise. Yes, so your mother told me. I'm glad that you did, Joe. If you're as much like your father on the inside as you are on the outside, you ought to make a good lawyer.

Joe. Thank you, ma'am. Daddy was a good lawyer. And I

199

thought it was the natural thing to do; a legal mind kind of runs in the family.

LOUISE. I declare it's a pity that Joe, senior, couldn't live to see you grow up. He was so proud of you.

JOE. I wish I could remember Daddy better. Mother says he had the strongest mind and the clearest vision. . . .

LOUISE. He was a born lawyer, and he was just as fair as the day is long.

JOE (fervently). That's my idea of greatness. To be fair, to be above prejudice, to have an unerring sense of elemental justice!

LOUISE (quietly). It's a great thing to have.

JOE (rising). I want to be able to stand on a mountain and look at the whole show and see all sides dispassionately. To be ruled by no emotion!

LOUISE. We couldn't live without emotion, Joe.

JOE. But emotion doesn't have to obscure the truth. I want to be so just that I could judge the most charming person in the world without being biased—so just that I could judge my own mother!

LOUISE. My! What law book did you get that oration out of? —I wish your mother'd come on home.

JOE. So do I. I sure do want to see her. What's she doing these days?

LOUISE. Oh, she's flirting outrageously with Colonel Haywood, whom she has no idea of marrying.

JOE (laughing). The one with the bay window?

LOUISE. You ought to see the way Agnes "strings" him. She smiles up at him like he's the only man on earth. She'd put a sixteen-year-old school girl to shame!

JOE. You know I marvel at mother. The way she keeps so young, and she's such good company.

LOUISE. Yes, Agnes is a good companion.

JOE. She's the best I've ever seen. And she's pretty. No wonder the Colonel fell for her.

LOUISE. Well, Agnes always had plenty of beaux, but she's devoted her life to you, Joe.

JOE. She's been wonderful. She's been a mother and father

both. . . . (*Meditating.*) And she's got a conscience like a man's. She's the soul of honor!

LOUISE. But she always gets what she wants.

JOE. Because she's lovely. Everybody falls for her charm. She could get away with murder.

LOUISE. Yes, . . . I believe she could.—I wish she'd come on; it's getting late, but I've *got* to see her.

JOE. If you're in a hurry, I'll take a message.

LOUISE. Thank you, no. I'd better wait. But—(*hesitating*)— Joe. . . .

JOE. Ma'am?

LOUISE. I suppose I ought to tell you, too. . . . People are saying things about Agnes that I don't like.

JOE (*abruptly*). Do you mean that some one has said something uncomplimentary about my mother?

LOUISE. Hold your horses, Joe. You can't do me any good if you fly up.

JOE. Well, I shan't permit—

LOUISE. Please give me a chance to talk. Can't you think quietly about this?

JOE. I hope I am old enough to be cool.

LOUISE (*sitting on the sofa*). I hope so too. Come sit down, and let me tell you about it. You remember that lavender dress your mother had summer before last—the one with the fringe?

JOE. Yes'm.

LOUISE. Well, she had it dyed and she wanted a distinctive ornament for it.

JOE (*perplexed*). Well—what under—

LOUISE. But she couldn't find anything in town that wasn't ordinary.

JOE. Naturally.

LOUISE. Then day before yesterday, it seems, she went into the Metropolitan Clothing Store and she saw a very commonplace dress, ornamented with a beautiful beaded buckle.

JOE (*impatiently*). Did she buy the dress?

LOUISE. She didn't want the dress, Joe. She wanted the buckle; but when she asked the clerk to sell it to her, she refused to sell it without the dress.

JOE. Those clerks are the dumbest!

LOUISE. Agnes finally sent her to ask the manager, but the manager said that he wouldn't take the buckle off the dress.

JOE. And poor mother couldn't get anything?

LOUISE. Agnes was very much irritated. So she went to the back of the store with the clerk to ask the manager again to sell it.

JOE. And he refused *again*?

LOUISE. Yes, he refused again. So your mother just left them back there and walked out of the store. But, Joe,—the next time they looked at the dress *the buckle was gone!* (*There is a silence.*)

JOE. You reckon the sales-girl took it?

LOUISE. Probably. . . . Though she's a mighty nice girl. Leona King—you know her.

JOE. Yes, she was in my class at High School. Too bad.

LOUISE. But of course she doesn't admit it. She and old Herb Shine say that . . . Agnes *stole* the beaded buckle!

JOE (*dumbfounded*). That *my mother stole a buckle?* (JOE *rises, visibly angry.*)

LOUISE. Isn't it preposterous? But the worst part is that today Agnes walked into the "Metropolitan" wearing the spit image of the lost buckle.

JOE. Was old Herb Shine impertinent to her?

LOUISE. Oh, no. He hasn't nerve enough to be impertinent. He just asked Agnes where she got her buckle.

JOE. And what did mother say?

LOUISE. Why, she said she ordered it from Raleigh.

JOE. I reckon old Shine took a back seat then.

LOUISE. But he didn't. He and Leona started telling the town that Agnes stole—(JOE *starts toward the door.*) Why, Joe, where are you going?

JOE. I'm going to kill Herbert Shine!

LOUISE (*restraining him*). Now listen to me, Joe. You be calm, and wait—

JOE. Do you think I can be calm while the scum of the earth is slandering my mother?

LOUISE. You'd better wait and consult your mother before you do any killing. (MRS. AGNES MILLER *enters. She is a gracious woman of forty, combining the freshness of a girl with the poise of a matron. Her soft beguiling voice is very sweet, and her*

*arrogance is an inherent part of her charm. She wears a delicate
lavender gown with a vivid beaded buckle on the hip. She pauses
in the doorway when she sees* JOE; *then, with a little cry, she
rushes to him.*)

AGNES. Oh Joe! Where did you drop from, you precious lamb,
you. . . . (*Embracing him.*) Oh, you're so strong; you'll break
every bone in my body. . . . Why didn't you let me know you
were coming? I'd have had a party for you.

JOE. I didn't want a party, Mother. I wanted to see *you.*

AGNES. Aren't you the quintessence of gallantry? (*She holds
him at arm's length.*) Stand off there and let me look at you . . .
just let me look at. . . . Isn't he beautiful, Louise? (LOUISE *smiles
indulgently.*) Do you know I haven't seen him since Easter?—
Isn't he perfectly lovely? Son, you're so beautiful I just can't
stand it! . . . Look at me straight in the eyes and tell me the
truth, Joseph.

JOE. Yes, Mother, my word is as good as my bond.

AGNES. Are you getting enough to eat?

JOE. Yes'm, absolutely! On my honor!

AGNES (*surveying him*). I don't know . . . you look a little
wan. Don't you think so, Louise?

LOUISE. Well, no—not particularly, Agnes.

AGNES. But you're perfect anyway. You're just perfect! Why
are you so perfect, son?

JOE (*joking*). Because Miss Louise is my godmother, I guess.

LOUISE. No, I don't take any of the credit, Joe.

AGNES. But what have I ever done to deserve such a son?

JOE. If you had your deserts—

AGNES. Did you ever see a boy so unconscious of his own
beauty? (JOE *admits this.*) See how straight he holds himself!
I love him to distraction! Come here, angel, and kiss your poor
old down-trodden mammy.

JOE (*kissing her fondly*). Mother, you look like a full-blown
rose.

AGNES. Isn't it a blessing to have a dear appreciative child
in your old age? Especially when he's all you've got in the world.
Lou, do you think you could ever love one of yours like I love
Joe?

LOUISE. Oh, I think I love 'em enough. But I *know* that if

I raved about my six like you rave about Joe they'd think I was crazy.

AGNES. But he's so perfect!

LOUISE (laughing). They all are.

AGNES (going over to the table, discovers JOE's pipe). I thought I smelled this horrible old thing. That's all right, Joe. If you can't "smell up" your own mother's house, whose house can you smell up? (Removing her hat.) Don't you like my dress? (JOE and LOUISE exchange glances.)

JOE. Yes, mother, but—

LOUISE. Agnes, I came to tell you about that dress. Everybody is talking—

AGNES. What's the matter? Has some old gossip-monger discovered that it's about a hundred years old?

LOUISE (hurriedly). Agnes, I might as well tell you. . . . Mr. Shine and Leona King say that you stole that buckle!

AGNES. That I stole this buckle!

LOUISE. They say that you went in their store.

AGNES. Yes, I went in their store. I admit I went in their store. I went in their store because there are no decent stores in this town to go in!

LOUISE. And you wanted them to sell you a beaded buckle.

AGNES. Yes, it was the only pretty thing in the store, and they refused to sell it to me without a tacky little dress. Refused to sell me a buckle! When it's only my patronage and that of my friends that has kept the doors of that store open at all. It's the insolence of it that I despise. I can remember when old Herb Shine was—

LOUISE. They say that after you left they looked at the dress and the buckle was gone!

AGNES. And therefore I took it. I took their beaded buckle! It's pitiful how the insignificant love to slander their superiors. I suppose they will attempt to blackmail me.

JOE (passionately). I'm going to beat up that swine—

AGNES. No, Joe, no! You can't do that and get all this in the papers. Your mother's name in the papers in such a story. We can't court publicity. We'll have to hush this thing up. Of course that little Leona has lied to all her friends, and that stratum of Glendale society considers me a thief—

JOE. The low-down blood-suckers—the gully dirt—the—

LOUISE. Joe, I thought it was you who were orating to me about level-headedness. Calm down and try to see their point of view.

JOE. They have no point of view—they—

LOUISE. Oh, yes, they have. The buckle is gone. Of course it's ridiculous for old Shine to say that Agnes took it, but he thinks he's right. There's nothing to be mad about.

JOE. Mad! Of course I'm mad! I'm fighting mad! I'm mad because they have displeased my mother!

AGNES. I'll have to see them myself. I'll have to see that this thing is stopped immediately. It isn't fair to Joe to allow his mother's name to be—

LOUISE. I wouldn't go down there if I were you, Agnes.

AGNES. No, indeed. They shall come up here, and I shall tell them to be quiet. I go down there indeed! They must come to me. I'll make them go down on their knees! I'll—(she sweeps to the telephone.) One, seven, eight, please. May I speak to Mr. Shine? . . . How do you do, Mr. Shine? This is Mrs. Joseph Conroy Miller of Myrtle Hill. I wish you and Miss King to confer with me at my home immediately. . . . No. . . . To-morrow will not do. . . . No, I shall not be free to see you this evening. . . . Very well, Mr. Shine, but I think it would be to your advantage to come immediately. . . . I shall expect you in a few minutes, then. Thank you. (She hangs up the receiver and turns to LOUISE and JOE.) The idea of their refusing to sell me a buckle in the first place. I needed that buckle to complete my costume! What does he keep his messy little store for anyway, if it's not to serve me?

JOE. Oh, Mother, I can't stand it!

LOUISE (by the window). Agnes, there goes Mrs. Berkeley looking like she's full of a mean tale.

AGNES. Oh, I bet she's spreading the buckle story. We'll call her in. (She rushes to door.) Oh, Mrs. Berkeley, come in a minute. (To JOE.) Joe, she's a newcomer trying to break into society and she has the most abominable tongue in town. (MRS. BERKELEY at the door.) Why, how do you do, Mrs. Berkeley. Come in, I want to show you my jewels.

MRS. BERKELEY (*observing the buckle*). Your jewels? . . . How do you do, Mrs. Bailey.

AGNES. Yes; my child, and my first roses! This is my son Joseph. How do you like him?

MRS. BERKELEY (*coyly*). I'm afraid that, if I told him, I might embarrass him.

JOE. I am not easily embarrassed. . . . I go to the University.

AGNES. He's really quite nice when you know him. But oh, Mrs. Berkeley, I have a choice bit of gossip. (*She motions her to a chair.*)

MRS. BERKELEY. What is it? Do tell me, my dear.

AGNES (*sitting beside her*). It's about this beaded buckle. It seems I stole it.

MRS. BERKELEY. You stole it!

AGNES. So I hear. It seems that I went into the Metropolitan Store, knocked the clerk down, snatched the buckle, and ran out of the store with the whole works crying after me, "Stop thief!" Can you imagine that?

MRS. BERKELEY. How absurd.

AGNES. Yes, it would be amusing, if it were somebody else. The little sales-girl evidently took it. I'm not going to say anything about it, though. I really feel sorry for her. Starved for beauty, I suppose. (*Sweetly.*) Of course all this is confidential.

MRS. BERKELEY (*eagerly*). Of course.

AGNES (*rising and taking the roses from vase*). And Mrs. Berkeley, as you go, I want you to take these; they're the first from my garden.

MRS. BERKELEY. Why, they're lovely. It's awfully sweet of you.

AGNES. Oh, can't you and Mr. Berkeley drop in for bridge tonight?

MRS. BERKELEY (*flattered*). We'd be very pleased to come!

AGNES (*she has ushered her to the door*). I shall expect you then—about eight. And remember, don't breathe that buckle story to a soul.

MRS. BERKELEY. Oh, no! That's confidential. Good-by. So glad to have seen you. (*She goes out, passing by the window.*)

LOUISE. That settles her. She'll spread your version.

JOE. She looks like a cat.

AGNES. She'll spread my side; but there'll always be people in town who'll believe that I stole that buckle!

LOUISE. It's horrid for you. But I believe old Shine and Leona will soon need more sympathy than you do.

JOE. If mother'll let me alone, Shine will.

LOUISE (*starting out*). Well, I'll run before the fight begins. My cook got married last week and—

AGNES. Louise, you're just lovely to come tell me. You're the living example of true friendship.

LOUISE. Oh, Agnes, don't take on so. I've got to run and fix supper.

AGNES. I don't see how anybody can be a cook and a lady at the same time. But you could step right off of an ash can and say the right thing at the right time— Oh, by the way, dear, the Colonel is coming to dinner this evening, and he has a plebeian passion for boiled onions. And oh, Lou, should you mind if I sent them over to your house to be boiled? They make the house smell so bad.

LOUISE. Why—Agnes Miller! You certainly can flatter and insult in the same breath. But, no, I don't mind. Send them along. Bye bye. (*She goes.*)

AGNES. Louise is pure gold! But, Joe, isn't it strange how some people can be born and bred with no conception of honor? Like that little Leona King—people who don't even know it's wrong to lie, or, if they do, as your Greatuncle Sam said to your Great-uncle Fred, "The worst of it, they don't give a damn!"

JOE. Mother, say "damn" again. You do it so charmingly!

AGNES. Why, dear, you know I never said "damn" in my life! . . . Joe, did you think your own mother would ever be called a thief?

JOE. Mother, please let me *kill* that man.

AGNES. No, no, not for the world. But—as if it would have been stealing if I had taken his old buckle! Why, the thing wasn't worth two dollars and it's only my patronage—and then to be rewarded in this way!

JOE. That stripe of trash doesn't know the word gratitude.

AGNES. By the way, dear, what's the law about libel?

JOE (*hesitatingly*). We haven't taken that up yet. (*There is a knock at the door.*)

AGNES. Answer it, Joe. And wait, dear, be kind and firm. Hold up your shoulders and remember that you have the best blood of North Carolina in your veins. (*A second knock.* JOE *opens the door.* HERB SHINE *and* LEONA KING *enter. He is old and wizened.* LEONA *is pretty in an unrefined way.*)

AGNES (*sitting on the sofa*). Good afternoon, Mr. Shine. How do you do, Leona?

SHINE (*bowing and scraping*). Good evenin', Mrs. Miller.

LEONA (*coyly*). How'do. Heyo, Joe.

JOE (*formally*). How do you do, Miss King.

AGNES. Won't you sit down? (*They sit.*) I called you here, Mr. Shine and Leona, because I hear that you have been maligning my character.

SHINE (*embarrassed*). You don't want to believe all you hear, Mrs. Miller.

AGNES. Am I to understand that you have not said, Mr. Shine, that I took from your store a beaded buckle?

SHINE. Wal now, Mrs. Miller—

AGNES. Mr. Shine, do you think that there is any sane person in Glendale who would believe that I stole a buckle from you? Don't you realize that to refuse to sell me a buckle in the first place was insolence? Don't you?

SHINE. Mrs. Miller, we've always been good friends—and I'd like to have given you the buckle but—

AGNES. Mr. Shine, I have never taken a gift from you and I never expect to. You know, I suppose, that it is from me and my friends that you get your bread and butter. Your little old store isn't any good. You never keep anything fit to wear. We always have to go to Raleigh in the end. But we keep on trading with you out of kindness—that's all that keeps you out of bankruptcy. And, in offending me, you have offended the best people in Glendale.

SHINE (*cringing*). They ain't any reason to get offended, Mrs. Miller. I've allus been your friend. 'Twas jus' two winters ago that I knocked five dollars off'n your winter blankets.

AGNES. There is no use mincing words. You two have borne false witness against me. You are guilty of a horrible crime . . . the crime of libel! My son, who is a law student at the University, has informed me that I can have you put in jail for sixty days, and heavily fined.

SHINE. Oh, Mrs. Miller, I hope you don't believe I've said nothin' against you. I don't know who started that lie about me, but you know I never said that you—

AGNES. I'm glad you understand how serious libel is. My duty to society is to have you sent to the penitentiary. My son has urged me to prosecute you to the full extent of the law.

LEONA (impertinently). I never heard of that law before.

AGNES. There are a great many things you have never heard of before, Leona, and one of them, I regret to say, is the truth. I don't want to cast doubt upon you, but are you sure that you don't know where that beaded buckle is?

LEONA (stiffening and glaring at AGNES's belt). No'm, I haven't said I didn't know where the buckle was—

SHINE (taking courage). She saw you—

JOE. You're a liar!

SHINE. Wal—it's better for me to lie than for you to lose your manners. (AGNES gives JOE's hand an admonishing squeeze.)

AGNES. I could have you both put in jail tomorrow. But I'm not going to prosecute you. I'm not even going to have my friends boycott you, but I want you to know that I could. I need only speak the word, and no lady would ever set foot in your store again.

SHINE. Let's don't have no hard feelin's, ma'am. It's sho' kind of you to do that way arter what Leona said.

LEONA (insisting). Well, the buckle was gone.

AGNES. And when I walked in with a similar buckle on my dress you jumped to the conclusion that I had stolen it. Leona, I permitted my son to go to the Public High School. I am not a stickler for caste, but I am forced to speak of it to you. Don't you understand that I am well known in Glendale? That my family for generations has stood for honor and integrity? Don't you see that any one of consequence would laugh at the idea of my stealing a buckle?

LEONA (weakening). Well, I couldn't see where it went to.

AGNES. I was terribly hurt that it was you who said these things, Leona, because you are the only clerk in town who has any taste. I had always felt perfectly safe when I traded with you, but now . . .

LEONA *(showing signs of breaking down).* Well, you know how sometimes when you're worried you . . . s-s-say things. . . .

AGNES *(impulsively).* Yes, dear, I know. But we mustn't let our tongues run away with us. We must always be sure that they are telling the truth.

LEONA *(crying).* I didn't mean. . . .

AGNES. I'm glad you're sorry, Leona. Now we can be friends again. I've liked you ever since you were a little girl with such pretty hair—I see you've still got it—and it's all for your own good that I'm saying this. I would hate for you to get into trouble, and the easiest way to do it is to begin talking about people behind their backs and stooping to petty dishonesties—

LEONA *(snivelling).* I wasn't dishonest—

AGNES. Of course you weren't intentionally, but it wasn't right to slander me, Leona. Don't cry, here, take my handkerchief and keep it—to remember me by.

LEONA *(sobbing and blowing her nose).* It smells so sweet!

AGNES. Mr. Shine, I told you that I got this buckle from Raleigh. *(She takes a paper from purse.)* Here is a bill for it. *(SHINE reaches for it.)*

JOE *(rushing toward him).* Can't you take my mother's word? You look at that bill and I'll break your neck! *(The bill slips to the floor.)*

SHINE *(placating).* Naw . . . now, it don't make no difference; and, Mrs. Miller, if any of your friends speaks o' this fool story again, you kin tell 'em thet . . . now's I think about it, I believe I *saw that buckle slip through a hole in the floor!*

LEONA *(relieved).* Yes, there *was* a hole in the floor.

AGNES. Very well, I suppose that's just what happened. I knew you would explain things to me and that we could be good friends again. Thank you so much for coming. And now—good-by. Good-by, Leona.

SHINE and LEONA *(going).* Good-by.

JOE. Mother, you are the most diabolically clever person! Why, they reacted so to your charm that they left here feeling that you had paid them a compliment.

AGNES *(laughing gaily and sinking down on the sofa, she*

looks adoringly at JOE *who is standing by the door).* Well, what's charm good for, if it doesn't get reaction? Oh, dear, I'm so sorry all this happened while you were at home. Come sit down by me and tell me everything. (JOE *starts to obey but stoops to pick up the bill. She raises her hand to detain him, but immediately recovers her composure.* JOE *looks at his mother with an amused chuckle.)*

JOE. Mother, this isn't the bill for the buckle. It's a bill for my new "Tuck!"

AGNES. Is it, dear? I declare . . . I was about to show them the wrong bill! But you saved me. You reacted wonderfully, too!

JOE (*trying to be casual).* But, Mother . . . where *is* the bill for the buckle?

AGNES. The bill for the buckle? (*She laughs merrily.)* There is no bill for the buckle! (JOE *stands looking questioningly at her, then walks away a little.)* What's the matter, dear? Was that very wicked?

JOE. But, Mother. . . .

AGNES. Joe, what are you thinking, darling? (JOE *turns to her, takes her face between his hands and looks into her eyes wonderingly.)*

JOE (*smiling whimsically).* When I look at you, Mother, I can't think. I only know that I love you . . . that you are the most adorable woman in the world!

CURTAIN

WASH CARVER'S MOUSE TRAP

A Carolina Mountain Comedy

BY

FRED KOCH, JR.

A PLAY BY PROFF'S SON

Seldom do the sons of famous fathers follow the parental paths, and for a while it looked as if not a one of Professor Koch's four sons would pursue playmaking. Soon after leaving college, each one entered a field considerably removed from the drama. For one son, however, though the way was circuitous, it eventually led to the theatre.

Fred Koch, Jr., was born September 15, 1911, in Grand Forks, North Dakota, where his father was teaching English at the University of North Dakota. Aged seven, he came to Chapel Hill when Proff transferred there in 1918 to found the Carolina Playmakers. He attended the local schools and graduated from the University in 1933 with a major in sociology. A year later the Emergency Relief Administration sent him to spend four months in Graham County on the Tennessee border in the extreme western part of the state. There in the Smoky Mountains his job was to investigate several hundred families on relief.

In the summer of 1935 he made a turn toward playmaking, when he toured New England and Canada with a puppet show. With the help of his wife, he subsequently organized a show of traveling puppeteers and zigzagged throughout North Carolina for the State Board of Health in the interest of "better dental care." His interest in the theatre now firmly established, he began writing plays and took a master's degree in dramatic art at the University in 1938. As a graduate student, he held a Rockefeller Foundation fellowship in playwriting. Besides "Wash Carver's Mouse Trap," he wrote another mountain comedy, "These Doggone Elections." His full-length "Smoky Mountain Road" was produced in Chapel Hill in July 1940 while he was teaching in the summer term. In 1939 he had gone to the University of Miami as chairman of the drama department, and there he has remained. Other teaching assignments include two summer terms at the University of Virginia and one at Huckleberry Mountain Workshop near Hendersonville. In recent years he has been guest director of the Parkway Playhouse at Burnsville. A musical comedy, "Southern Comfort," for which he wrote the lyrics, was produced in Miami in 1955.

Explaining the background of "Wash Carver's Mouse Trap,"

Koch writes of his tour of duty in the mountains of North Carolina: "I became pretty well acquainted with the mountain people and, in return for their patience in answering good-naturedly the endless questions called for in the investigation blanks, I listened sympathetically to their woes. I found them, on the whole, the most interesting people I ever met . . . as happy a lot as may be found anywhere.

"When the rainy weather set in after the clear skies of the colorful Indian summer, the country roads were well-nigh impassable. Although I kept chains on my car, I was frequently mired in the red clay of the little-traveled roads. Sometimes I had to walk miles to get help. But on Mouse Branch road I never had to walk or wait. Almost before my little A-model Ford had given up the struggle to get through the quagmire road, the real Wash Carver of Mouse Branch appeared with his mules, ready to pull me out. This happened every time I came that way and I concluded rightly, I think, that Wash Carver had bogged up the bottom on purpose to catch the likes of poor me.

"The city people of the play I learned to know well in traveling with my puppet show through the summer camps of New England. I often wondered what would happen if a couple of them got caught in Wash Carver's 'mouse trap.' This little play is the result of my wondering."

THE CHARACTERS

Wash Carver
Jen Carver, *his wife*
Harry Goldstein
Rosie Goldstein, *his wife*

SCENE

Wash Carver's cabin on Mouse Branch road, off the scenic highway to the Great Smoky Mountains of western North Carolina.

TIME

Eight o'clock on a rainy summer night of 1934.

WASH CARVER's *cabin is tucked away in a remote cove of the Great Smoky Mountains of western North Carolina. It perches high over Mouse Branch road, a rough, dirt road, passable in dry weather, in wet weather "not even jackassable," as* WASH CARVER *would say. A few miles away this straggling dirt road runs into the wide paved highway that takes tourists from Asheville into the Smoky Mountains Park.*

The scene is the living room of WASH CARVER's *two-room cabin. There is a rough, but clean and homey, look about it. The smooth-worn planks that wall the room are well over a foot wide, having been cut long before the days of second-growth "toothpick" timber. A door in the right of the rear wall opens onto the* CARVERS' *front porch. To the right of the door a rough board ladder leads to the loft. To the left of the door is a homemade wooden bed. In the right wall is a fireplace hung with several strings of "leather britches" (dried string beans), some twists of home-grown tobacco, and strings of small red peppers. In the left wall, opposite the fireplace, is a door leading into the cook-room and a window overlooking the road. Under the window is an old-fashioned family trunk. The soft grey of the walls is brightened by gay-colored magazine pictures and the shifting lights of the wood fire.*

As the curtains open JEN CARVER *is seated in front of the fireplace, by the center table, mending by lamplight a bedspread of antique design. She is a sturdy, middle-aged mountain woman, dressed in a plain, loose-fitting cotton print. Standing and looking intently out of the window, with foot propped on the trunk, elbow on knee, and chin cupped in hand, is* WASH CARVER, *guardian of Mouse Branch road. He is a tall, lean, slow-moving and slow-talking man with weathered face and shrewd blue eyes. He wears a faded work shirt and dark cotton trousers, stuffed into mud-bespattered brogans.*

JEN (*righteously*). I'm a-tellin' ye, Wash Carver, ain't no good goin' t' come of it.

WASH (*innocently*). Kin I help it if they git stuck up?

JEN. I seen ye, Wash Carver, drivin' that load o' wood back-'ards an' for'ards, a-geein' an' a-hawin', an' a-whoain' an' a-backin' till them wagon wheels had cut the bottom plumb out'n that road. Jist so folks 'u'd git stuck up.

217

WASH. Reckon a feller's got a right to haul his wood down the public road.

JEN. Well, ye sure picked a fine time to do it, an' the road plumb drownded with rain, an' all them tourist cars turned through here on that detour.

WASH (a little irritated). Reckon ye think I made it rain. Reckon ye think I.put up that detour sign, jist so them cars 'u'd git stuck up.

JEN. I don't reckon nothin', Wash Carver. All I know is ye done got that bottom in sich a shape a hog couldn't git through 'thout gittin' mired up to the ears. (With disgust.) Eight cars stuck up since dark!

WASH (coming over to the table and pulling some bills and change out of his pocket, begins to count). Well, I pulled 'em all out, didn't I?

JEN. Yeh, ye pulled 'em all out. An' ye charged 'em a-plenty fer it too.

WASH (gloating, his spoils laid out before him). Seven dollars an' sixteen cents cash money. And that last feller I pulled out give me a can o' smokin' terbaccer an' a pearl-handled pocket knife. That ain't a bad haul fer a little extry work, is it? (Exhibiting the knife proudly.) Ain't that pearl purty? Look at it shine! Always did love pearl.

JEN (regarding it with disapproval). Hope ye cut your throat with it. It 'u'd serve ye right. A-stickin' folks in the mud an' a-chargin' 'em all that money to pull 'em out.

WASH. How come you to git so blamed sanctified? Last I recollect you warn't so bad at stickin' folks yerself—a-puttin' water in the milk, an' lard in the butter.

JEN (without a wince). Don't see as that's got a thing to do with this.

WASH (with the wisdom of many such fruitless encounters). Well, mebbe not. (Pocketing his spoils.) Ain't had so much luck since time I won that bedspread you're a-mendin' over to the Indian Fair. Jen, you ort to a-gone with me to that Fair. I remember same as yisterday how I won that spread. I kin see that feller now, standin' back there amongst all them purty doll babies and bedspreads, a-spinnin' that big, red wheel with the numbers on it round and round. (He illustrates with his hand.)

Seems like somethin' jist told me to slap a dime down on that "thirteen." (*In his enthusiasm he whacks the table with his big hand, rocking the lighted lamp.*) Well sir, them—

Jen. I've heard ye tell it more times than they is fleas on a dog, Wash Carver—(*mimicking him*)—how them little nails went clinkin' around, how it stopped on "thirteen," an' how you won this here bedspread fer only a dime—an' you needn't go a-knockin' the lamp off'n the table to fresh up my memory on it neither! (*Squelched, Wash goes back to his post by the window.*)

Jen (*rising*). I don't know as ye didn't git stung a-payin' a dime fer it. (*Crossing to the bed she spreads the cover on it.*) I ain't never liked this spread. Hit's as coarse as a old feed sack. Ain't fitten to bed down a sick calf. Why, it already looks fer all the world like one o' them ol' wore-out homespun bedspreads. Ye ort to a-had sense enough to a-picked me out one o' them shiny, pink kind, like Lovey Crisp has got.—Talkin' about luck, now Lovey Crisp was lucky. Sold all her maw's old homespun bedspreads to one of them fancy tourist places in Asheville for five dollars apiece. It shore beats me how anybody'd give five dollars fer one o' them ol' homespuns when the mail order sells them shiny, pink kind with the ruffles fer only ninety-eight cents. (*With a sigh.*) I shore wish you'd git me one.

Wash (*excited*). Jen, yander comes another autimobile! He jist turned that first curve by the branch. (*Overcome with curiosity Jen goes to the window. The powerful beams of the automobile headlights shine through the window brilliantly illuminating their faces for a moment.*) Lord, his light's brighter 'n a June bug. Must be one o' them new cars. (*Turning suddenly, he catches Jen watching eagerly too.*) What you lookin' at?

Jen (*starts and turns away guiltily*). Wash Carver, I ain't a-studyin' yer doin's.

Wash. He's a-slowin' up fer that first bad place by the willer tree. . . . (*Breathlessly.*) Looks like he's got out o' the ruts. (*The excitement is too much for Jen; she cannot resist going to the window to see for herself now.*) God a'mighty, he's slidin' like a greased eel . . . look . . . look at him . . . look! He's stopped. (*A long blast from a high-powered horn breaks the spell. Wash slaps his knee and shouts gleefully.*) Listen at 'im holler. Mouse Branch road has trapped another'n! Wonder who it is this time,

Jen. Hope it's one o' them rich fellers that wears diamond rings and smokes big, ten-cent seegars. *(With sudden inspiration he takes the lamp to the window, waves it several times, then sets it down on the window ledge.)*

Jen. Wash Carver, you bring that lamp right back here this minute an' set it on this table where it belongs. If it falls off'n that window and ketches the house afire, they'll see your house sure enough.

Wash. Aw Jen. . . .

Jen. If you don't fetch that lamp back, Wash Carver, I'll— *(And he does! Then sits by the table, takes off his shoes, crosses the room barefoot, and conceals them under the bed.)*

Wash. Jen, fer Lord's sakes, don't ruin ever'thing. There ye stand slap in the middle o' the room like a preacher layin' fer the devil. Set down, and act natural!

Jen *(stubbornly)*. I'll not be a partner in yer sinful doin's, Wash Carver.

Wash *(rushing to the bed, he pulls off the spread and forces* Jen *into the chair by the fireplace.)* Here, act like common. Make out like you're a-mendin' the bed-kivver.

Jen. You're as crazy as a slew-foot gander! Ye know I jist got done mendin' this bed-kivver.

Wash. Don't make no difference. Jist make out like you're a-sewin' on it. *(More gently.)* Come on, Jen. I'll give ye half o' what we git out'n this un'.

Jen *settles back with a snort.* Wash *takes up the Bible from the table, opens it at random and pretends to read. After a bit he looks at* Jen, *who now smiles triumphantly.*

Wash *(disappointed, looks toward the window)*. Don't look like they're a-comin'. Told ye the lamp ort to been in the window so's them pore folks could see where the house's at. Woman, you ain't got no heart at all! *(He gets up and tiptoes to the window.)* Them pore folks must a-sunk plumb to Chiney!

Jen. Well, I hope they got out. *(Voices are heard outside.* Wash *hurries back into his chair.)*

Wash *(motioning* Jen *frantically)*. Set down, woman, set down!

Jen *(still standing)*. If you think ye kin drive me around like one o' yer blamed mules, ye— (*The sound of footsteps on the porch checks her. Unwillingly she slips into her chair and begins her mending.*)

ROSIE (*outside, her whining voice unmistakably "East-Side-New-York"*). Harry . . . Harry Goldstein. . . . Wait for me, Harry!

HARRY (*outside, of the same species, his voice rasping with exasperation*). For Christ sake, Rosie, I told you to stay in the car!

ROSIE (*outside, wailing*). Oh, Har-r-ry. (*She draws out his name, accenting both syllables.*)

HARRY (*outside*). Rosie, will you shut up! (*He knocks sharply on the door. Neither* JEN *nor* WASH *makes a move to answer.*)

ROSIE (*outside, innocently*). Why don't you ring the bell, Harry?

HARRY (*outside*). For Christ's sake, Rosie, 'cause there ain't any bell!—Why don't you go hop a street car? (*He pounds frantically on the door.*) Hello . . . hello there inside. . . . I want some help! My car's stuck!

WASH (*casually*). Jen, seems like I hear somebody at the door. (*Calling over his shoulder.*) Jist pull the latch an' push the door.

ROSIE (*outside*). What did he say, Harry?

HARRY (*outside*). How do you think I can hear what he said with you talking? Shut up, Rosie!—Hello there inside; I'm stuck in the mud.

WASH (*gets up at last and ambles to the door*). Why, come on in! Jist come right in!

HARRY *steps inside. His nervous movements, his unmistakable East-Side accent, and his oily, well-groomed appearance stamp him immediately as a city "furriner." He is obviously out of his element, as much out of place as the mud on his polished shoes and on his striped trousers.* ROSIE, *his wife, eases in behind him. She is considerably younger, or at least a certain silliness in her manner makes her seem so. She is dressed in ridiculous hiking togs. Both* ROSIE *and* HARRY *stand a moment struck by the strangeness of the room and the spectacle of* WASH CARVER *standing in his bare feet, his big toes upturned.*

Wash (*in the typical manner of greeting strangers*). Don't believe I know you. (*He studies a minute.*) Seems like I've seed your face som'ers, but I don't believe I can call yer name right off.

Rosie (*eagerly stepping forward*). Goldstein—Mr. and Mrs. Harry Goldstein from New York. Harry and I are touring through your be-a-utiful Smoky Mountains. (*Aside to* Harry.) Oh, Harry, isn't this romantic? It's just like that movie we saw at Radio City last week. Aren't you glad now we came to the mountains? (*Back to the* Carvers.) Harry wanted to go to the seashore but I—

Harry (*finally explodes*). Rosie, for God's sake—(*To* Wash.) Listen, I'm stuck.

Wash (*innocently*). What say?

Harry. I'm stuck, *stuck!* My new car's sunk in the mud!

Wash (*incredulous*). Stuck? Well, you don't say. Where at?

Harry. Where? By that damn brook down there where the road is all wet. (Wash *looks puzzled.*) About two blocks from here.

Wash (*uncertainly*). Brook . . . two blocks. . . . Oh, yeah, you mean where Mouse Branch runs acrost the road through that bottom. You know, I was just a-telling' Jen here how them cars a-comin' through this detour had got that bottom mighty slickery. (*Hospitably.*) You all jist take chairs an' rest yerselves awhile.

Harry. Good Heavens, man, rest? We haven't time to rest. We've got to make Asheville tonight.—How far is it to the nearest garage?

Wash (*scratching his head*). Garage, did ye say? Let me see now. Pap Wilkins runs a sort o' fillin' station like, if that's what ye mean. (Harry *nods impatiently.*) Hit's jist yan side o' the gap o' Sugar Loaf Mountain. Ye remember that time, Jen, when me and Pap went bear huntin' up Little Snowbird and that derned cow almost—

Harry (*in no mood for a mountain yarn*). The garage! How far is it?

Wash. Oh, let me see now. From here to Grady Mashburn's mill is about a quarter. Then on to Sweetwater church . . . that's another quarter, or maybe that 'u'd come nearer to bein'

a half, don't ye think, Jen? Well, anyhow, I'd say from here
to Red Hog knob is upwards of three mile. Now from Red Hog—

HARRY. Please! please! The garage? How far is it?

WASH. Makin' a chanc't guess I'd say it was ever' bit o' five
mile from here. (HARRY *wails.*) Without you knowed the short-
cuts it 'u'd take you upwards of two hours o' stiff walkin' to
make it to Pap's. I reckon Pap's done gone ter bed by this time
though, ain't he, Jen?

JEN. Hunh? I don't know nothin' 'bout Pap's bed habits.

ROSIE. Five miles! Oh Harry, that's entirely too far for you
to walk with your blood pressure. . . . Maybe he'd let you use
his telephone, Harry!

HARRY. Rosie, will you please shut up! (*To* WASH.) Has this
Pap fellow got wrecker service?

WASH (*enjoying the game hugely*). Wrecker service? (*He
pretends to be puzzled.*) Oh, he's got 'im a wife if that's what
you mean! (WASH *guffaws loudly at his own joke, then seriously.*) Naw, Mister, Pap Wilkins ain't got nothin' but a T-model
Ford an' a monkey wrench. You-uns just stay here and spend the
night with us. They's a extry bed up in the loft. (*He motions
toward the ladder.*) Jen and I 'u'd be plumb glad to have ye
stay, wouldn't we, Jen?

JEN (*sourly*). I reckon. . . .

WASH. Course we would! Course we would, plumb glad!

ROSIE. Oh, Harry, let's stay. (*Nudging him.*) Southern hos-
pitality, Harry!

HARRY (*pacing the floor*). My God, Rosie! This is terrible.
(*To* WASH.) Listen, I've got to get out of here at once. I'll lose
five hundred dollars worth of business if I'm late back to New
York. (*In despair.*) Rosie, I told you we should have went to
the beach. (*Back to* WASH.) Listen, you've got to help me out.
Great God, Rosie, I'd give ten dollars to get out of this dump!

WASH (*quickly*). Ten dollars?

HARRY. Yes, five dollars.

WASH (*sitting on the bed and scratching his head, he drawls.*)
I was jist a-figgerin'. I got a team o' mules been pullin' chestnut
stumps on some new ground top o' Old Whiteface. (HARRY
starts impatiently.) Say ye had a Ford or a Chevrolet?

ROSIE (*irrepressible*). It's a Packard. It's the latest model—

a blue one. Harry wanted a Buick but. . . . (HARRY *turns sharply and she stops. Innocently.)* What's the matter, Ha-r-ry?

WASH. Packard. That's one o' them big, high-priced cars, ain't it? *(Shaking his head.)* I'm afeard it 'u'd strain the mules. Ye know, that least mule o' mine's got a sore place on 'er back. I was jist a-tellin' Jen awhile ago that—

HARRY *(pacing the floor, stops abruptly).* Listen, you've got to help me. I've got to get out. My God, my business! Every minute is money to me. I'll pay you extra . . . extra!

WASH *(shaking his head).* Them big cars is awful heavy.

HARRY. Listen, I'll give you ten dollars to pull me out, ten dollars!

WASH *(looking up).* Ten dollars? *(He pretends to study a minute. Then suddenly.)* You know, I jist remember.—Jen, ain't there an old block 'n' tackle in the shed right under them feed sacks?

JEN *(with a snort).* Not as I know about.

WASH *(unperturbed).* Now, come to think on it, I know there is. *(He hauls out his shoes from under the bed and begins putting them on.)* You know, with that block an' tackle, them mules kin more'n like make it. Ye say ye'll give me ten dollars?

HARRY *(reluctantly).* Yes, ten dollars . . . if you pull me out.

ROSIE *(petulantly).* Harry, I think that's an awful lot of money to spend. . . .

HARRY *(with a wail).* Rosie, I suppose you think I want to spend it!

ROSIE. Harry Goldstein, if you spend ten dollars on your old car I'm going to buy one of those homespun bedspreads for Rachel's room. You know I promised Rachel I'd buy her a spread and here you go spending all the money on your old car.

HARRY. For cryin' out loud, Rosie!—We're stuck in the mud . . . stuck in the mud! We got to get out! You want to stay here all night?

ROSIE. Harry, you're so unreasonable. Yes, I'd much rather stay here than go with you. *(Mincing over to MRS. CARVER.)* You'll let me stay, won't you, Mrs. . . . Mrs. . . . .

JEN. Carver. I reckon ye kin stay.

WASH *(going to the door).* Well, Mister Gold . . . Goldpine—

HARRY. Gold*stein.*

WASH. That's right, Goldsign.—Don't know as I ever heard that name before.—Well, Mr. Goldmine, I'll go put the gears on them mules, an' we'll jist see if they can't yank that big Packard o' yourn out'n the mud. (*He illustrates.*) Same as a stump. (*He goes out.*)

HARRY. Come on, Rosie.

ROSIE. I'll do no such thing, Harry Goldstein. It was you stuck that car in the mud; now you can just get it out yourself. I'm going to stay right here and talk to Mrs. Carver.

HARRY. Rosie, for—! (*His patience utterly spent, he gives her an annihilating look, turns and goes out, slamming the door in her face.*)

ROSIE (*with a hurt cry*). Oh, Harry! (*She turns and wanders down toward* JEN *with a puzzled expression.*) Now, what do you suppose I could have said, Mrs. Carver, to make Harry so angry? Harry is so unreasonable.

JEN. Reckon all men critters is that-a-way.

ROSIE. But your husband seems so nice, Mrs. Carver.

JEN. You jist don't know him like I do.

ROSIE. But he's so quiet and country-like. You know, Harry don't appreciate the country. All he cares about is business. Sometimes I say to him, "Harry, why don't you give up the jewelry business and buy a nice little farm where we could settle down with a cow?" But Harry don't care about nothing but business. (*Contemptuously.*) Selling cheap ten-cent-store jewelry—(*she indicates a string of imitation pearls she is wearing*)—like these pearls.

JEN. You mean them pearls cost only ten cents?

ROSIE. Oh yes, Harry sells thousands of them to Ten Cent Stores. (*With pride.*) He's the best salesman the company ever had. Mr. Greenberg, he's the President, says Harry could sell trunks to elephants. (*She giggles.*) Mr. Greenberg is so funny. (*Sighing.*) Oh, I guess I shouldn't complain, but sometimes Harry is so unreasonable. Only yesterday, in Knoxville, I had a chance to buy a real homespun bedspread for only ten dollars, and Harry wouldn't let me.

JEN (*taking the spread over to the bed, she starts to put it on*). I reckon all men-folks is ornery an' hard to git along with. I been a-tryin' to git my old man to git me one o' them shiny, pink bedspreads fer the last five years. This old spread ain't fitten—

Rosie (noticing the spread for the first time). Oh, Mrs. Carver, that's a beautiful bedspread! Do let me see it. (She takes it from the bed and examines it eagerly.)

Jen. I ain't never liked it much. It's too coarse an' common lookin'.

Rosie. Oh, I know, but all homespuns are coarse. I think it's exquisite! Did you make it?

Jen. Why no, I didn't make it. Hit's jist an old spread I got—

Rosie (interrupting her). Of course, you didn't make it. How stupid of me. It must be at least a hundred years old! I just love old antiques. (Holding it up.) You know, it's just the right color to match with Rachel's room—Rachel is my daughter, such a sweet girl! I'm furnishing her room in antiques, and this spread is just what I want. You'll sell it to me, Mrs. Carver, won't you?

Jen. Well, I'd like to sell it all right, but ye see—

Rosie. Oh, I understand so well. It's awfully hard to part with old things. But I'll pay you well for it. You know, I wanted so much to buy one of these hand-woven bedspreads yesterday in the tourist shop in Knoxville, but Harry said it might not be genuine. He was afraid it might be like the pearls he sells. It's hard to tell them from real ones. You don't know how much it would mean to buy an antique spread where you know it's genu-ine! I'll pay you well, Mrs. Carver.

Jen (struggling with her conscience). I'm awful sorry to tell you, but that spread—

Rosie (insisting). Mrs. Carver, I simply must have it! It's just the right shade for Rachel's room. (Opening her purse.) I'll give you ten dollars for it.

Jen (thunderstruck). Ten dollars! I'd like to sell it, but—

Rosie. I know that's not enough but. . . . (Looking in her purse and taking out the money.) Here's three more dollars, thirteen dollars in all. Now I know you're going to be a dear and let me have it, aren't you? (A long blast from the automobile horn.) Oh, there goes Harry. He must be un-stuck. Wouldn't you think he'd be gentleman enough to come for me, instead of blowing? *(Persuasively.)* Can't I have the spread, Mrs. Carver?

Jen *(bewildered).* Ye kin have it all right . . . but it ain't worth—

Rosie. You just don't know what they charge in the stores. It's worth every cent of it. And to buy it here in a real mountain cabin! *(A romantic sigh.)* When I look at it, I'll always think about the time poor Harry got stuck. Poor Harry! *(She folds the spread hurriedly and goes to the door.)* I'm sorry to hurry off. Thank you so much, Mrs. Carver. If you come to New York be sure to let me know. Good-by! Good-by, Mrs. Carver! (Rosie *hurries out. Her voice can be heard trailing off.)* Harry . . . I'm coming, Harry! Wait, Ha-r-ry! . . . Ha-r-ry! . . .

Jen *looks at the money* Rosie *has forced into her hand, then at the bed. Struck dumb at her good fortune, she sinks weakly onto the bed. She stares at the money, then at the door. She is undergoing a struggle. Suddenly she bolts for the door and calls.*

Jen. Mrs. Goldstein! . . . Mrs. Goldstein! . . . *(There is no answer. With a wide smile she closes the door, comes down to the table and resumes her seat by the fire still somewhat dazed as* Wash *comes stomping loudly onto the porch.)*

Wash *(entering).* Well, old woman, I pulled 'em out all right! *(Laughing.)* Easy as pullin' a blue tick off'n a hound dog. *(He looks out the window.)* Look at them lights move! Them folks sure is in a hurry. *(He sprawls on the bed.)* Bet ye cain't guess what I got.

Jen. There ain't no tellin'.

Wash *(gloating).* Jist seems like good luck's a-huggin' me tonight. That feller was a powerful good trader. He could out-talk a jaybird and trade the feet off'n a black snake. I sure had to talk 'im slick and trade 'im close. You got ter use yer head, ol' woman. *(Chuckling.)* You'll have to figger out somethin' better'n puttin' lard in the butter.

Jen. You're a-feelin' powerful high an' mighty, ain't ye, Wash Carver?

Wash. Got a right to. Ain't had so much luck since that time I won that derned old bedspread at the Indian Fair. *(He notices that the bed is uncovered.)* What's come o' that spread? What ye done with it?

JEN. That 'ere swift-talkin' woman tuck a likin' to it. *(Holding up the money gleefully.)* She give me thirteen dollars fer it!

WASH *(incredulous).* Thirteen dollars! Fer that old thing? Didn't ye tell her it didn't cost me but a dime?

JEN. Mebbe I did, and mebbe I didn't. She talked so fast I couldn't git a word in edgewise.

WASH. By God, Jen, she must a-been blind as a hoot owl.— What got into 'er?

JEN *(cryptically).* She jist took a likin' to the color.

WASH. Well, I'll be damned! *(Generously.)* Well, Jen. It looks like I've learnt ye to be a good trader after all. Them pore folks sure got skinned. *(A pause.)* Reckon, bein's how I won that spread, a part o' that money's mine, ain't it?

JEN *(firmly).* Not nary a cent, Wash Carver. You *give* me that spread, an' you know it.

WASH *(exploding).* Well, I'll be a suck-eared mule! If that ain't jist like a woman. It don't pay to be nice to 'em; it shore don't. *(He looks out the window.)* Wish't now I'd a-took the money instead.

JEN. 'Stead o' what?

WASH *(turning angrily).* Blamed if I give 'em to ye now! I'll take 'em to Bryson City an' sell 'em, an' it'll serve ye right.

JEN. Wash Carver, what air you a-talkin' about?

WASH. Somethin' I was aimin' to give ye fer a present.—Like a blamed fool I tuck to feelin' sorry fer ye.

JEN. Wash Carver, you're talkin' like a plumb fool!

WASH *(riled up).* Talkin' like a fool, am I? All right then, jist look! *(He digs into his pocket and pulls out a string of pearls. Triumphantly.)* Look at 'em! Pearls!

JEN. Pearls?

WASH *(holding them up, his eyes shining).* A whole string of 'em—*pearls! (With a contemptuous snort.)* And that feller thought he was a good trader.—I'll bet they're worth twenty dollars!

JEN. And how much did ye give fer them pearls, Wash Carver?

WASH. Besides givin' 'im the ten dollars I got fer pullin' 'im out, I just had to give 'im that sixteen cents I had in my pocket extry.

JEN. Sixteen cents extry? Ten dollars an' sixteen cents fer them pearls!

WASH. Yeh, why they ain't no tellin' how much they're worth! (JEN *bursts into laughter.* WASH *looks on, uncomprehending.*)

CURTAIN